AF471095

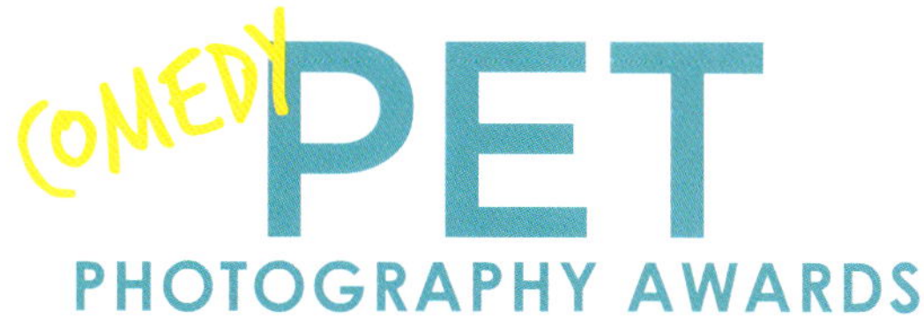

COMEDY
PET
PHOTOGRAPHY AWARDS

First published in the UK by John Blake Publishing
An imprint of The Zaffre Publishing Group
A Bonnier Books UK company
4th Floor, Victoria House,
Bloomsbury Square,
London, WC1B 4DA

Owned by Bonnier Books
Sveavägen 56, Stockholm, Sweden

www.facebook.com/johnblakebooks
twitter.com/jblakebooks

First published in hardback in 2024

Hardback ISBN: 978-1-78946-806-9

British Library Cataloguing-in-Publication Data:
A CIP catalogue record for this book is available from the British Library.

Design by www.envydesign.co.uk
Front cover image: Elke Vogelsang
Back cover image: Kenichi Morinaga

Printed and bound in Lithuania

1 3 5 7 9 10 8 6 4 2

Text copyright © Paul Joynson-Hicks and Tom Sullam, 2024
All images © individually credited photographers
Captions by Nathan Joyce

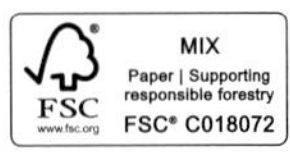

Every reasonable effort has been made to trace copyright holders of material reproduced in this book, but if any have been inadvertently overlooked the publishers would be glad to hear from them.

John Blake Publishing is an imprint of Bonnier Books UK
www.bonnierbooks.co.uk

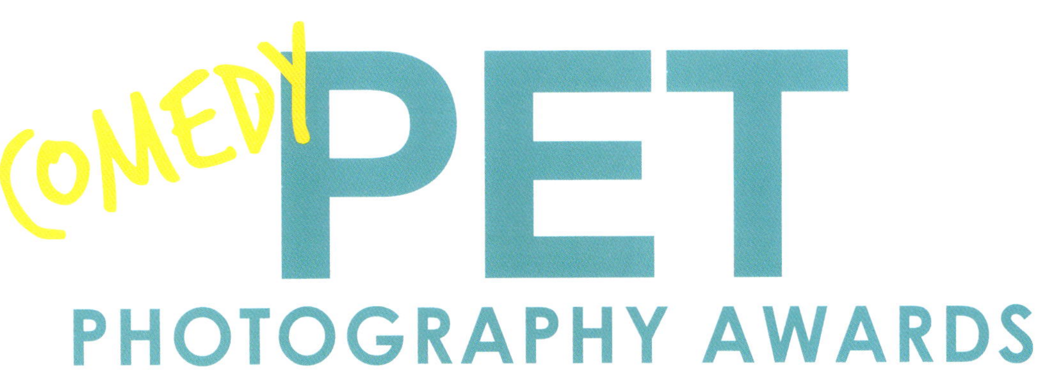

EDITED BY
PAUL JOYNSON-HICKS AND TOM SULLAM

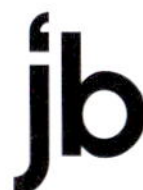

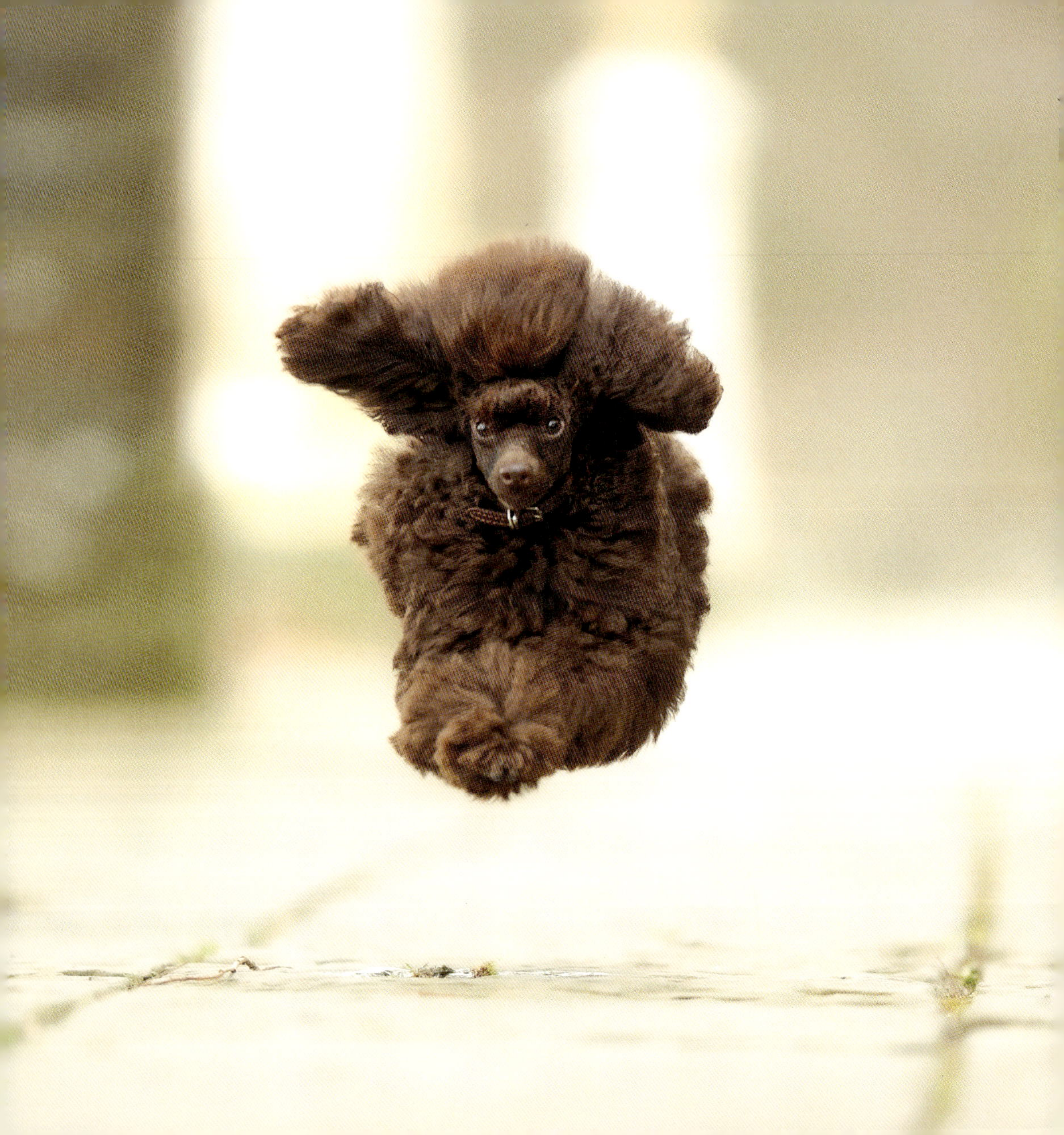

FOREWORD

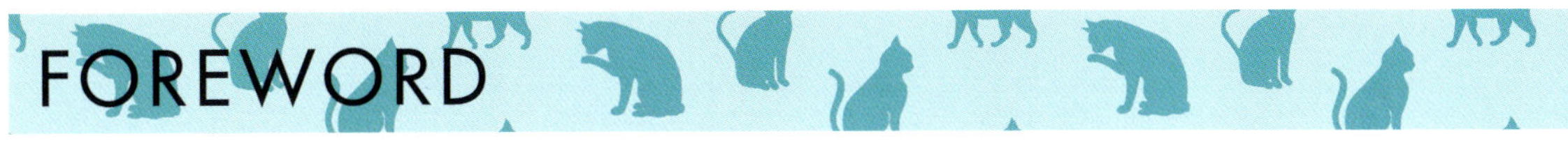

BY ELKE VOGELSANG, PET PHOTOGRAPHER

When I first read about the Comedy Pet Photo Awards back in 2020, I was hooked by the idea of a funny pet photo competition; one that supports animal welfare and has such a positive, upbeat vibe, and I knew immediately that I had to submit pictures of my very funny and entertaining Spanish greyhound mix, Noodles. It was meant to be.

She was one of a kind – I know, that's what all pet owners say about their pets, but she was. With her big floppy ears, cartoonish nose and goofy personality, she had all the makings of a first-rate comedian. However, her start in life was not so funny. She was rescued from death row in Spain and came to us at the tender age of six months, when she was just skin and bones. It was heartbreaking. But she loved life and every single human and dog that she met. She brightened our days with her outgoing, carefree and happy nature, so much so that we then adopted another beautiful and sensitive Galgo mix, called Scout. Incredibly, the two of them alerted me when my husband collapsed in the bathroom with a severe brain haemorrhage in 2009. These two abandoned strays became lifesavers and beloved family members. I can't put into words how much they mean to me and if you're a pet owner too, it will be a familiar feeling the world over. I guess that's why I try to express my admiration for pets in pictures as a professional photographer. They deserve it!

After my Noodles became the Overall Winner in 2020, I was asked to be a judge for future competitions and of course I said yes! Who wouldn't?! I can think of few things more entertaining than looking at funny, cute animal pictures all day long.

What makes me particularly happy about the competition is that Comedy Pets not only delivers a dollop of pure joy when you see the images, it also supports animal welfare through donations and by promoting adoption. Over a period of five years, a whopping £55k has been donated to various wonderful charities through sponsorship and donations from partners like Mars Petcare and Animal Friends and from competition winners keen to give something back. That is a lot of dosh! Comedy Pets is a wonderful community of animal ambassadors and by highlighting all the work that goes into helping keep pets safe and cared for around the world, we can make a difference. If you are ever in the enviable position of being about to choose a new pet, be sure to check out the shelters and rescue centres near you. There are many loving souls of all ages, sizes, with characters as big as houses and energy levels to match, that have much fun, entertainment and love to give. They will surprise you.

My pets are my joy, recreation and constant source of laughter, and all of them were once abandoned and rescued. The saying is true: one person's trash is another person's treasure. And thanks to this competition, we get to see some of the very best! Long may it continue!

Elke Vogelsang

INTRODUCTION

The Comedy Pet Photography Awards was created – and I will shamefully admit to it here in print – as a side show to the already established Comedy Wildlife Photography Awards. Our small team realised that as much as the world loves wildlife, more people can get involved when it means photographing their pets. It was an easy win, or so we thought. We had the capacity and the learned knowledge of how to run a competition, we had just brought in Michelle to help provide order, structure, insight and brains (and, as a bonus, a lot of humour), and so we were well placed to add another photographic competition. Seemed easy. Free throw. Open goal …

As it turns out, Paul and I have two left feet each. And we can't throw. And nothing is ever as easy as you think it is. It is only after the event that you can look back and enjoy the relative ease of being well on the way to your destination. At first, we skidded and slipped at the start line, and then bit by bit, with Michelle on board, we built and grew the fledgling, cheeky little sibling to the Wildlife competition. Comedy Pets now stands shoulder to shoulder with our Wildlife venture.

And so, as night follows day or chocolate follows everything, we just had to do a Comedy Pets book; a compelling collection of hilarious and joyous pet images, that have been entered into the competition since the very first one. From chicks to alpacas, ferrets to horses and of course cats and dogs, all providing the humour and positive imagery that is so addictive to us, not only as photographers but as pet owners.

And this is the crux. We have been absolutely blown away by the deep, real and unadulterated love that you pet owners have for your pets. At the risk of sounding overly dramatic, we are often on the edge of shedding tears when we hear your love and pride for your animals. Indeed, many of you who enter the competition are not even interested in winning a prize, you are just keen to see your best friend get some recognition for being the most positive thing in your life. And we know that feeling. The loyalty, the friendship, the unspoken words shared, these are all part of the fantastic beasts that we share our lives with. And our lives would be so much poorer without them. Aren't they just the best things ever? Yes, wholeheartedly yes. Our pets are our best friends, our family, our most loyal sibling, our most honest relationship.

Altogether, it brings me, Paul and Michelle so much joy to host this competition. Thank you all for buying this book, for loving pets, and for being the best friends your pets have got. We all play a part in animal welfare, and you are playing yours extraordinarily well. 2025 will bring us more laughs, we hope to see you in the competition then!

Tom Sullam
Co-Founder

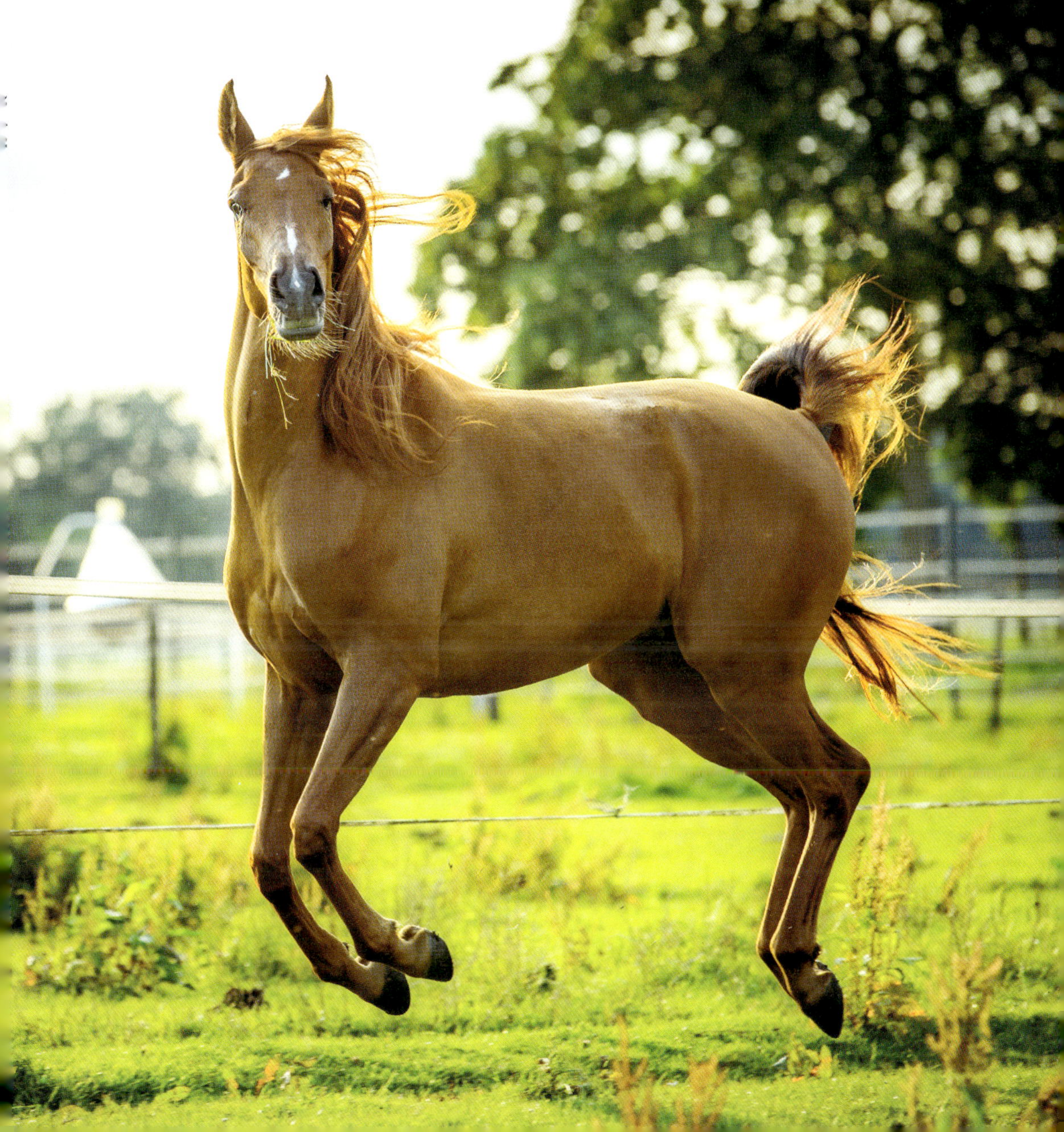

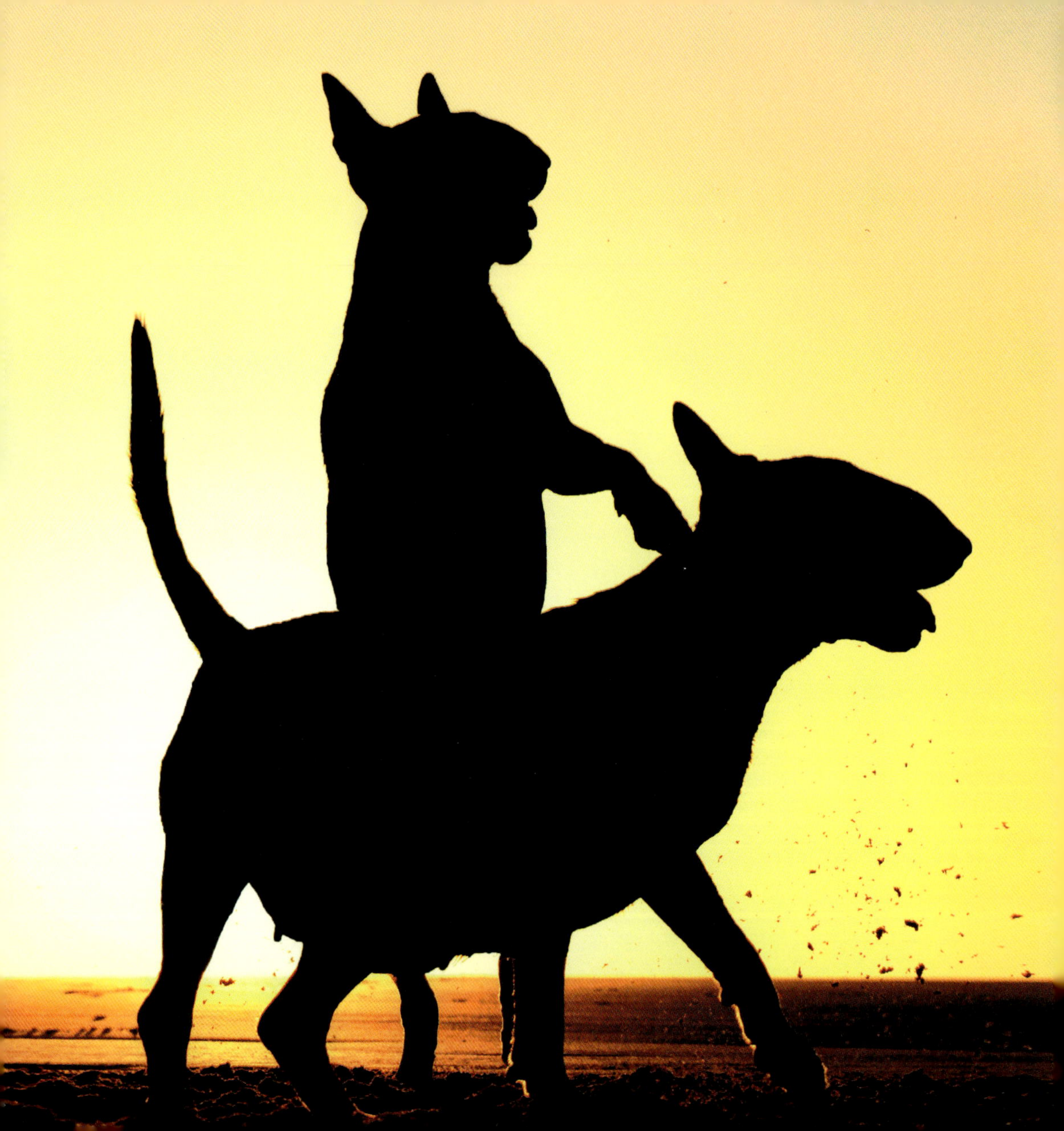

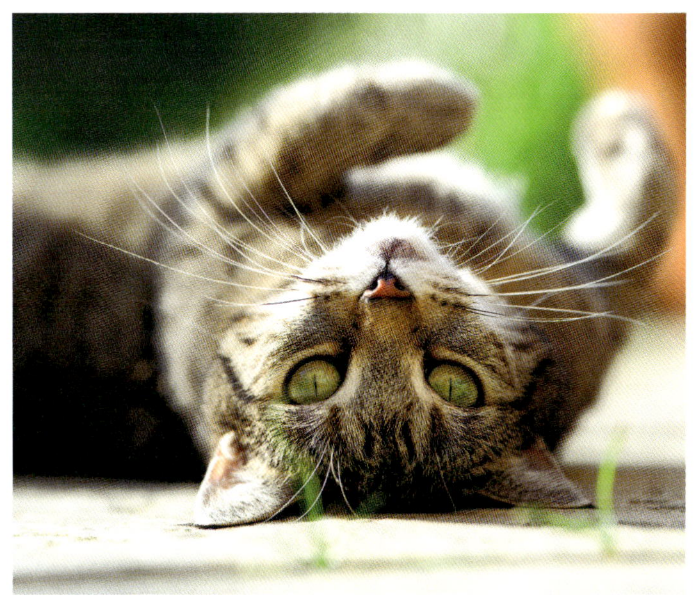

LOCATION: WYMONDHAM, NORFOLK, UNITED KINGDOM
Cats sleep for an average of 15 hours a day. And here's what they do for the rest of the time.
PHOTOGRAPHER: Jonathan Casey

LOCATION: ROCKANJE, NETHERLANDS
When I said 'pick you up at 6am', this isn't quite what I had in mind …
PHOTOGRAPHER: Alice van Kempen

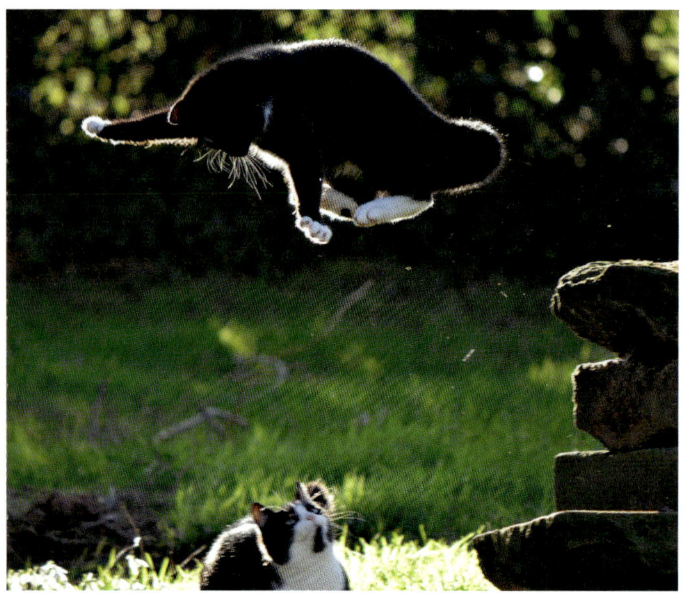

LOCATION: BIRMINGHAM, UNITED KINGDOM
Supercat waves to a fan.
PHOTOGRAPHER: Heather Ross

LOCATION: CANADA
There's nothing more humiliating than an un-met high five.
PHOTOGRAPHER: Chantal Sammons

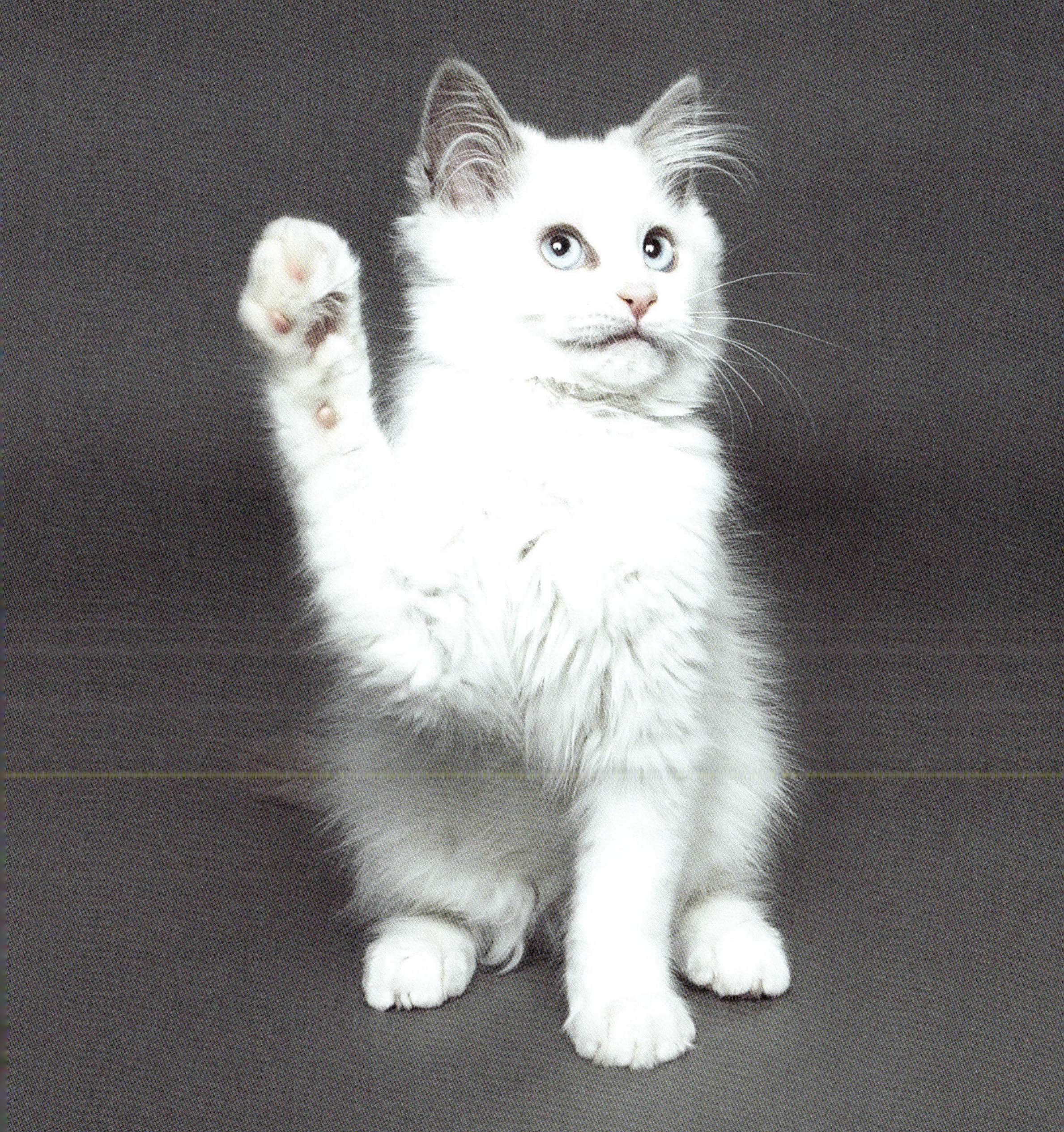

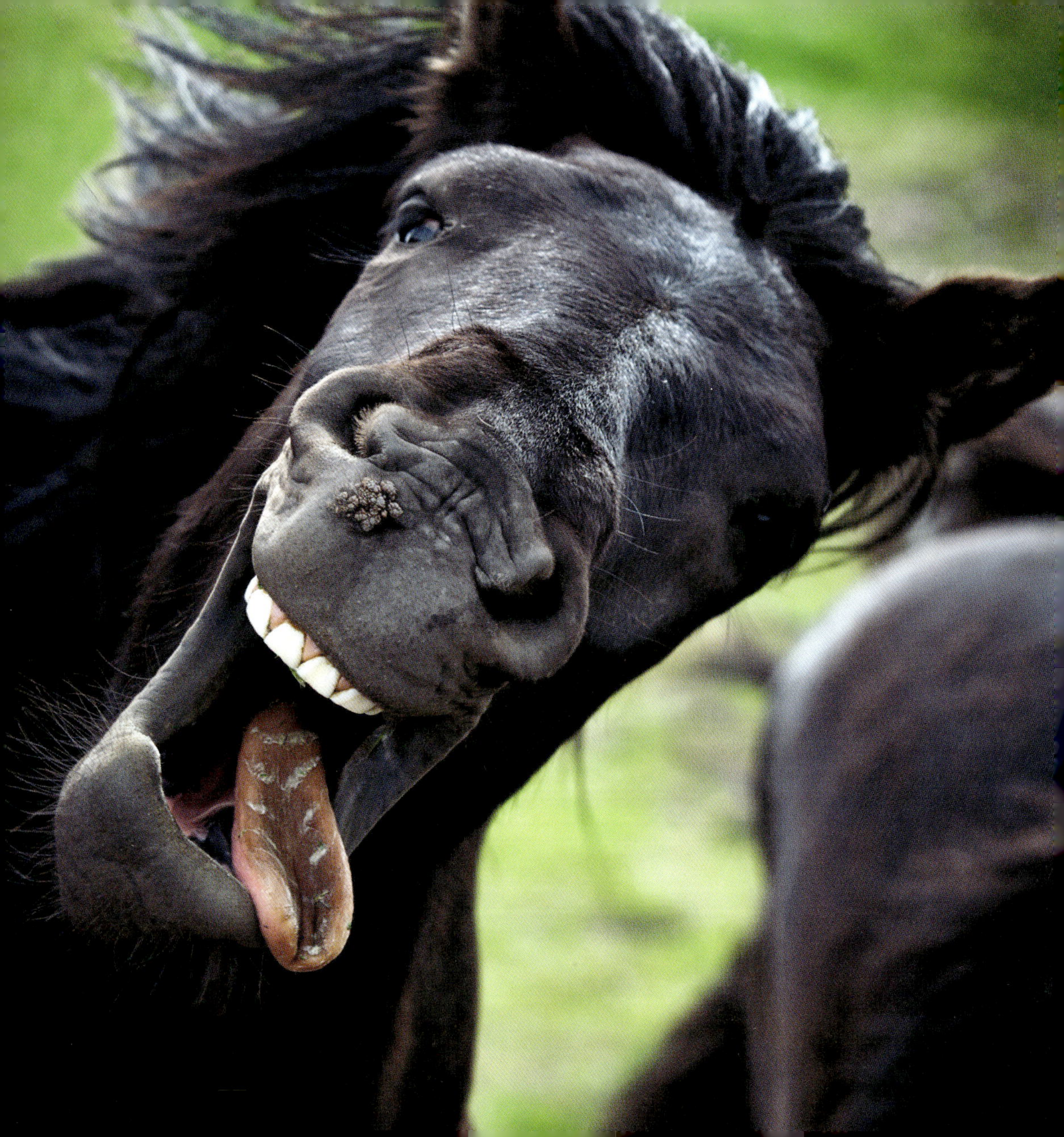

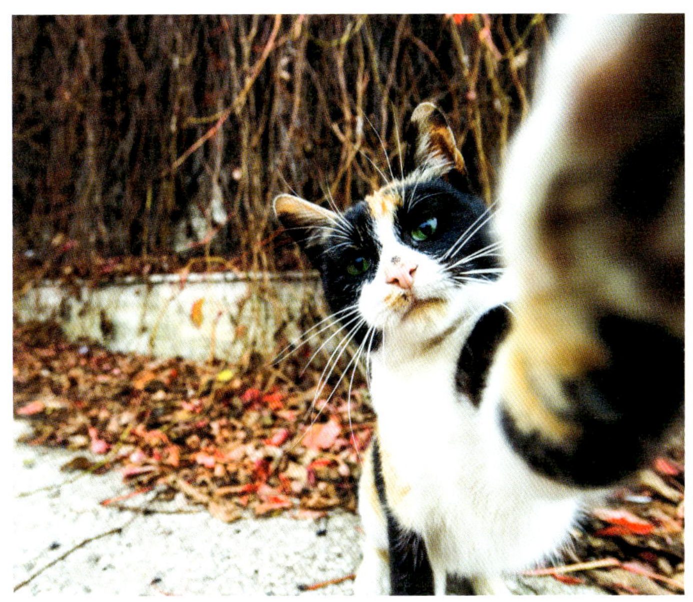

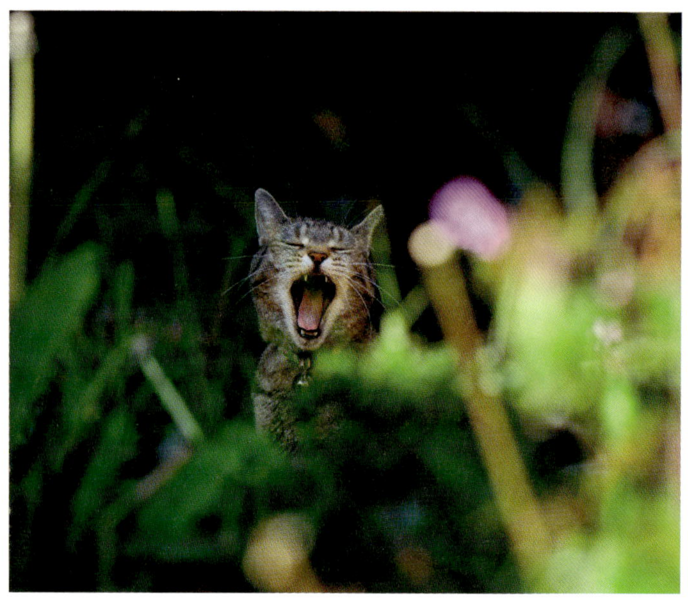

LOCATION: WYMONDHAM, NORFOLK, UNITED KINGDOM
Now try not to yawn!
PHOTOGRAPHER: Jonathan Casey

LOCATION: OGNA BEACH, NORWAY
Fido really mastered the 'I dig ya' Valentines card this year.
PHOTOGRAPHER: Anne Lise Gramstad

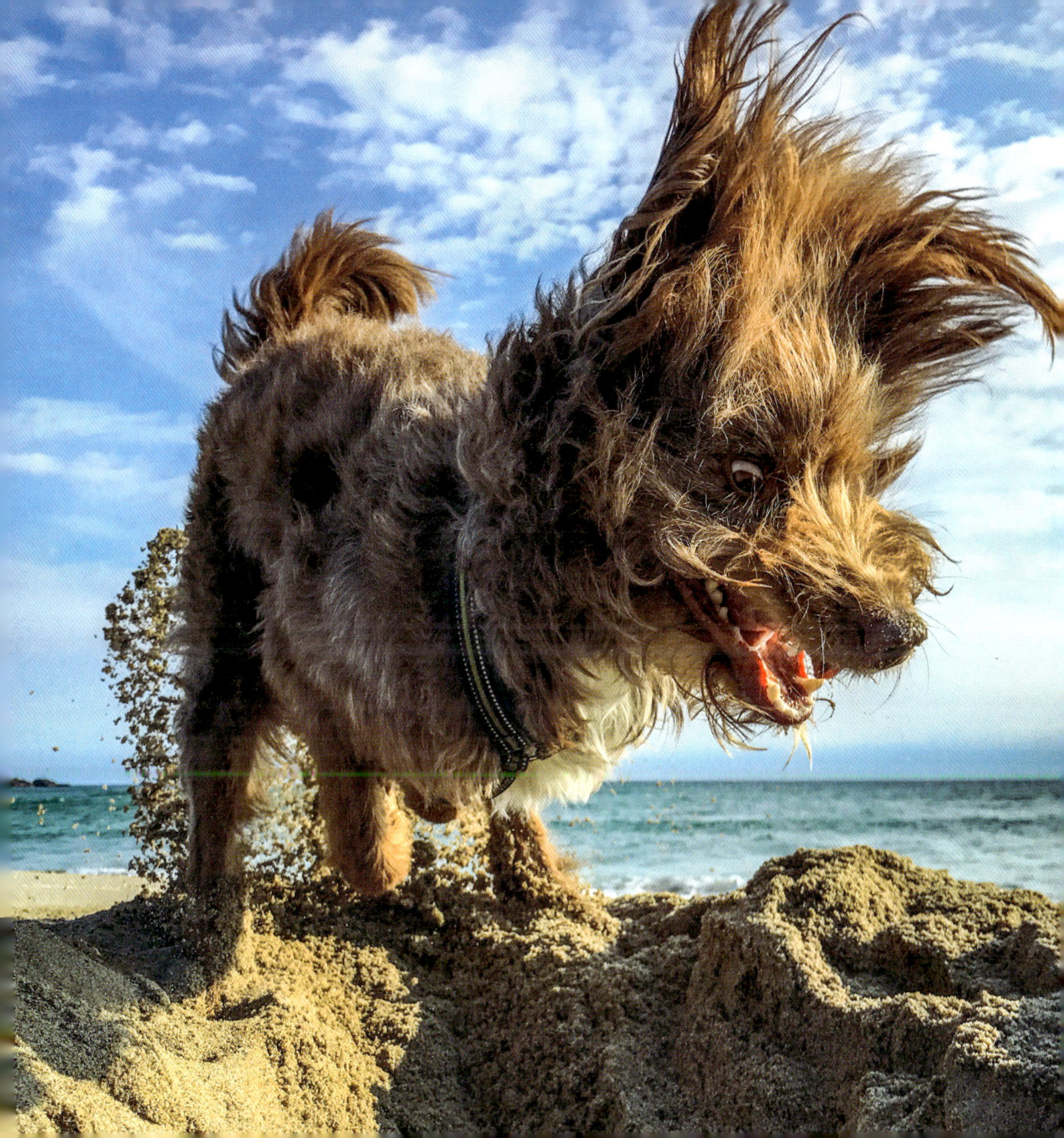

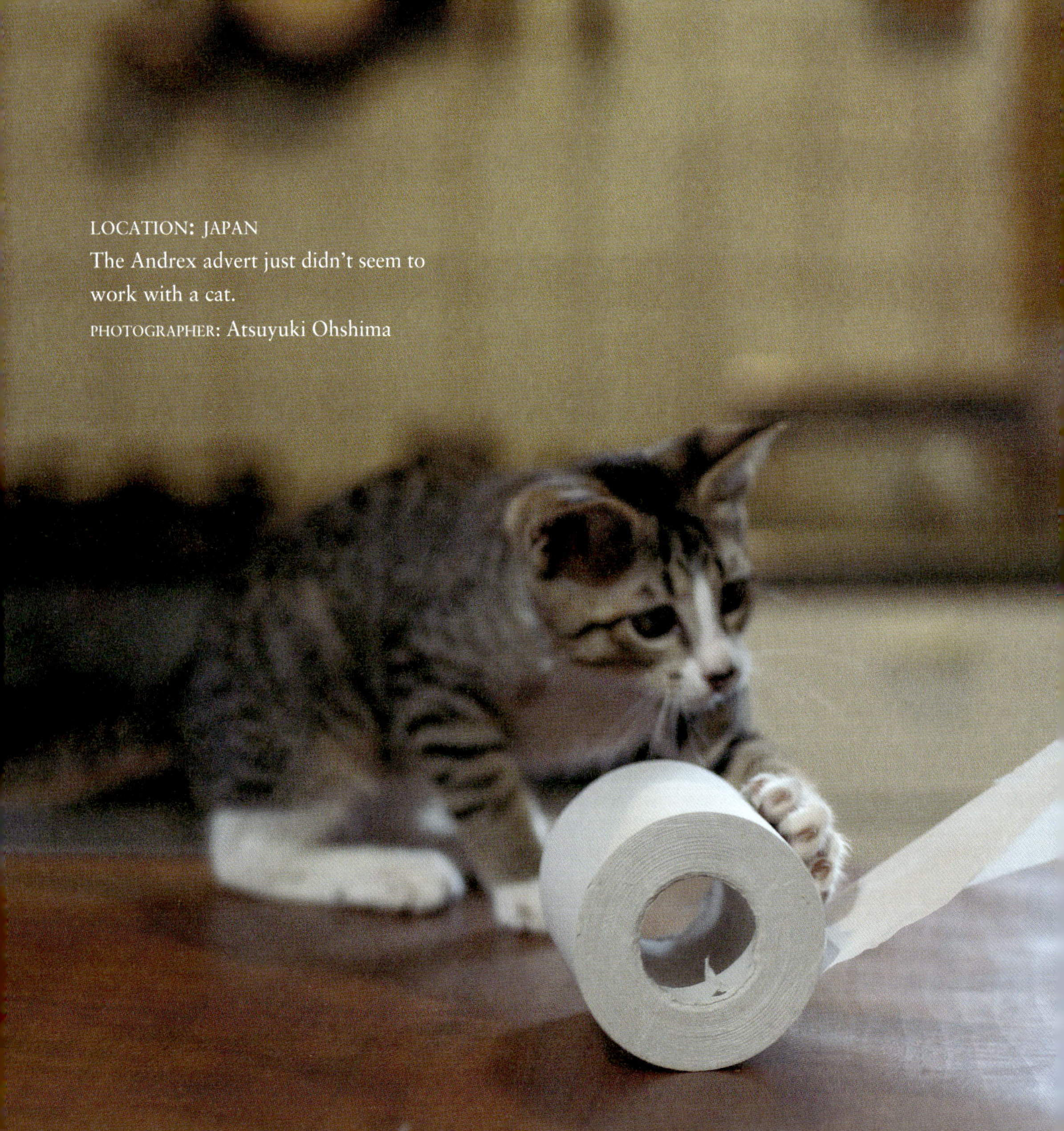LOCATION: JAPAN
The Andrex advert just didn't seem to
work with a cat.
PHOTOGRAPHER: Atsuyuki Ohshima

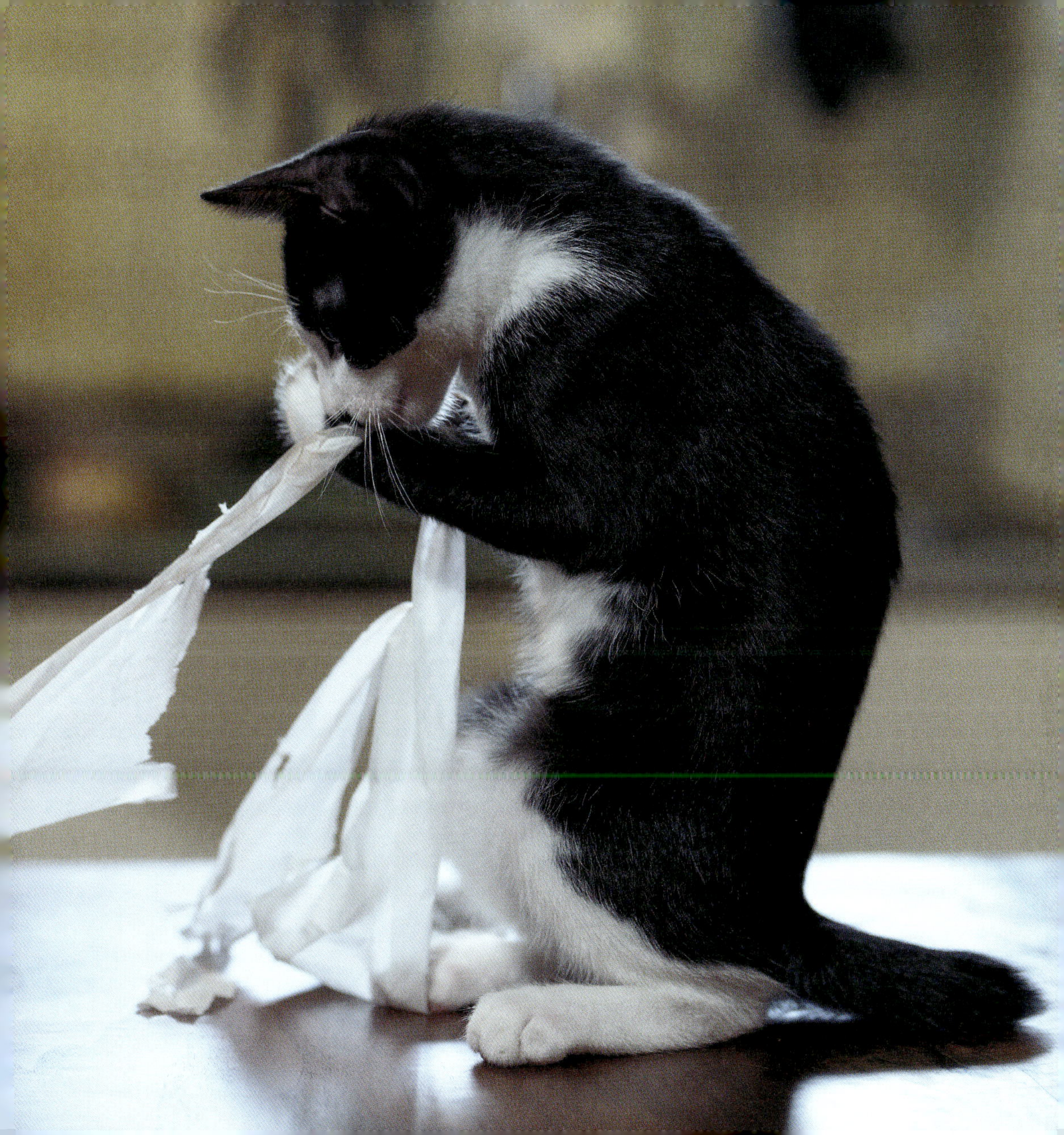

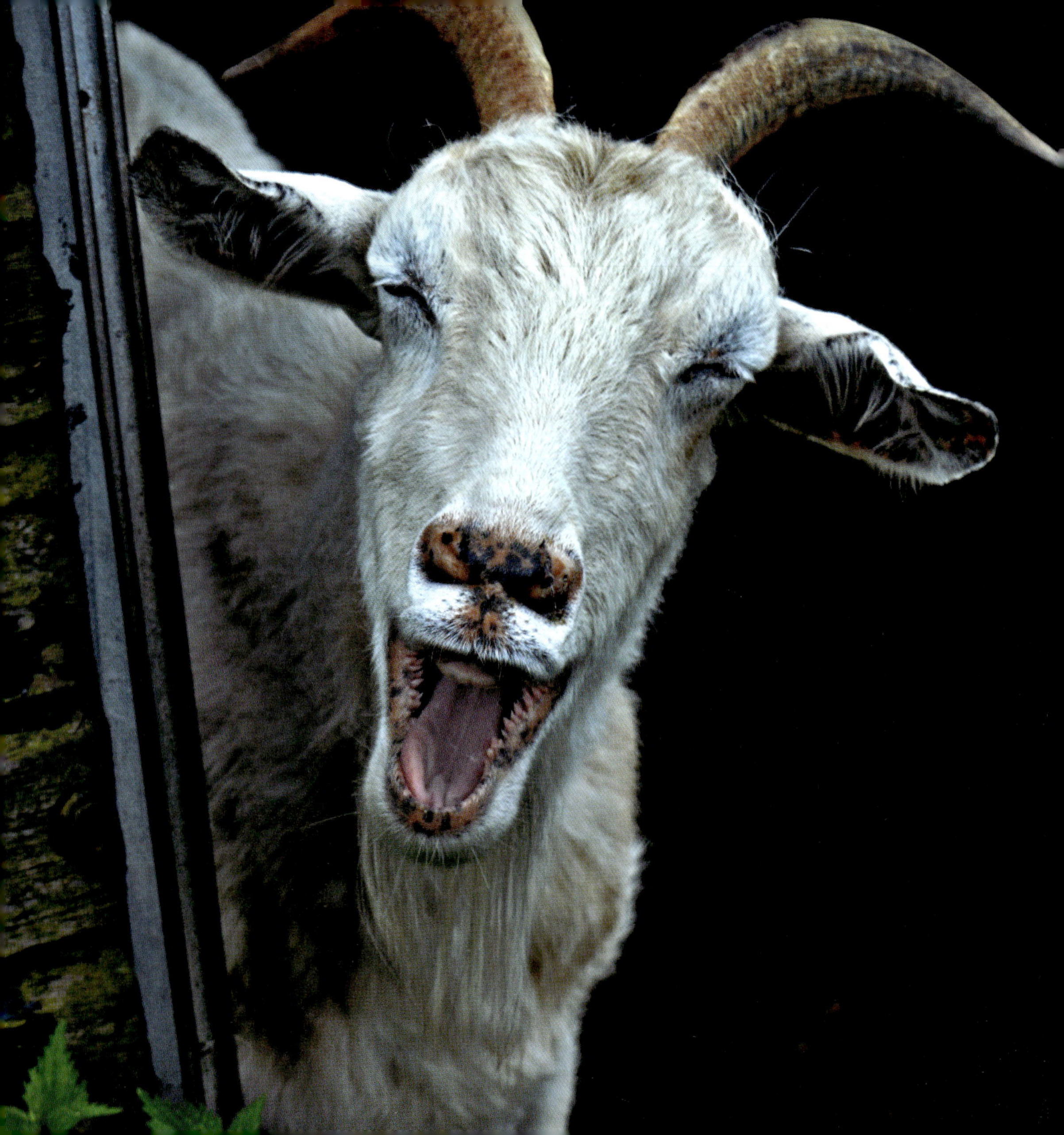

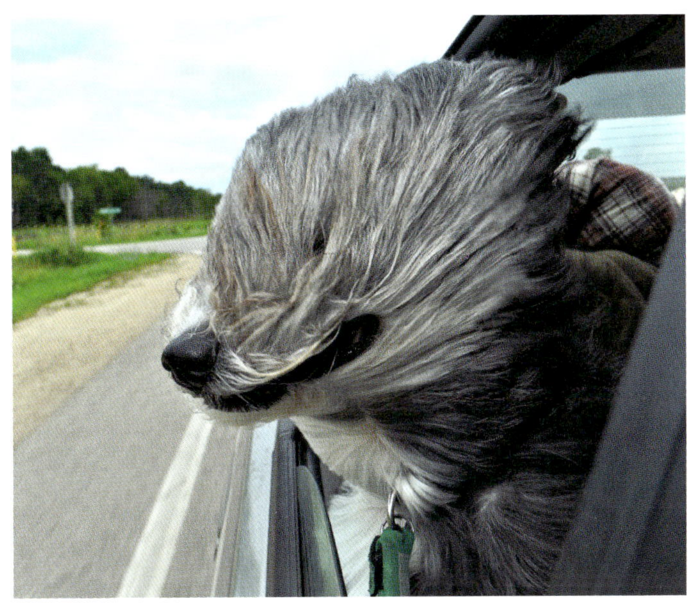

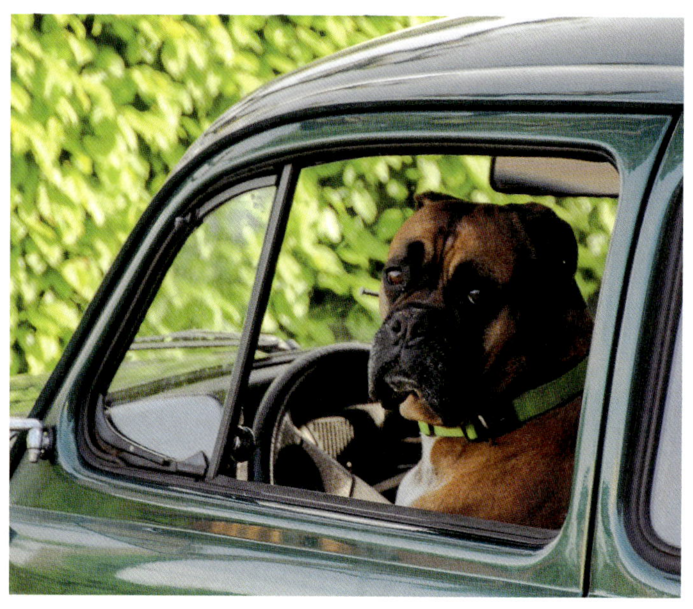

LOCATION: SWITZERLAND
Anything the matter, officer?
PHOTOGRAPHER: Theres Schlienger

LOCATION: COLUMBUS, UNITED STATES
This is going to go down a treat.
PHOTOGRAPHER: Connie Fore

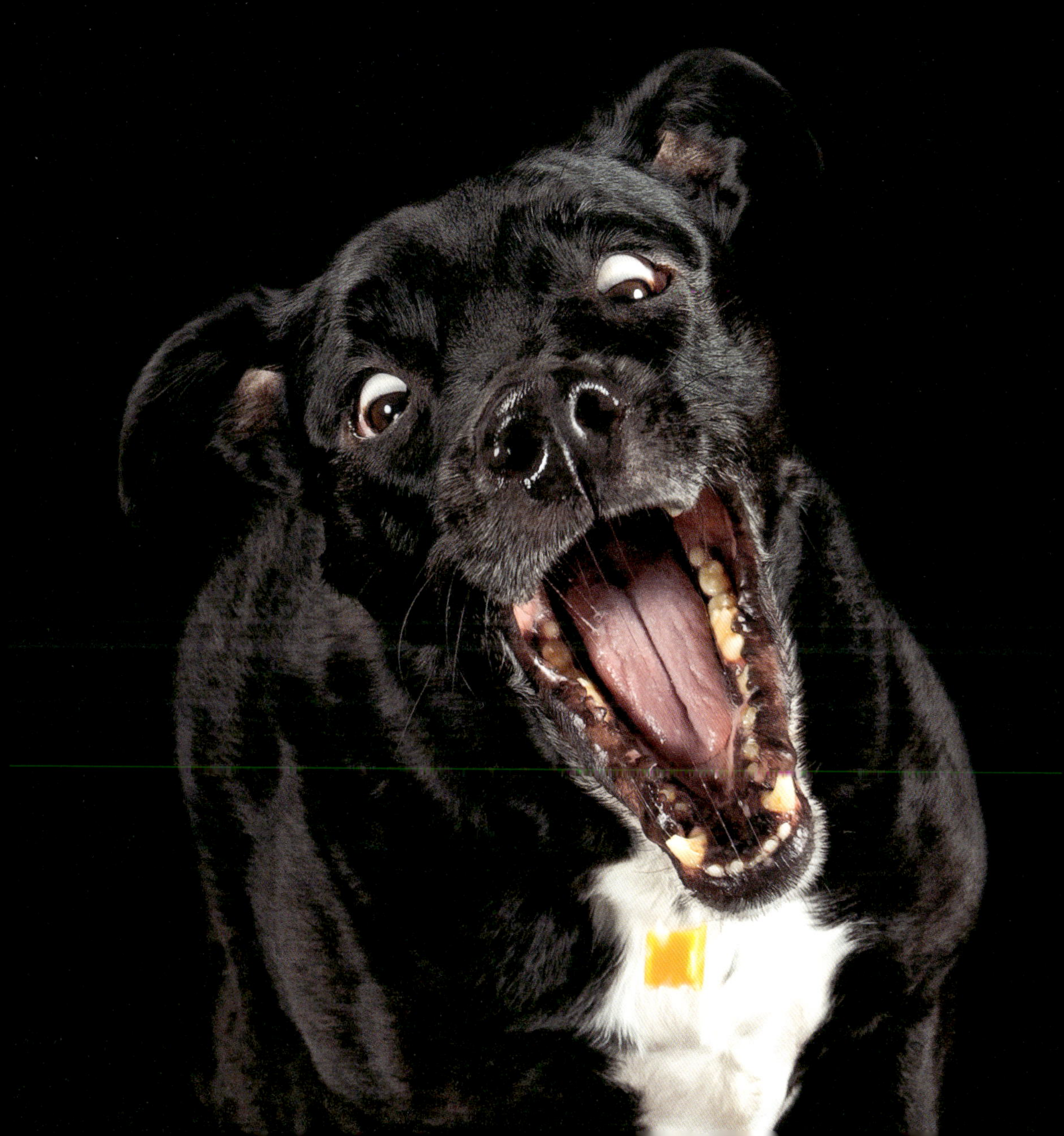

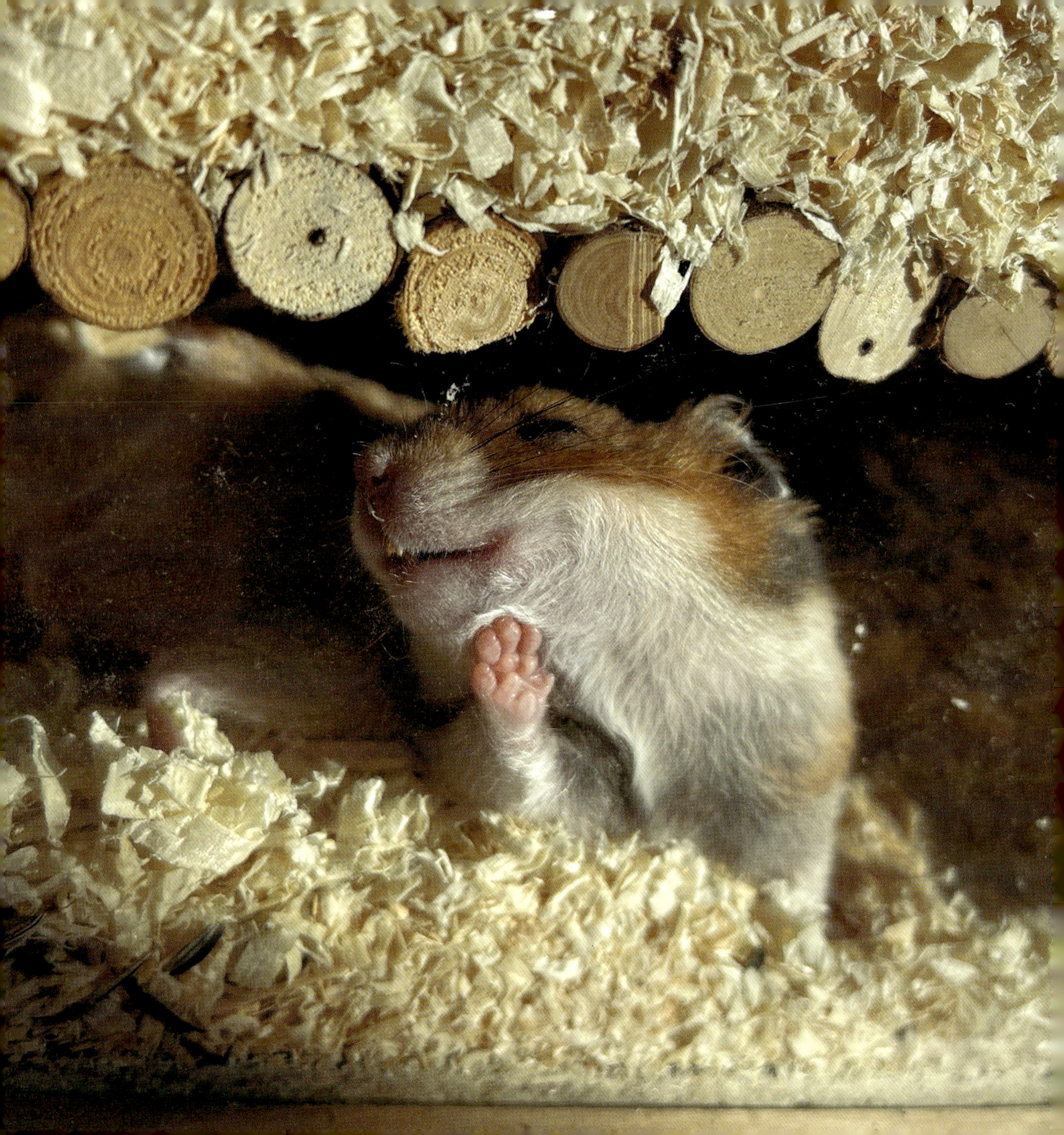

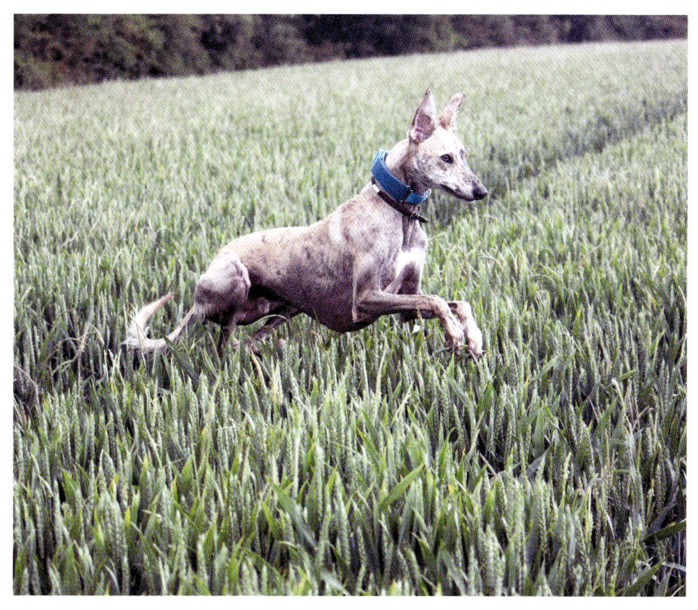

LOCATION: UNITED KINGDOM
Lurchers really go against the grain.
PHOTOGRAPHER: Katie Alder

LOCATION: GERMANY
They've gone all out on the hamster accommodation,
but where's a pillow when you need one?!
PHOTOGRAPHER: Alina Vogel

LOCATION: UNITED KINGDOM

That's the way to travel – wind in your whiskers.

PHOTOGRAPHER: Simon DeKnock

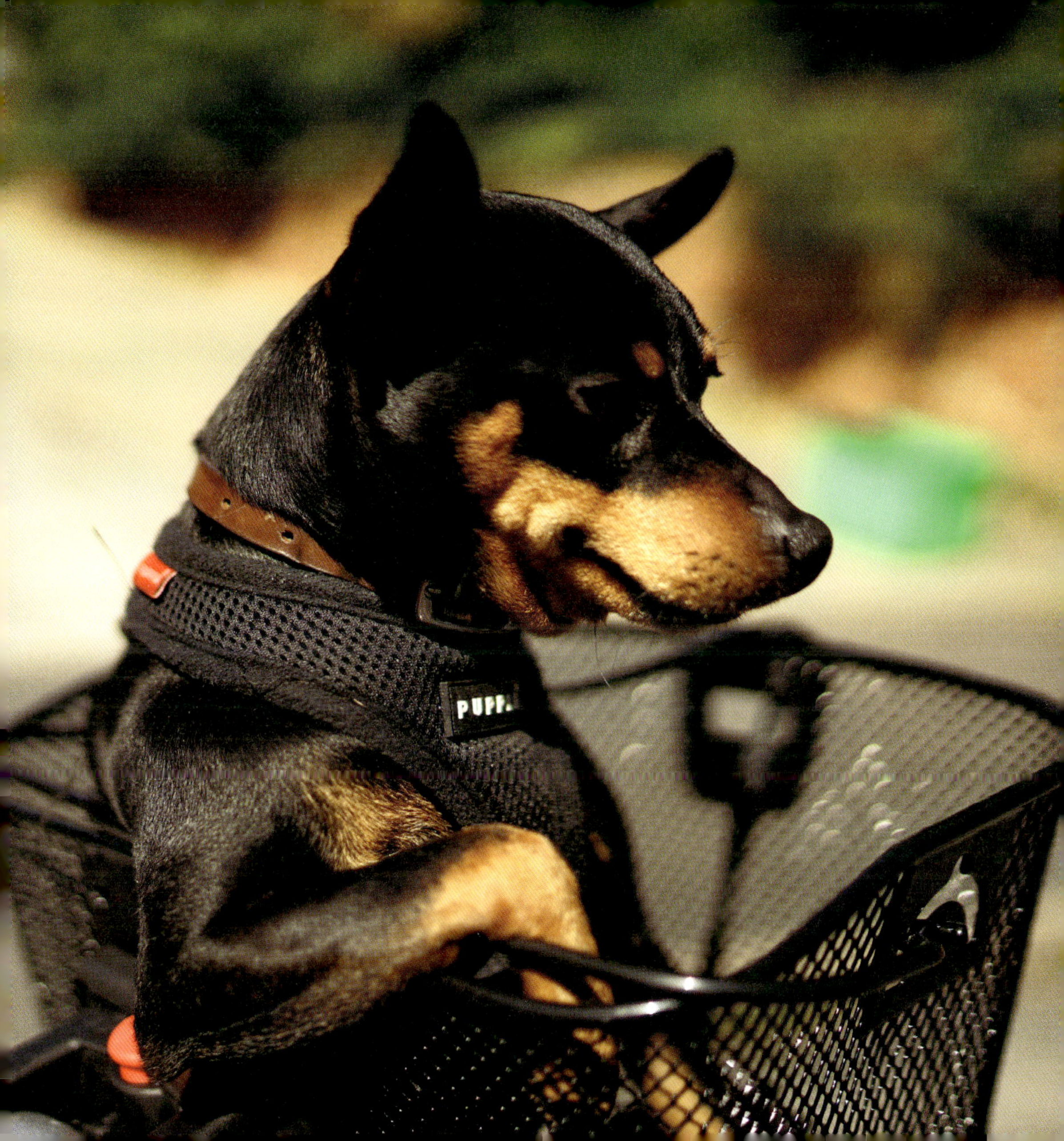

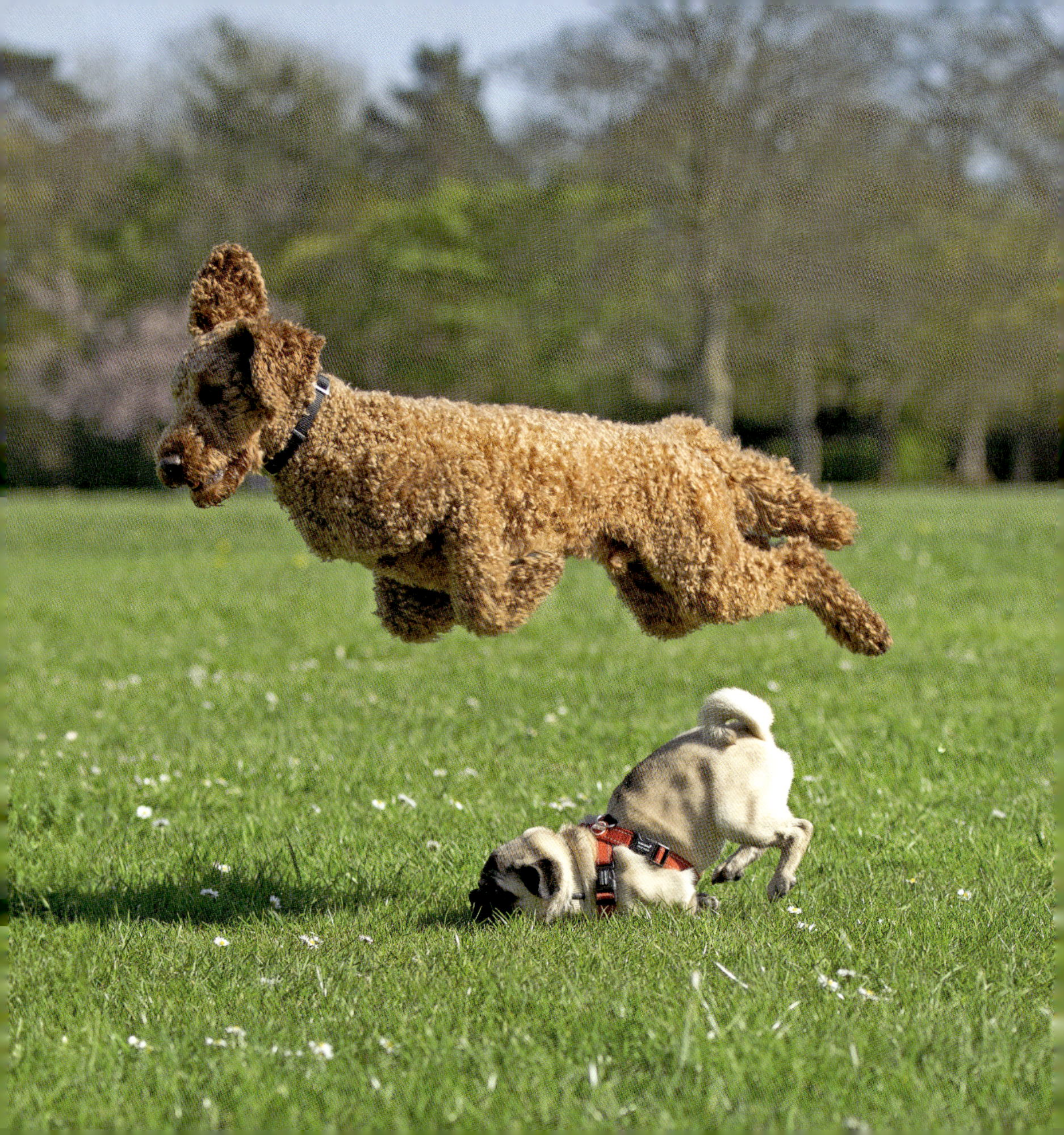

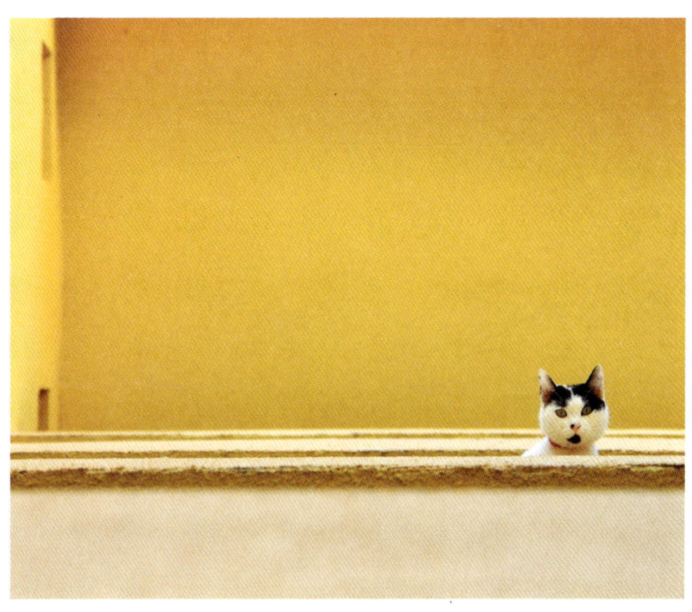

LOCATION: SUCEAVA, ROMANIA

Can I have my ball back purrlease?

PHOTOGRAPHER: Gabriel Constantin Marian

LOCATION: LANCASHIRE, UNITED KINGDOM

This Pug throws everything at the Poodle Javelin event.

PHOTOGRAPHER: Gill Woodcock

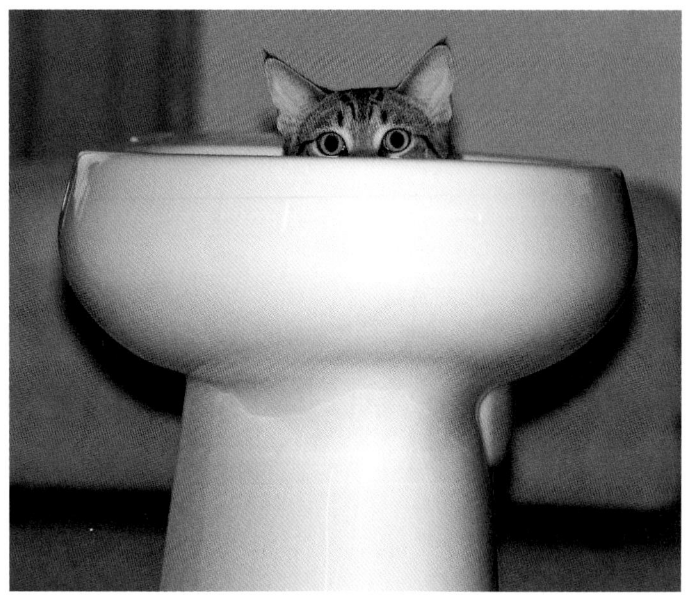

LOCATION: ILLINOIS, UNITED STATES
Can someone get meowt of here?
PHOTOGRAPHER: John Banas

LOCATION: SIOUX FALLS, UNITED STATES
There's something wrong with the throttle.
PHOTOGRAPHER: Annie McMillan

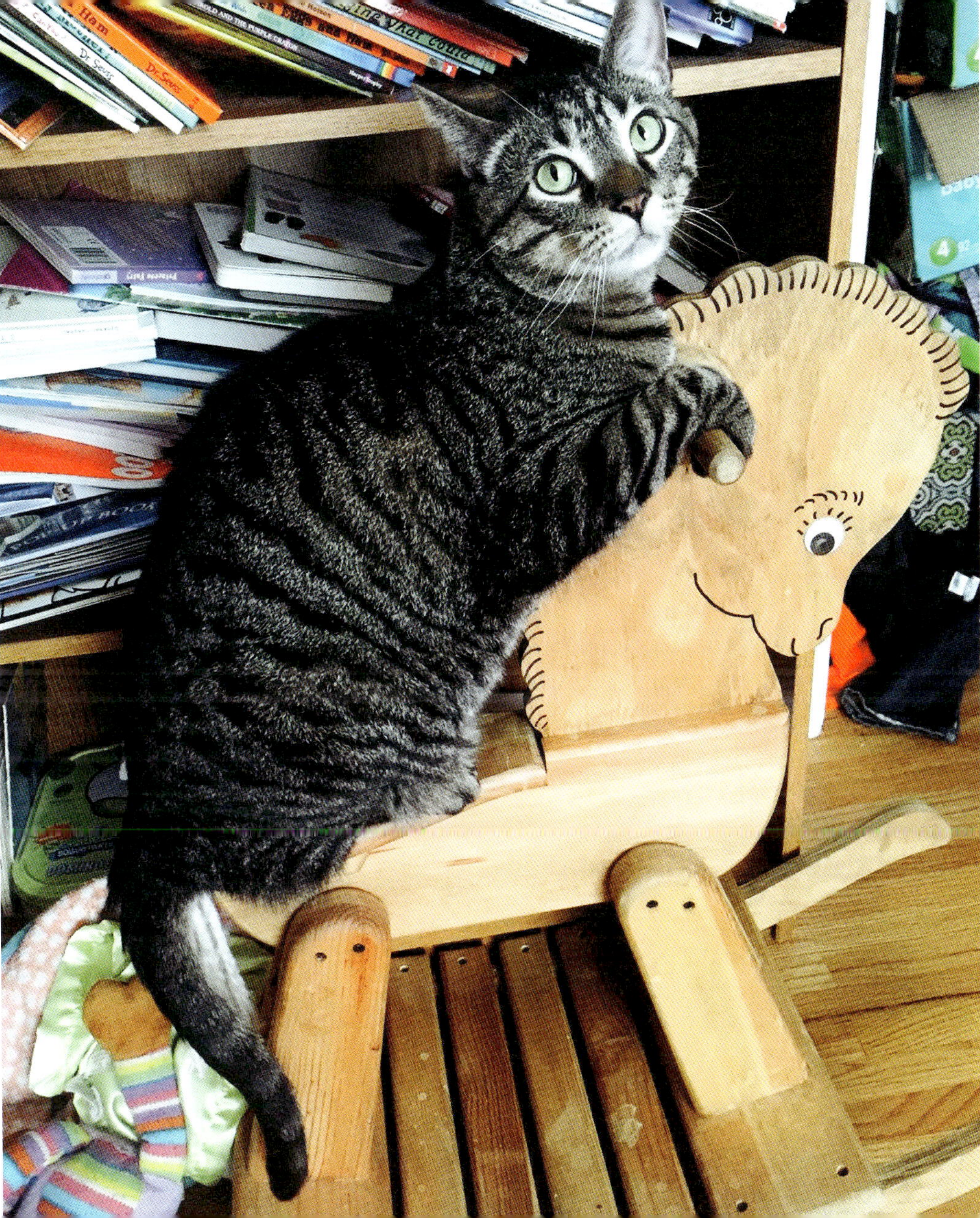

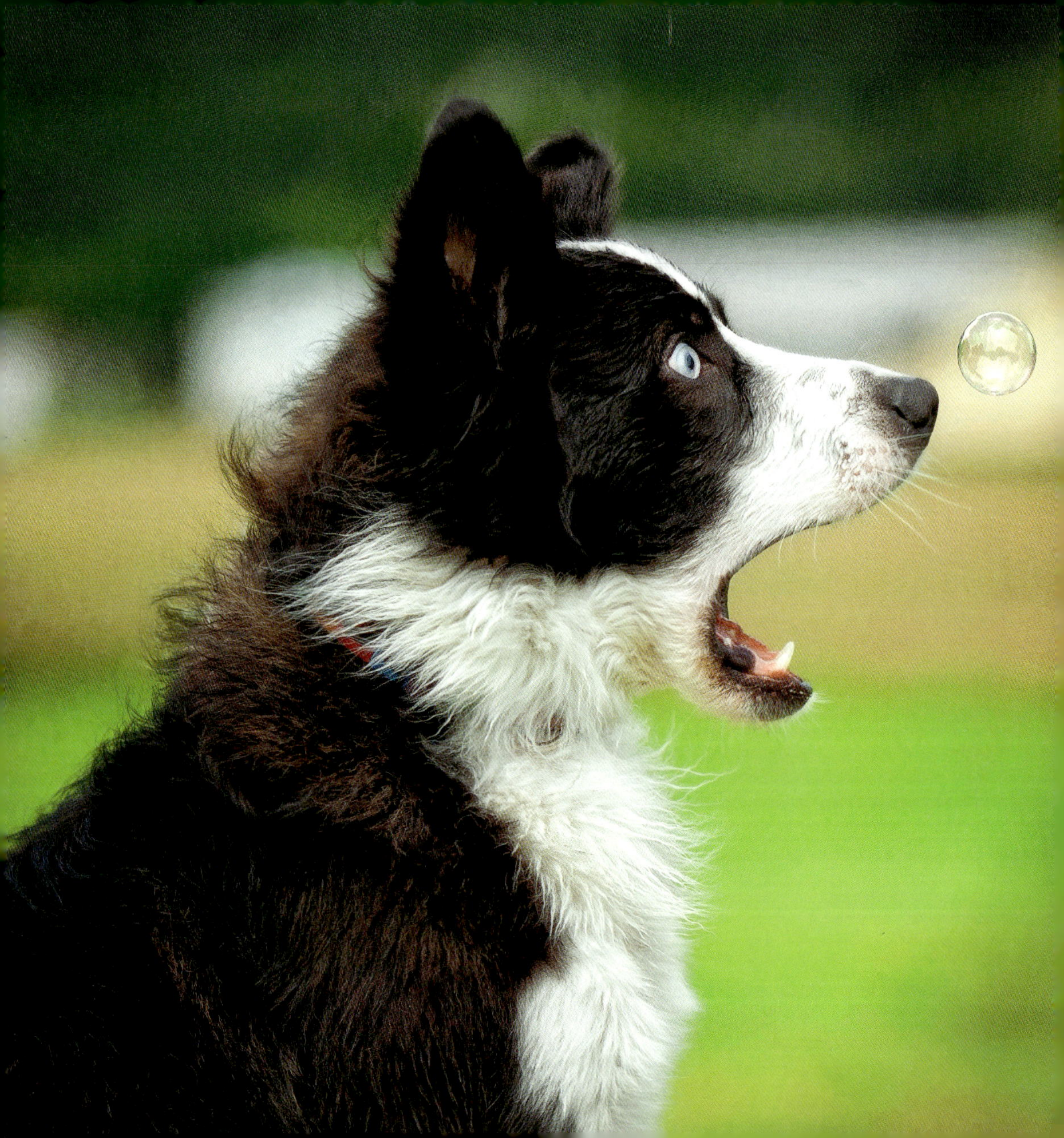

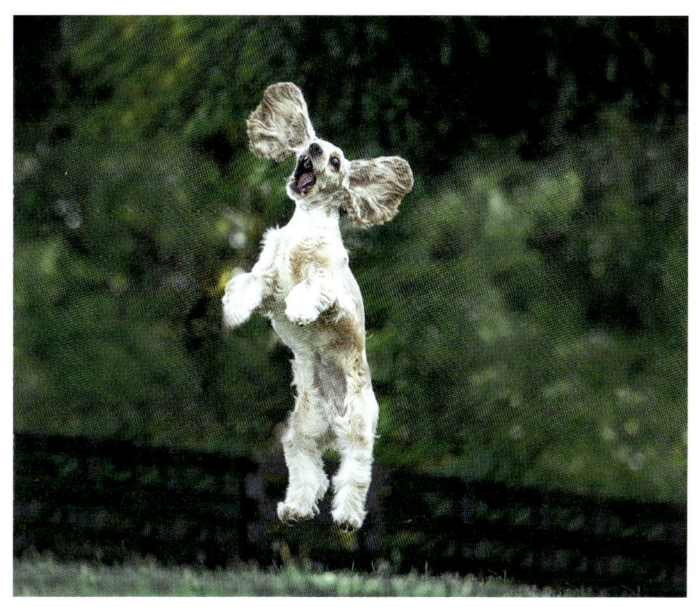

LOCATION: FRANKLIN, UNITED STATES
It's funny how much a leaping Spaniel looks like a novelty bow tie.
PHOTOGRAPHER: Jim Zuckerman

LOCATION: HARVARD, UNITED STATES
Wow – there's a tiny Collie in the bubble!
PHOTOGRAPHER: Connie Fore

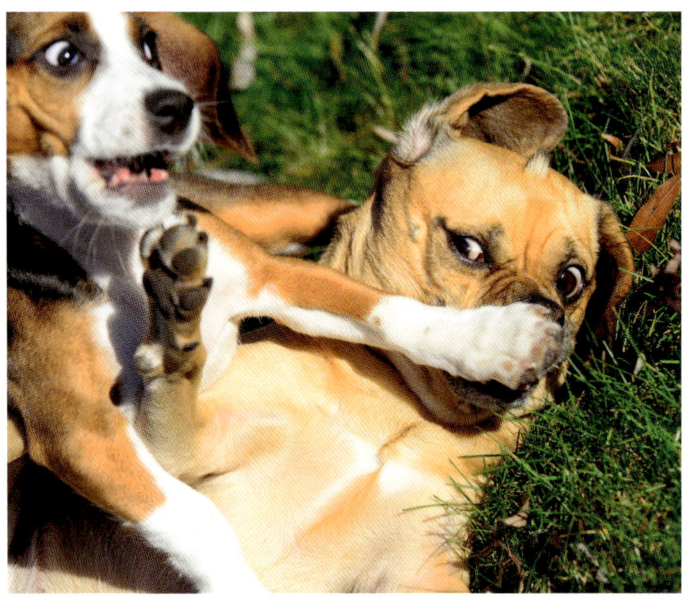

LOCATION: GRAND RAPID, UNITED STATES
Got your nose!
PHOTOGRAPHER: Nathan Schmidt

LOCATION: ALBION, UNITED STATES
This other cat keeps moving whenever I move!
PHOTOGRAPHER: Ariel Berry

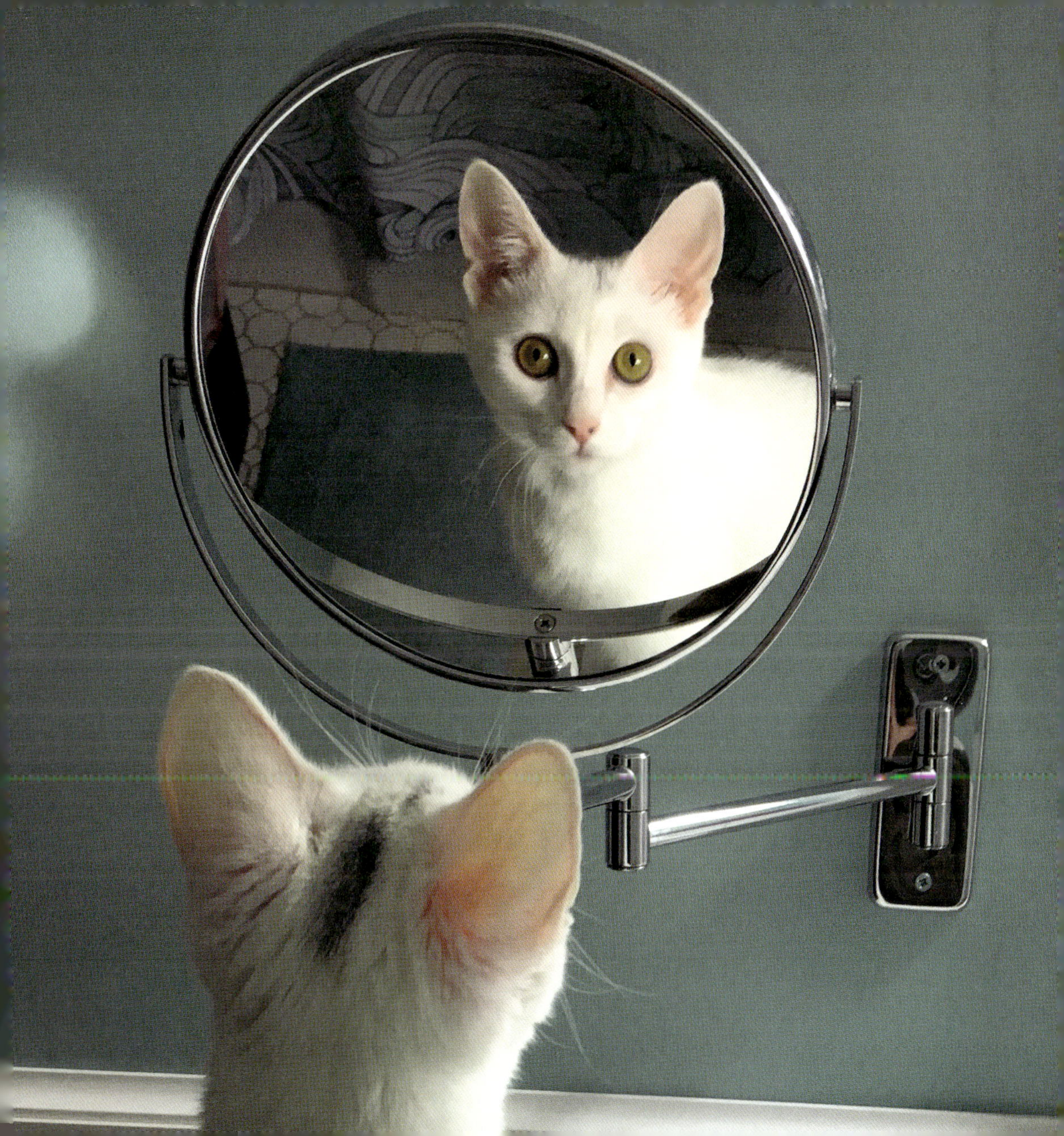

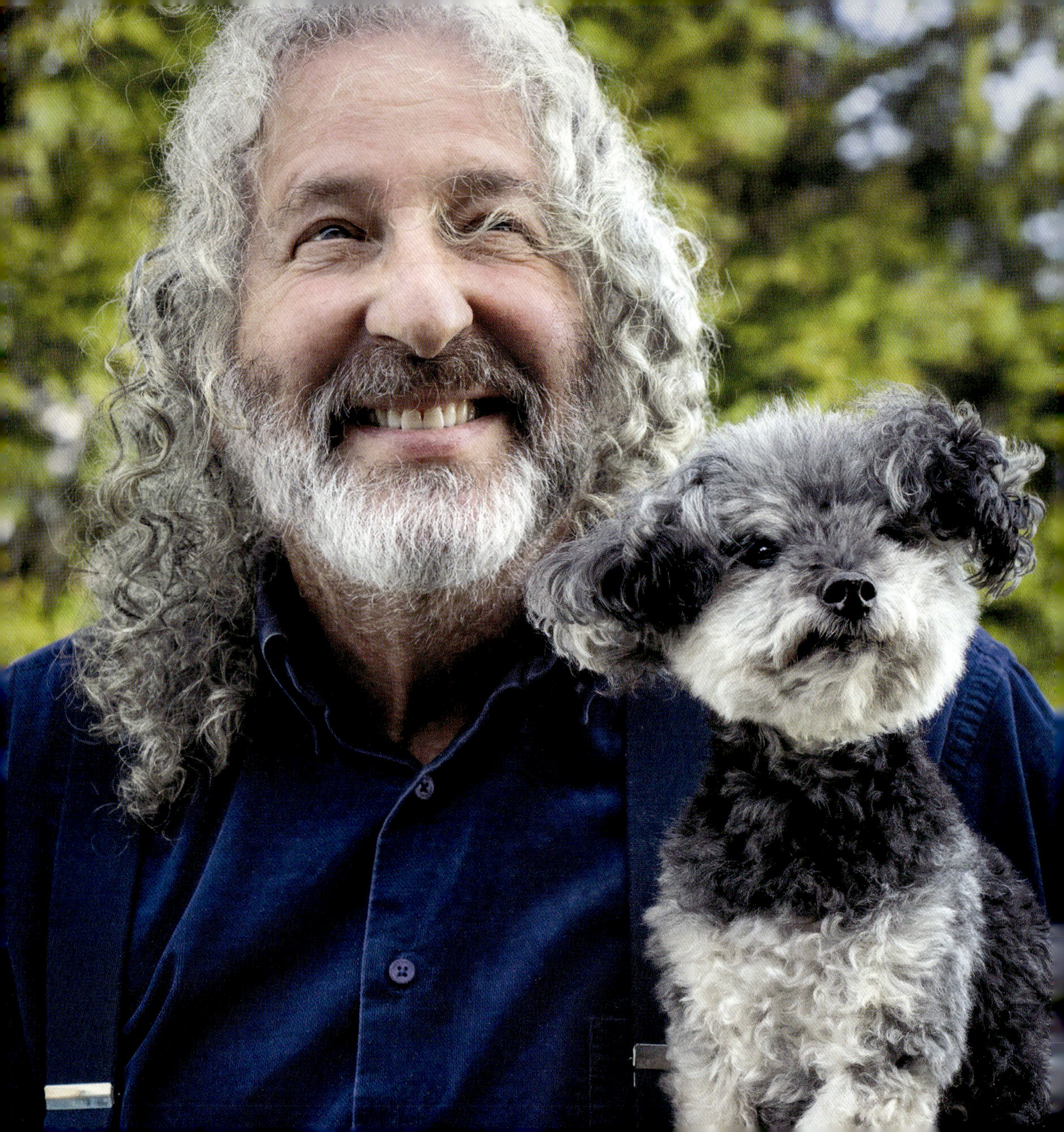

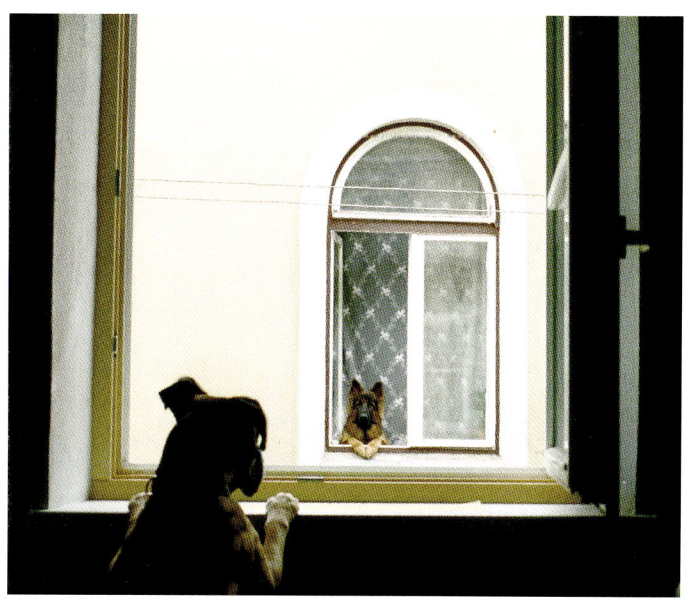

LOCATION: LITHUANIA
Good morning, neighbour!
PHOTOGRAPHER: Stasys Povilaitis

LOCATION: UNITED STATES
They say owners and their pets end up looking alike,
but I don't know if there's any truth in it.
PHOTOGRAPHER: Darya Zelentsova

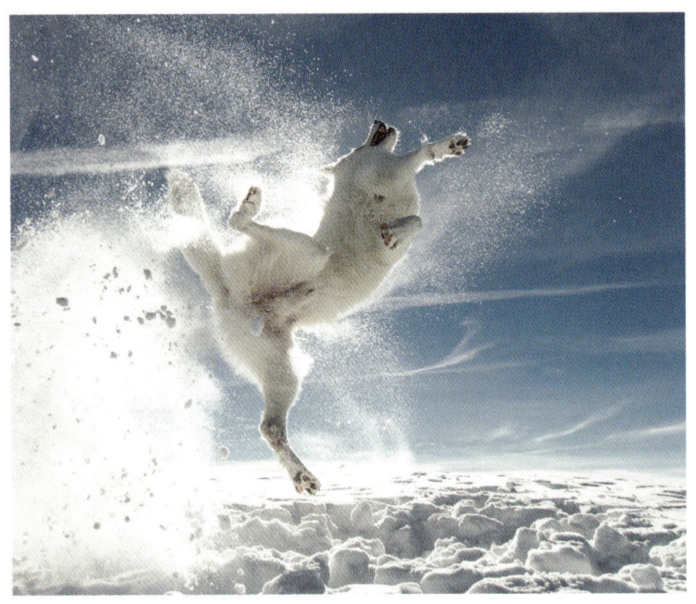

LOCATION: SWITZERLAND
They really do give it the beans for the
Arctic FoxTrot.
PHOTOGRAPHER: Sylvia Michel

LOCATION: ISRAEL
He's just heard the one about the donkey with two bottoms –
he was biased.
PHOTOGRAPHER: Nir Natan

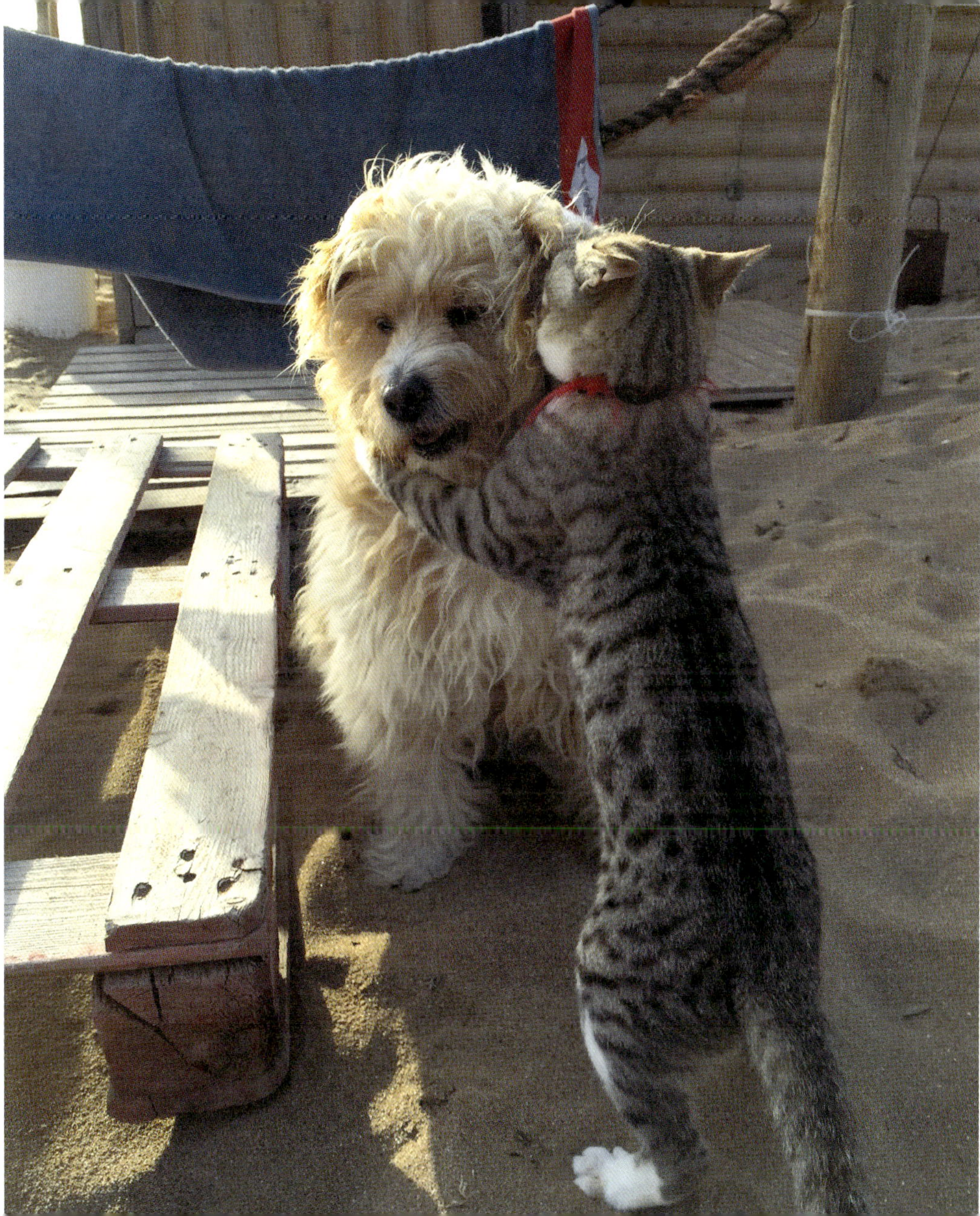

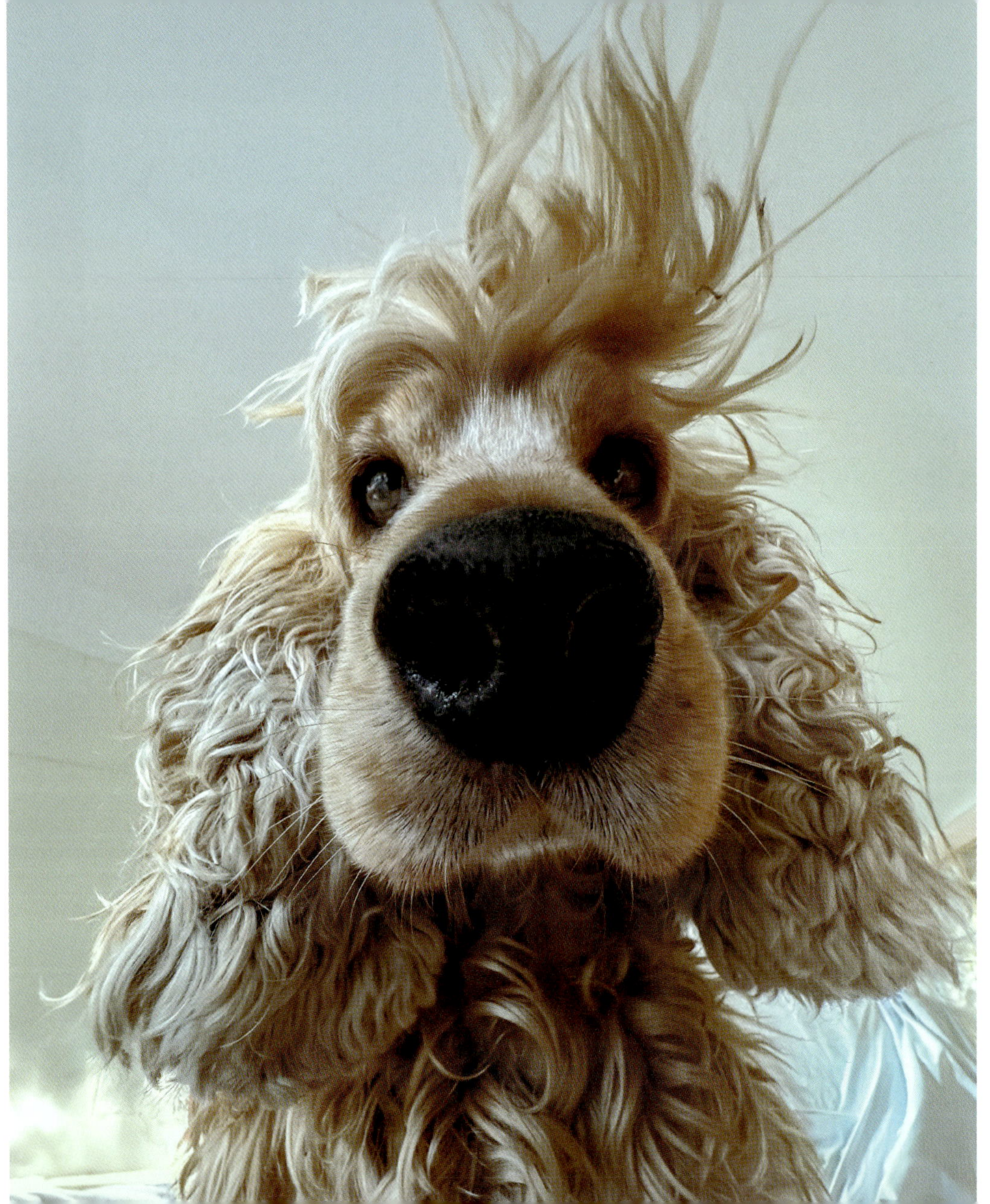

LOCATION: GENT, BELGIUM
You've heard of the downward dog.
Well here's the upward cat pose.
PHOTOGRAPHER: Brecht Van Gampelaere

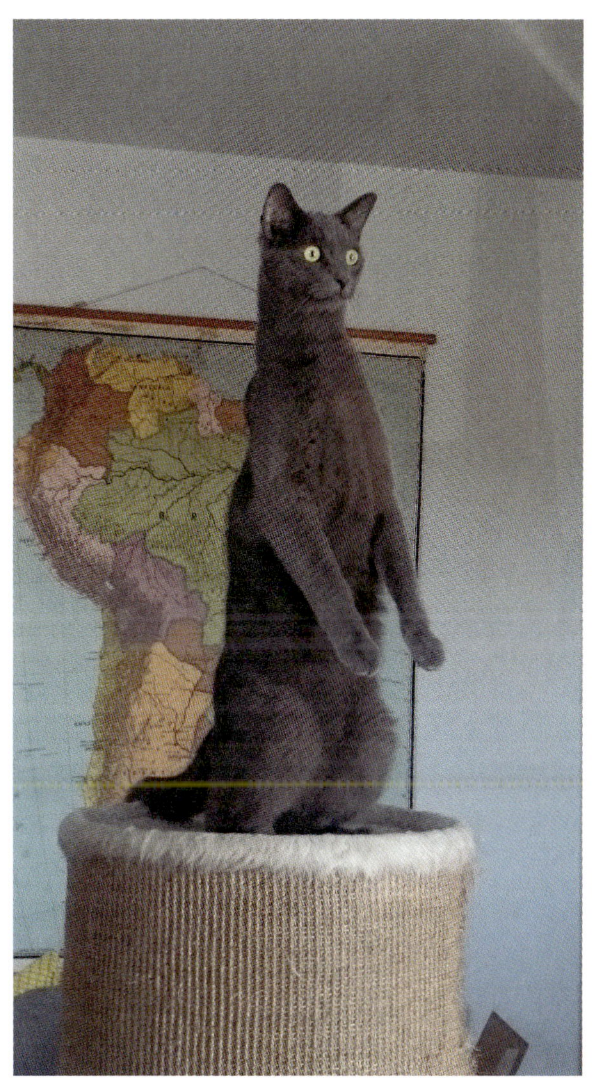

LOCATION: CHINA
Animal or human, this is how all
our first selfies look.
PHOTOGRAPHER: Lock Lui

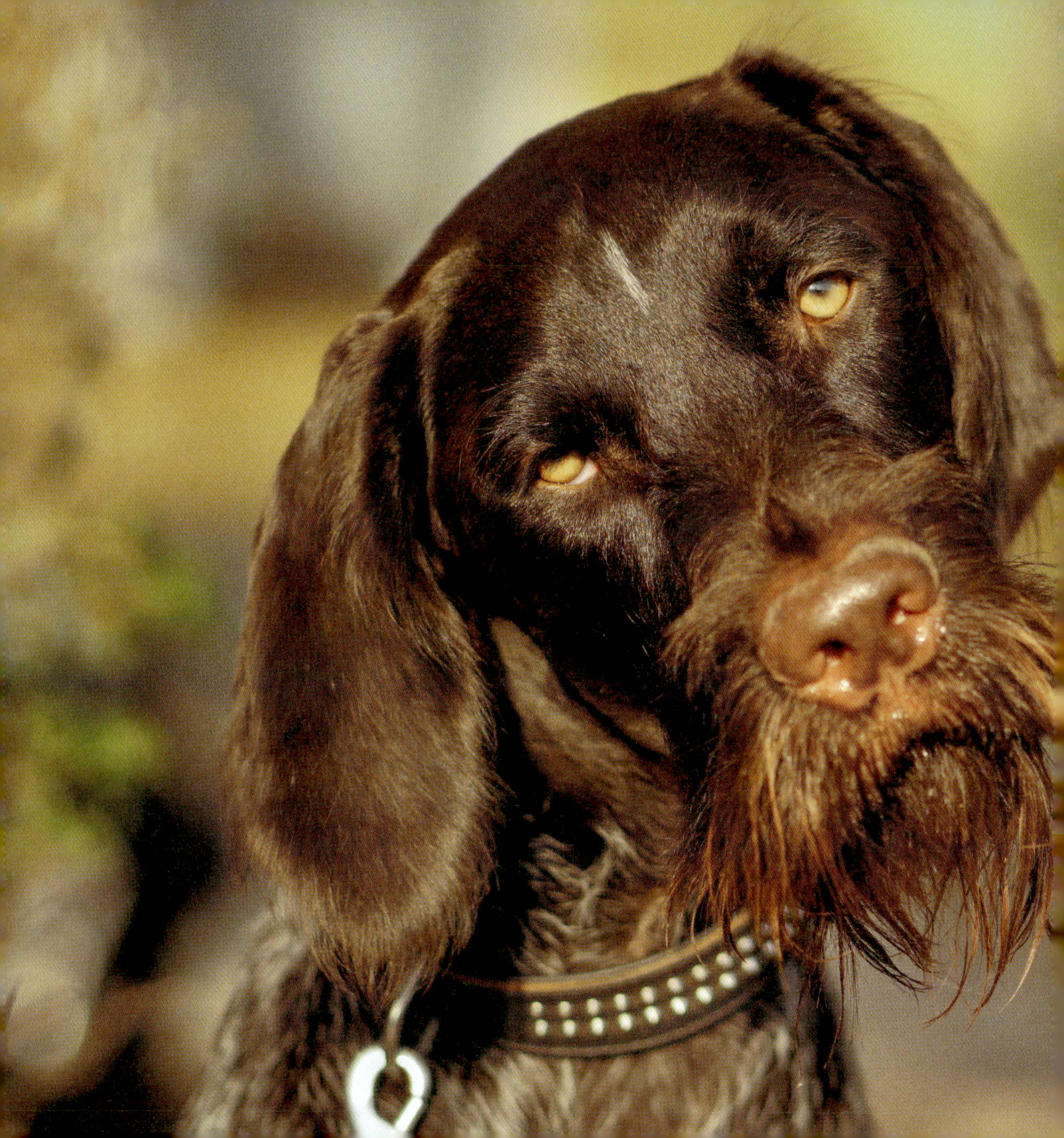

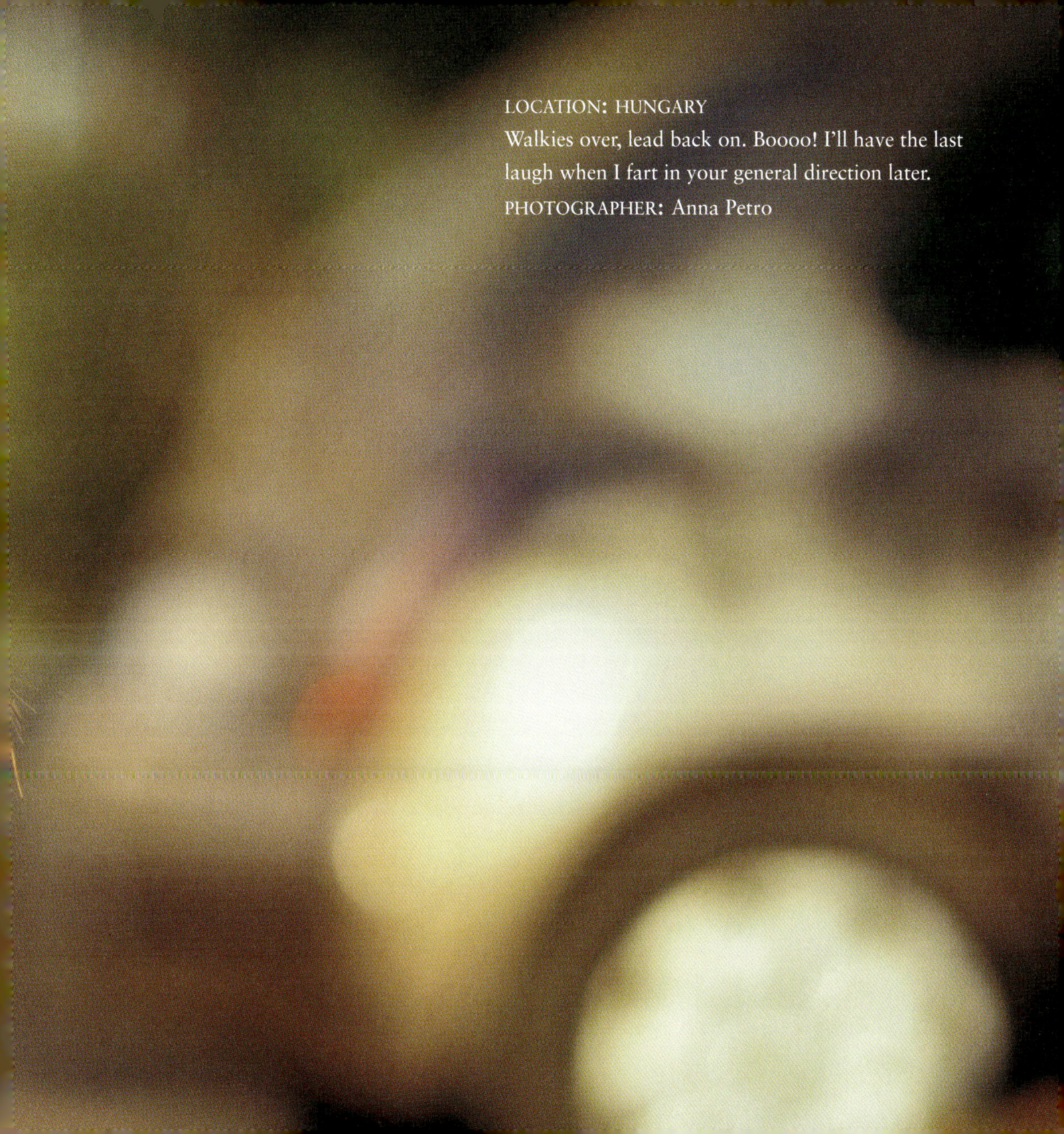

LOCATION: HUNGARY
Walkies over, lead back on. Boooo! I'll have the last
laugh when I fart in your general direction later.
PHOTOGRAPHER: Anna Petro

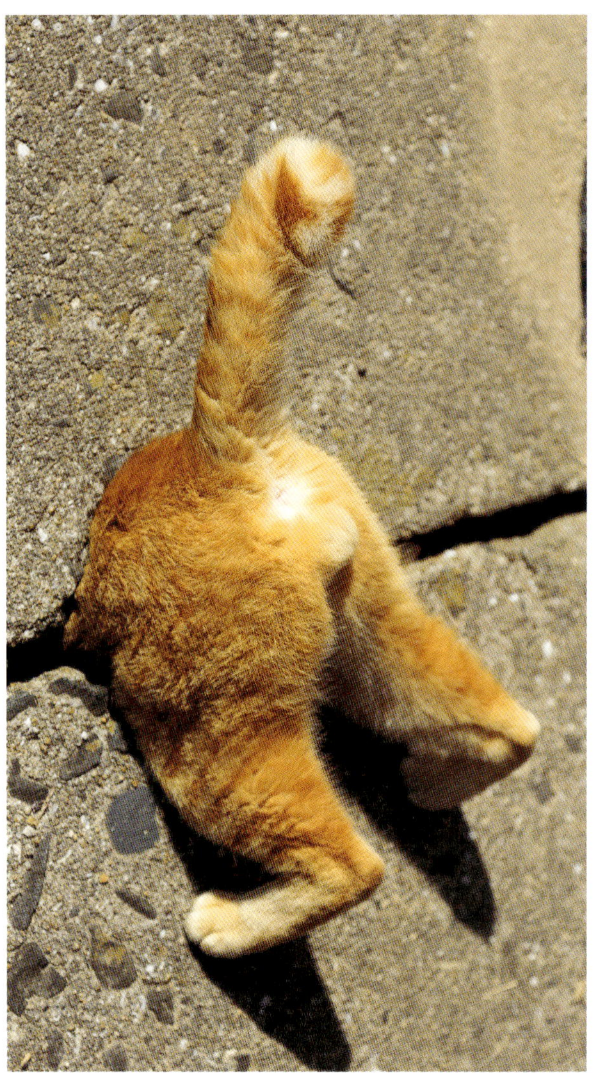

LOCATION: JAPAN
I think that's what's known
as a bum deal.
PHOTOGRAPHER: Kenichi Morinaga

LOCATION: GERMANY
Rocking the Kurt Cobain look for
karaoke night at the stables.
PHOTOGRAPHER: Annett Mirsberger

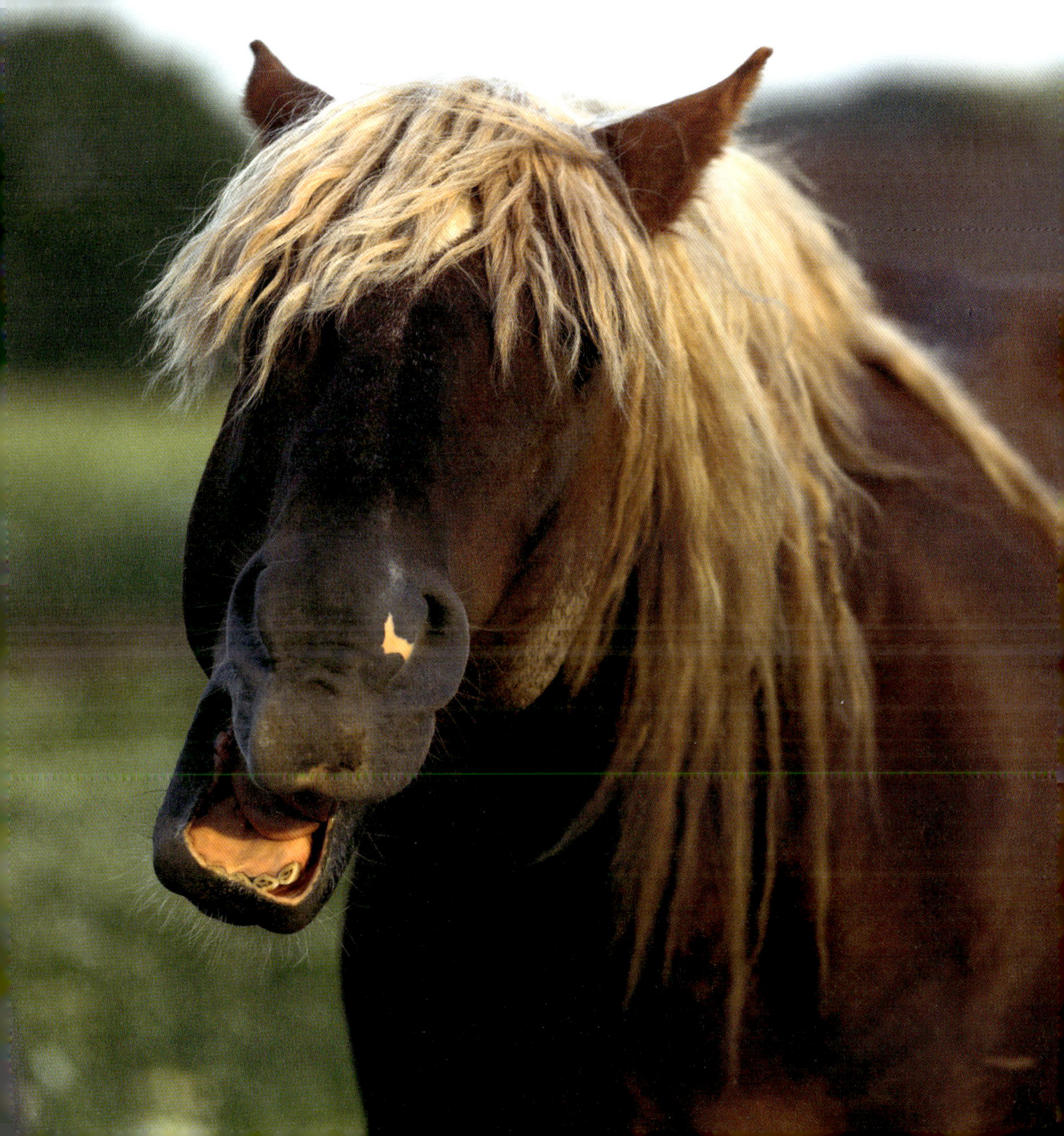

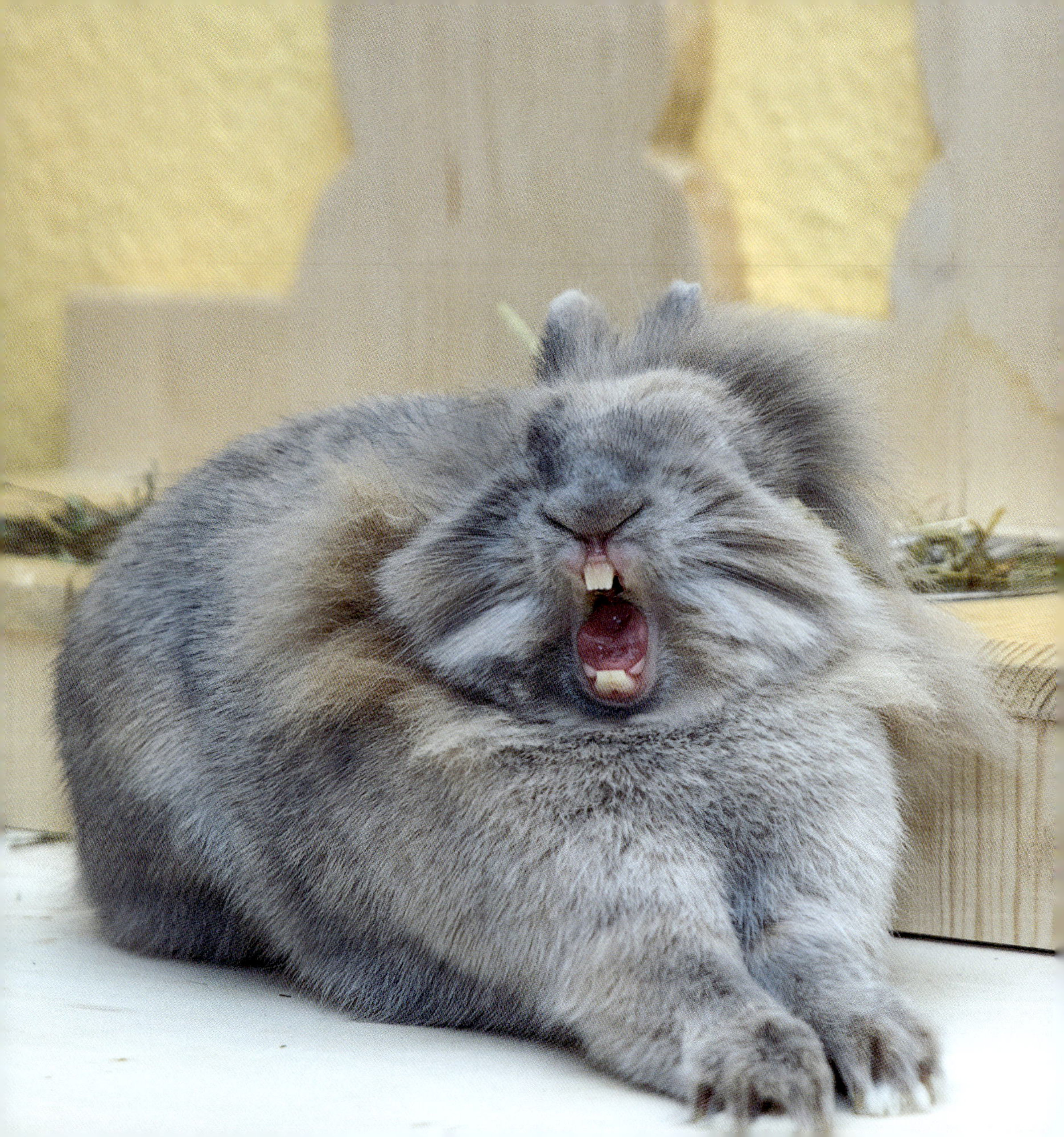

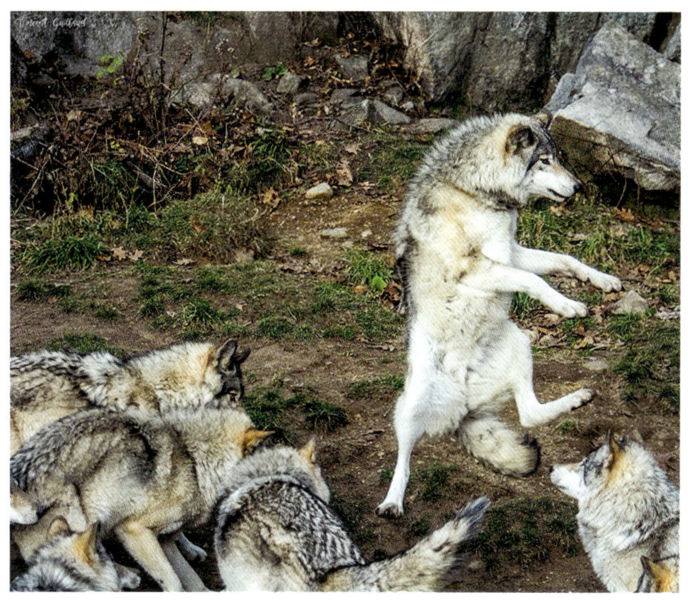

LOCATION: FRANCE

Dances with wolves.

PHOTOGRAPHER: Vincent Guilbaud

LOCATION: GERMANY

This drama queen was most displeased by the
lack of carrot in the amuse bouches.

PHOTOGRAPHER: Anne Lindner

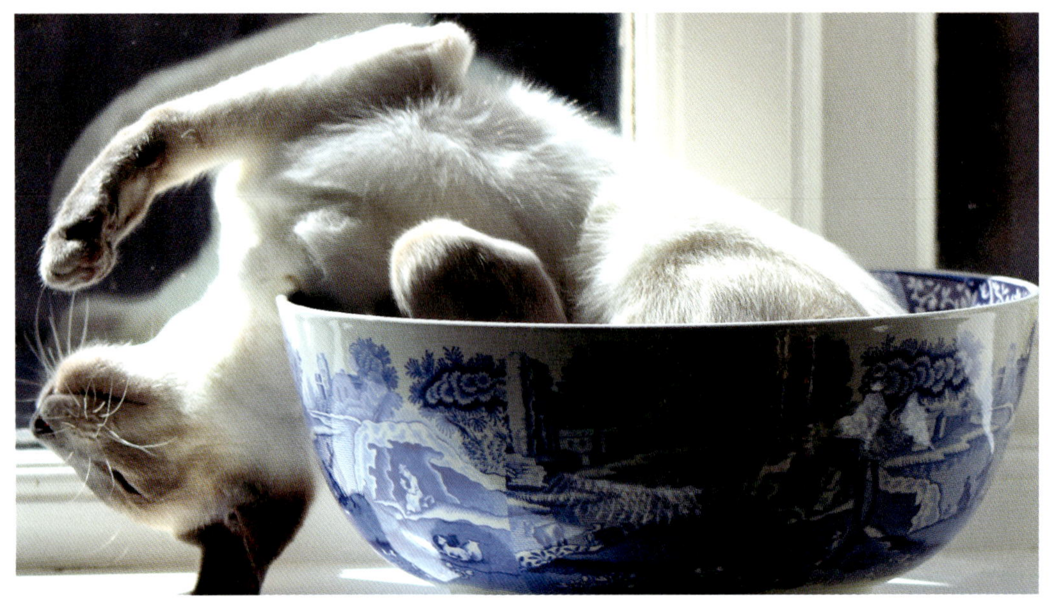

LOCATION: WILLINGHAM, UNITED KINGDOM
It's a new dawn, it's a new day, and I'm feline good.
PHOTOGRAPHER: Annette Edgar

LOCATION: NEW JERSEY, UNITED STATES
The famous shadow puppet duo call this creation 'Kangaroo vs Giant Butterfly'.
PHOTOGRAPHER: Barb Wentzel

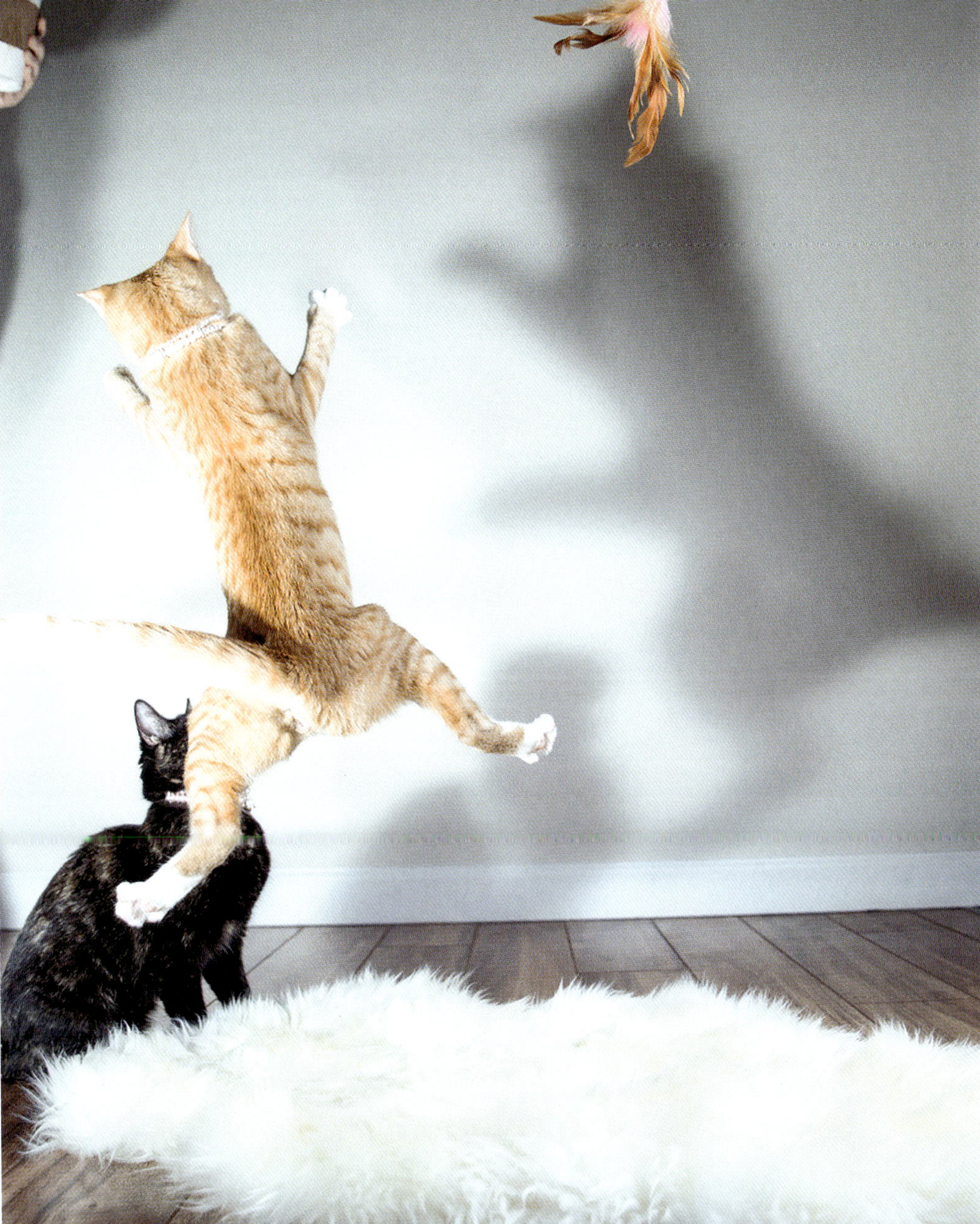

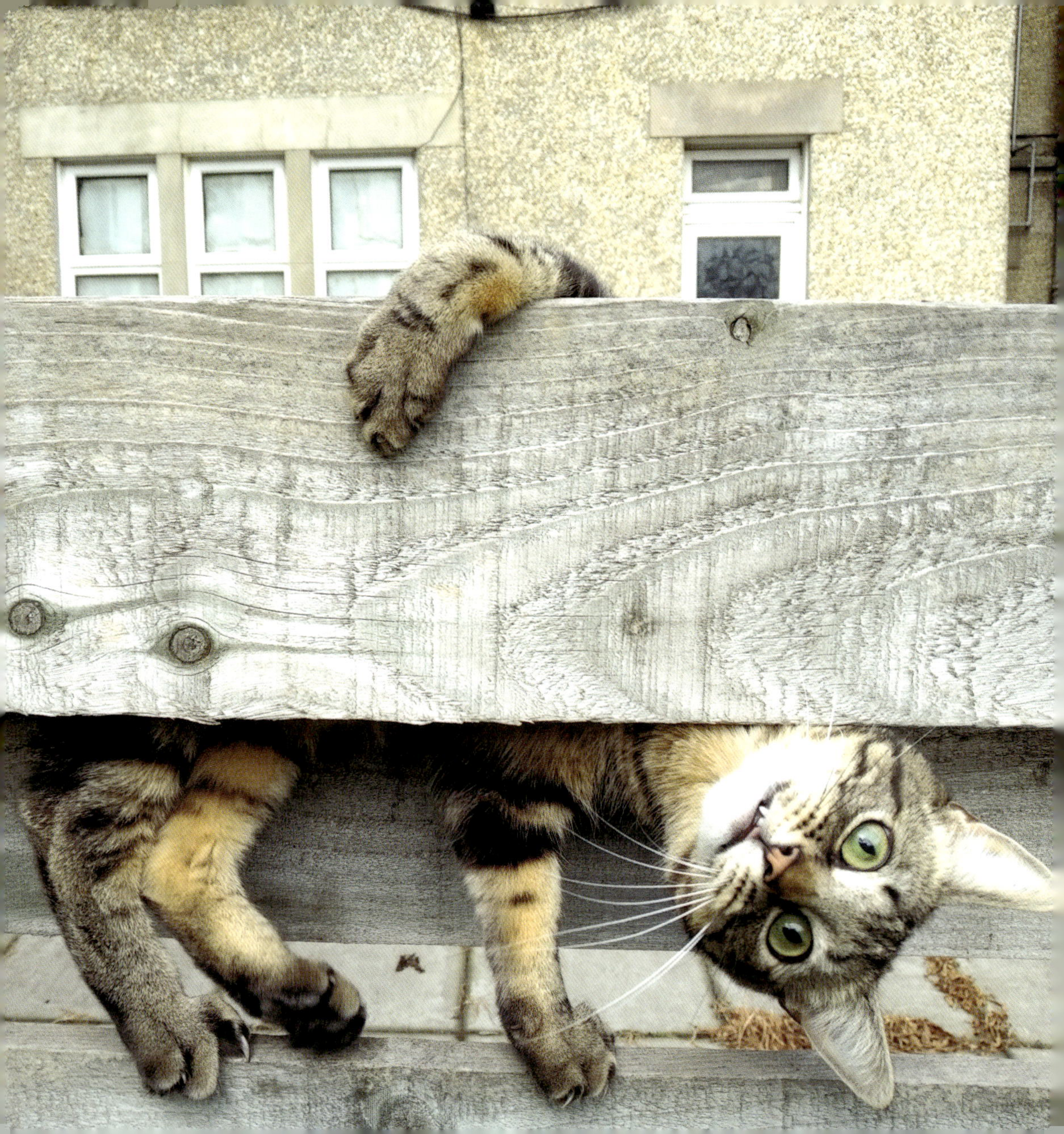

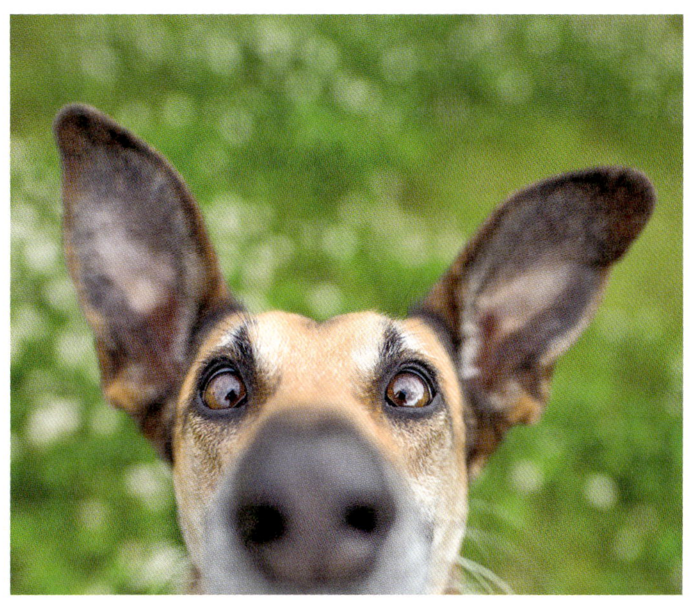

LOCATION: GERMANY

Sometimes it's better to have friends in low places.

PHOTOGRAPHER: Elke Vogelsang

LOCATION: SCOTLAND

Limbo dancing fail.

PHOTOGRAPHER: Malgorzata Russell

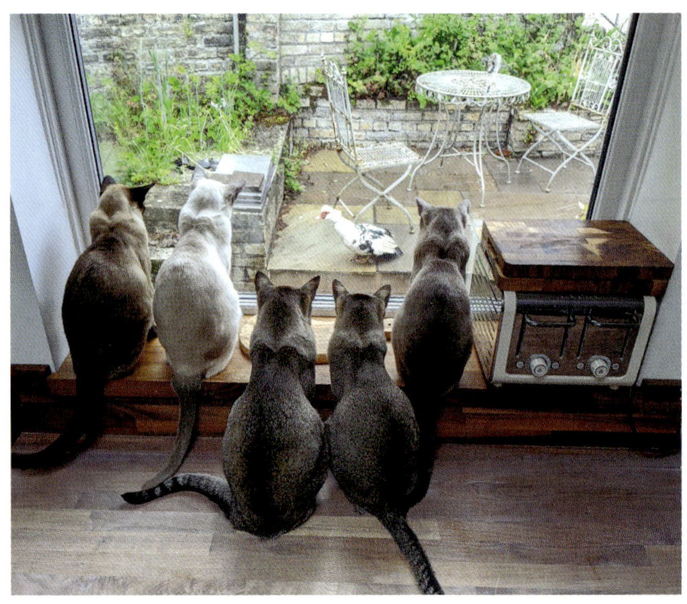

LOCATION: UNITED KINGDOM
There's a goose loose about this hoose.
PHOTOGRAPHER: Beth Noble

LOCATION: UNITED KINGDOM
It's much cheaper than a trip to the dental hygienist!
PHOTOGRAPHER: Lianne Richards

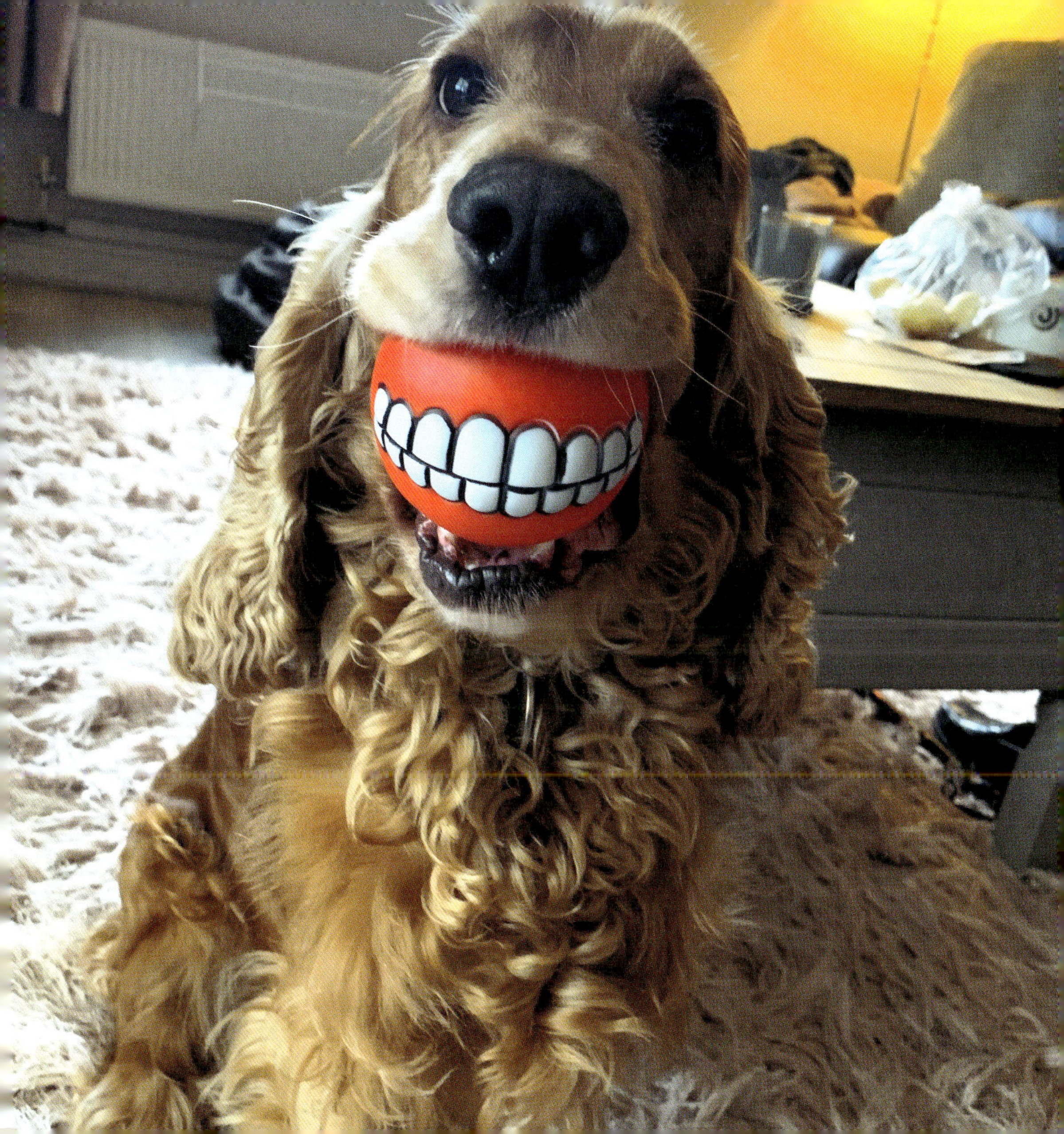

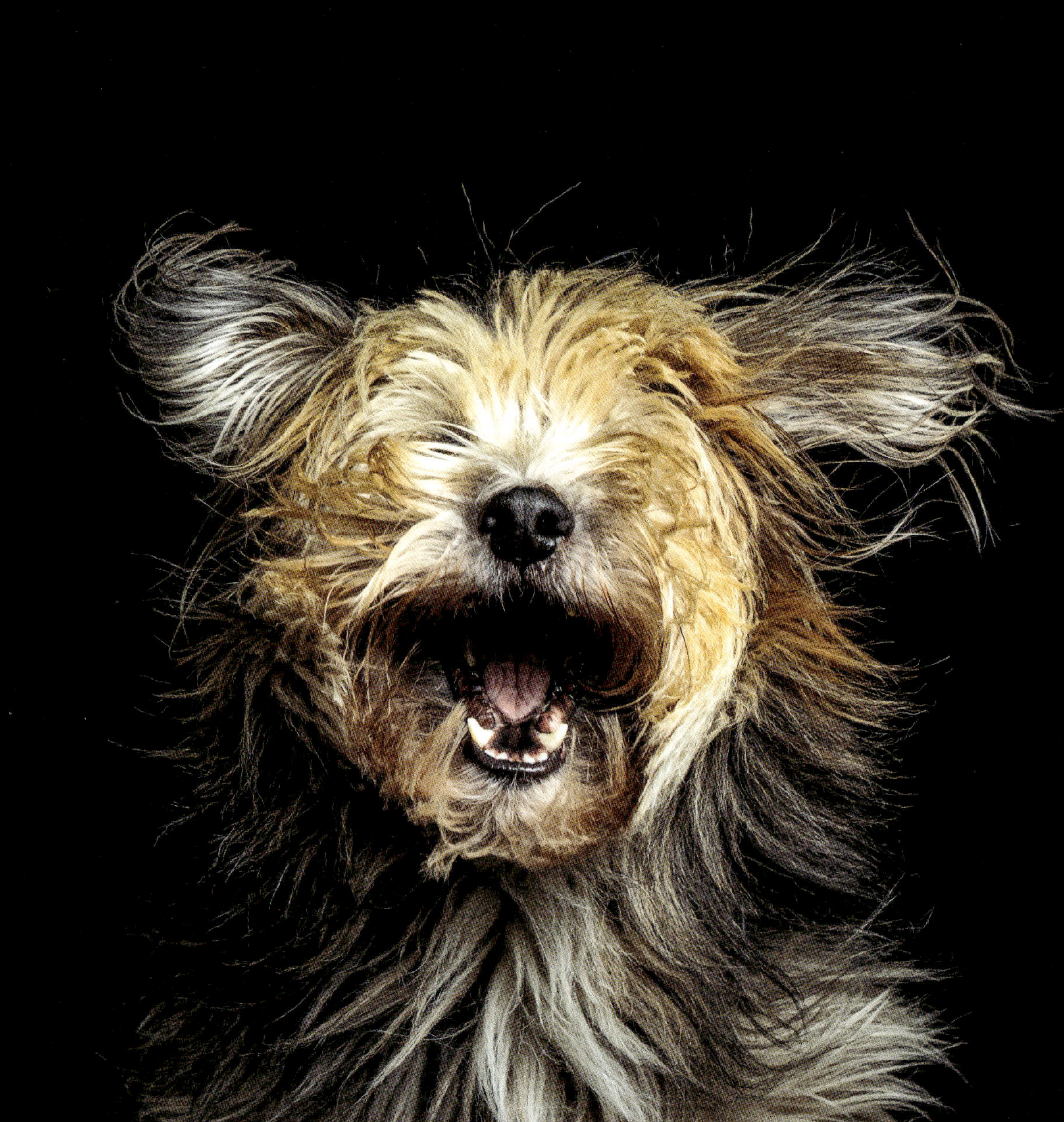

LOCATION: JAPAN
Hang on, which of us is hiding
and which of us is seeking?!
PHOTOGRAPHER: Yasuda
Aburanekomaru

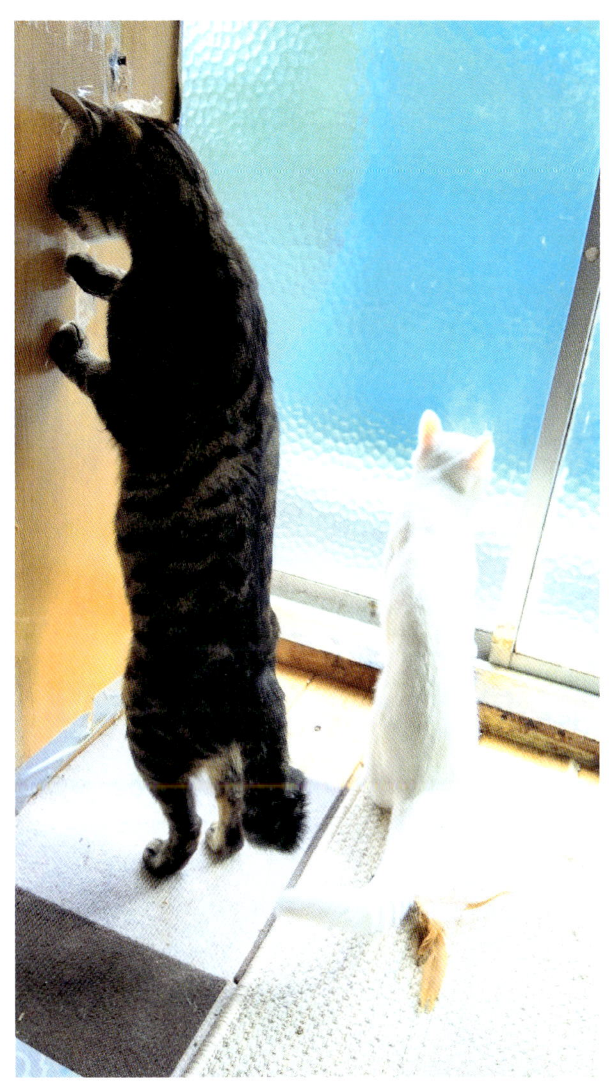

LOCATION: NETHERLANDS
Because she's woof it.
PHOTOGRAPHER: Hetwie van der Putten

LOCATION: SPAIN

Go-to goat relaxation.

PHOTOGRAPHER: Robert Prat

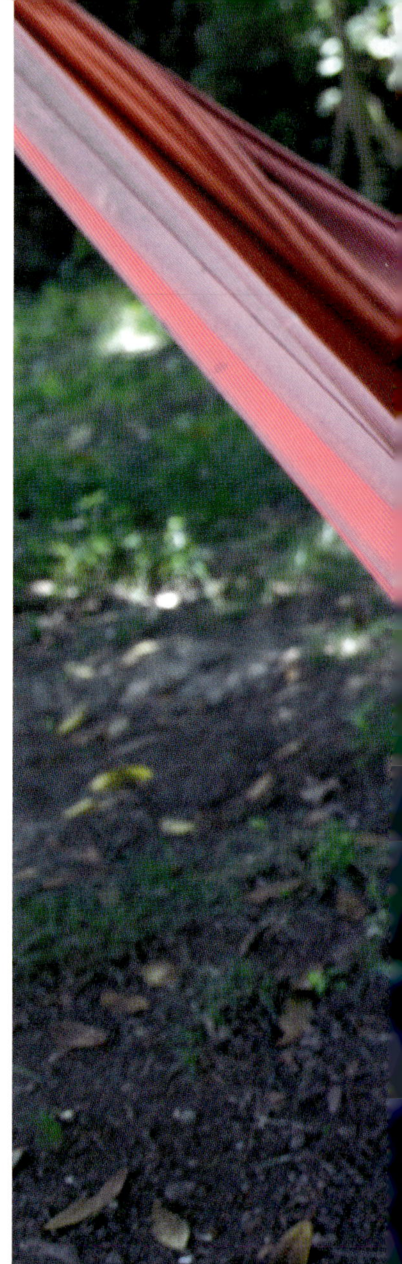

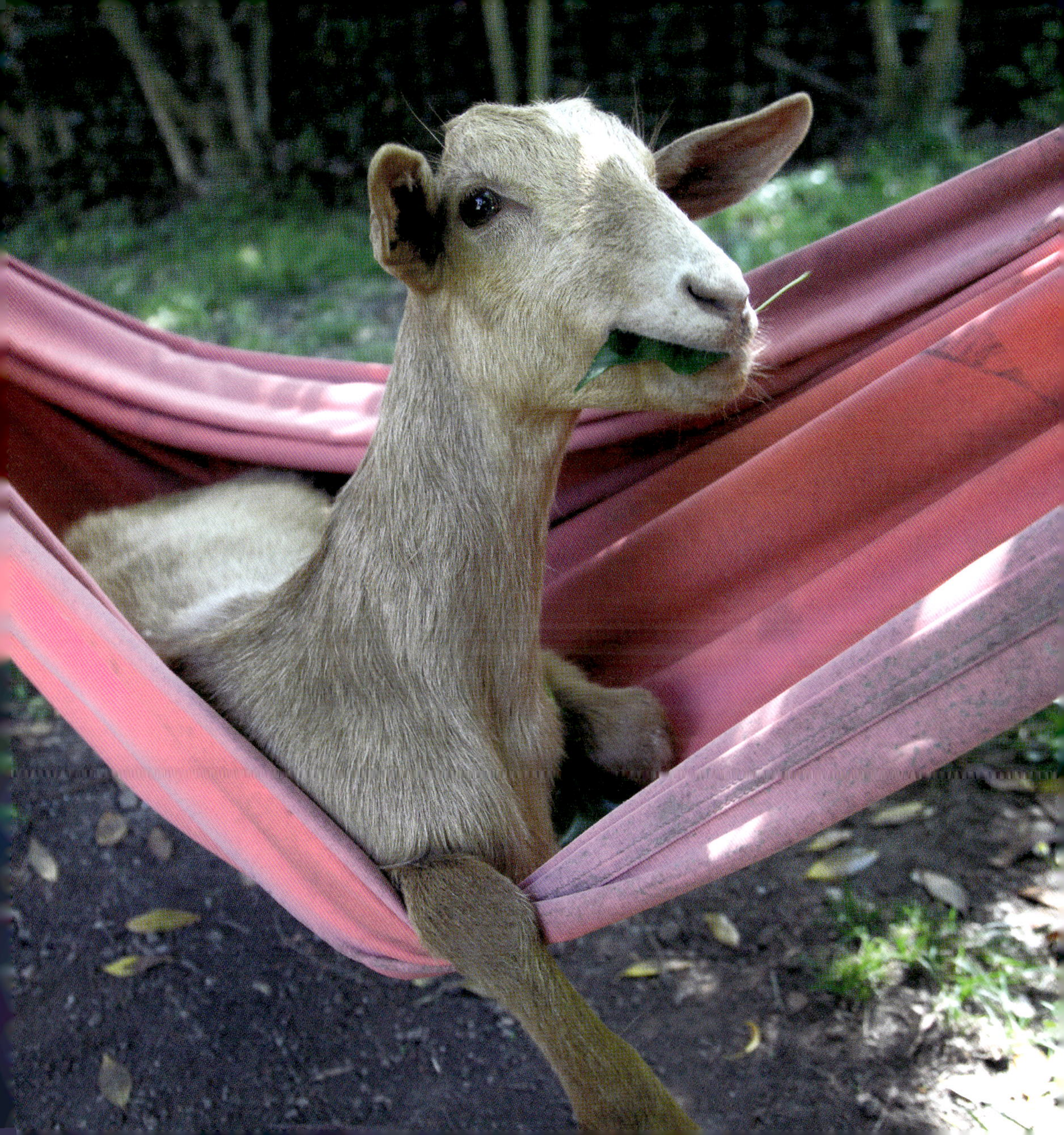

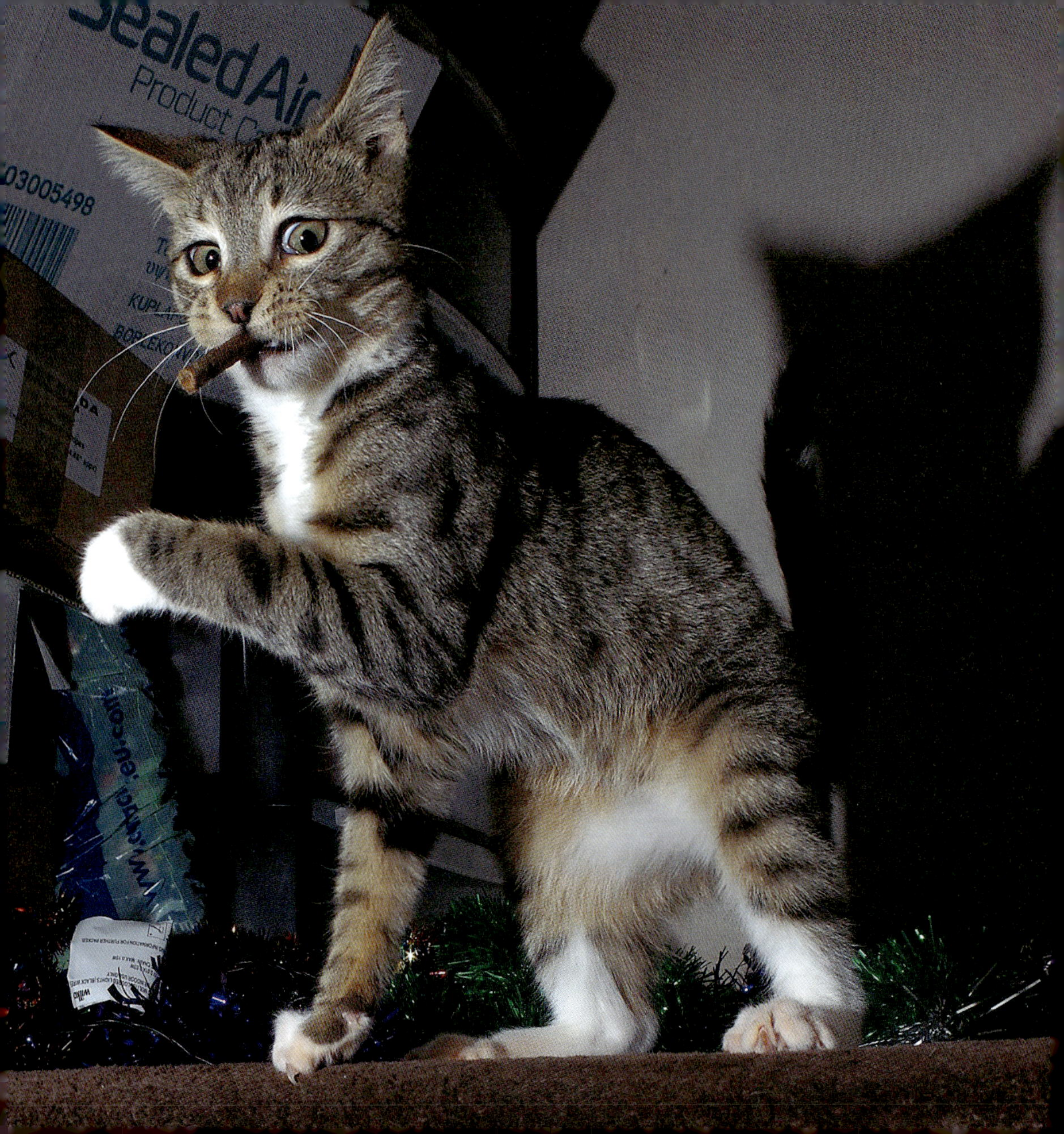

Sealed Air
Product Ca
C03005498

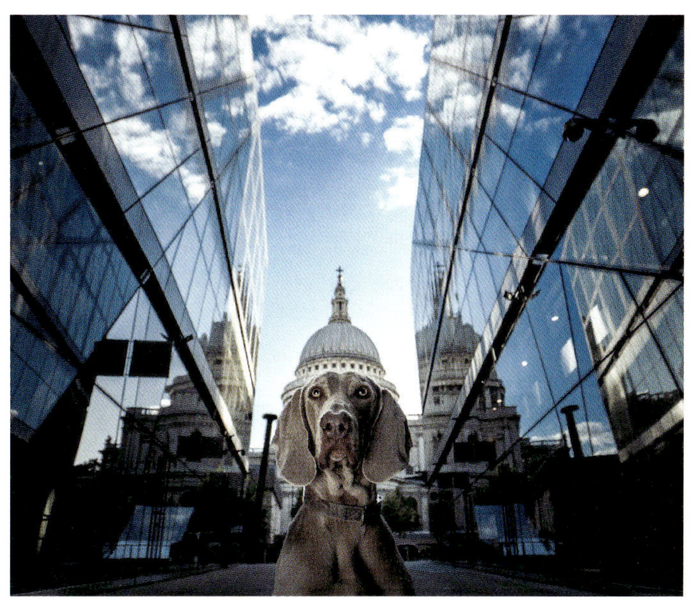

LOCATION: UNITED KINGDOM

Do you like my new hat?

PHOTOGRAPHER: Alex Class

LOCATION: WALES

Colombo the cat detective.

PHOTOGRAPHER: Iain McConnell

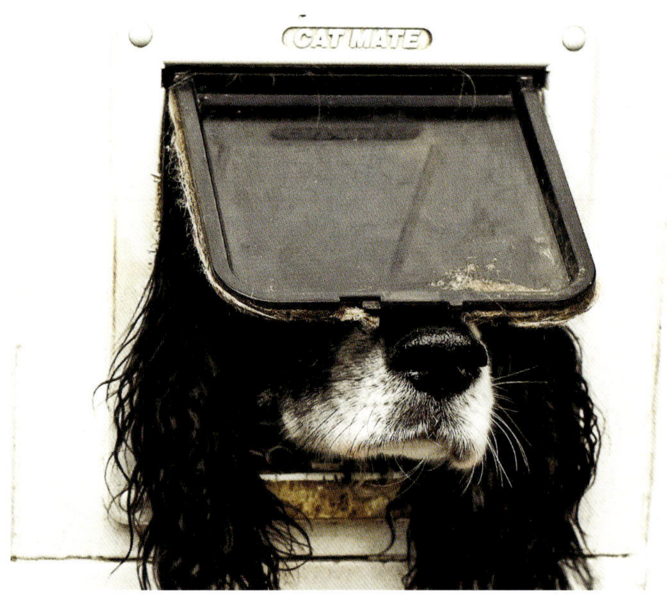

LOCATION: UNITED KINGDOM

I'm pretty sure these sunglasses appeared in *Star Trek*.

PHOTOGRAPHER: Sarah Haskell

LOCATION: GERMANY

'Squirrel!!!'

PHOTOGRAPHER: Elke Vogelsang

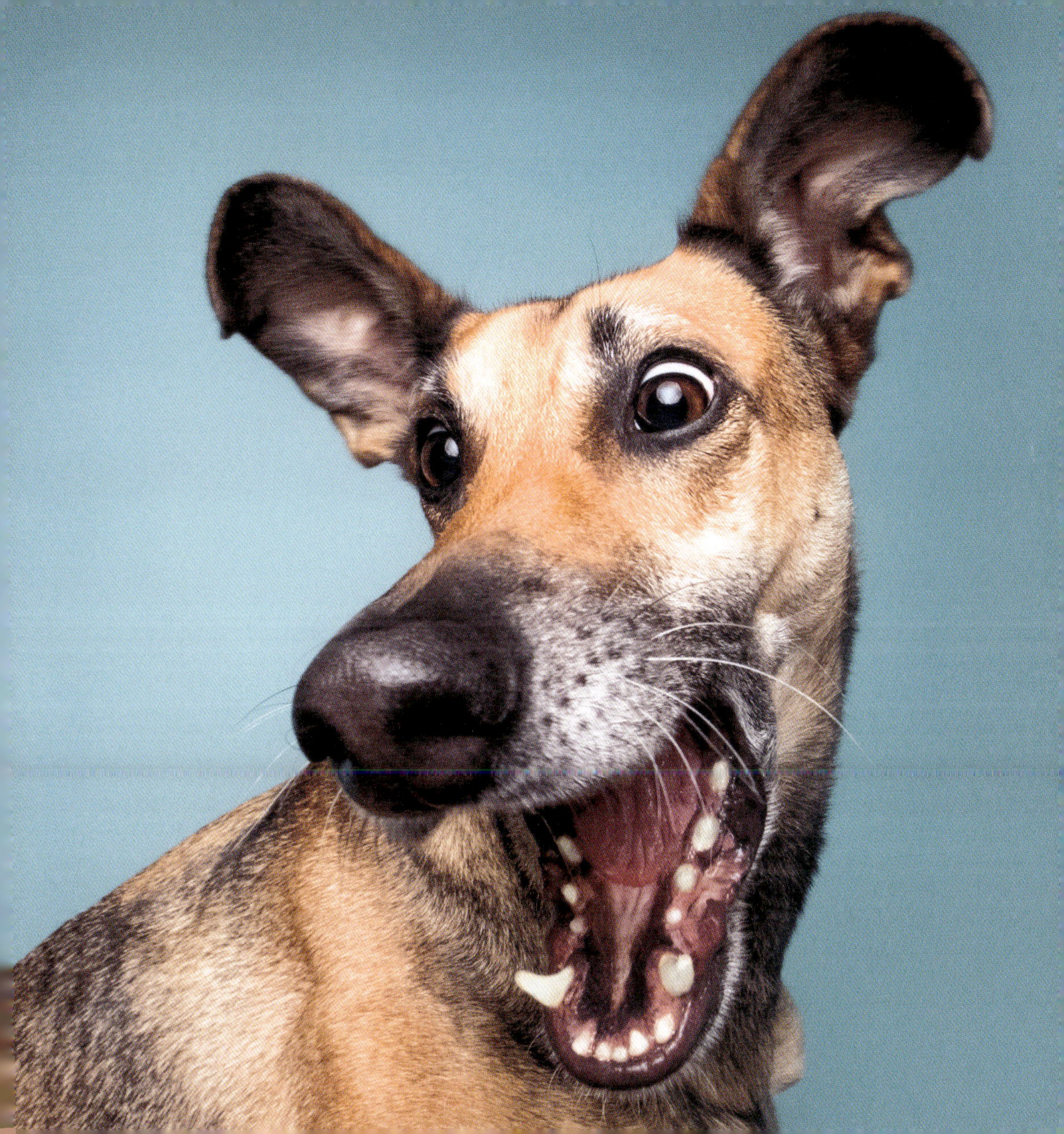

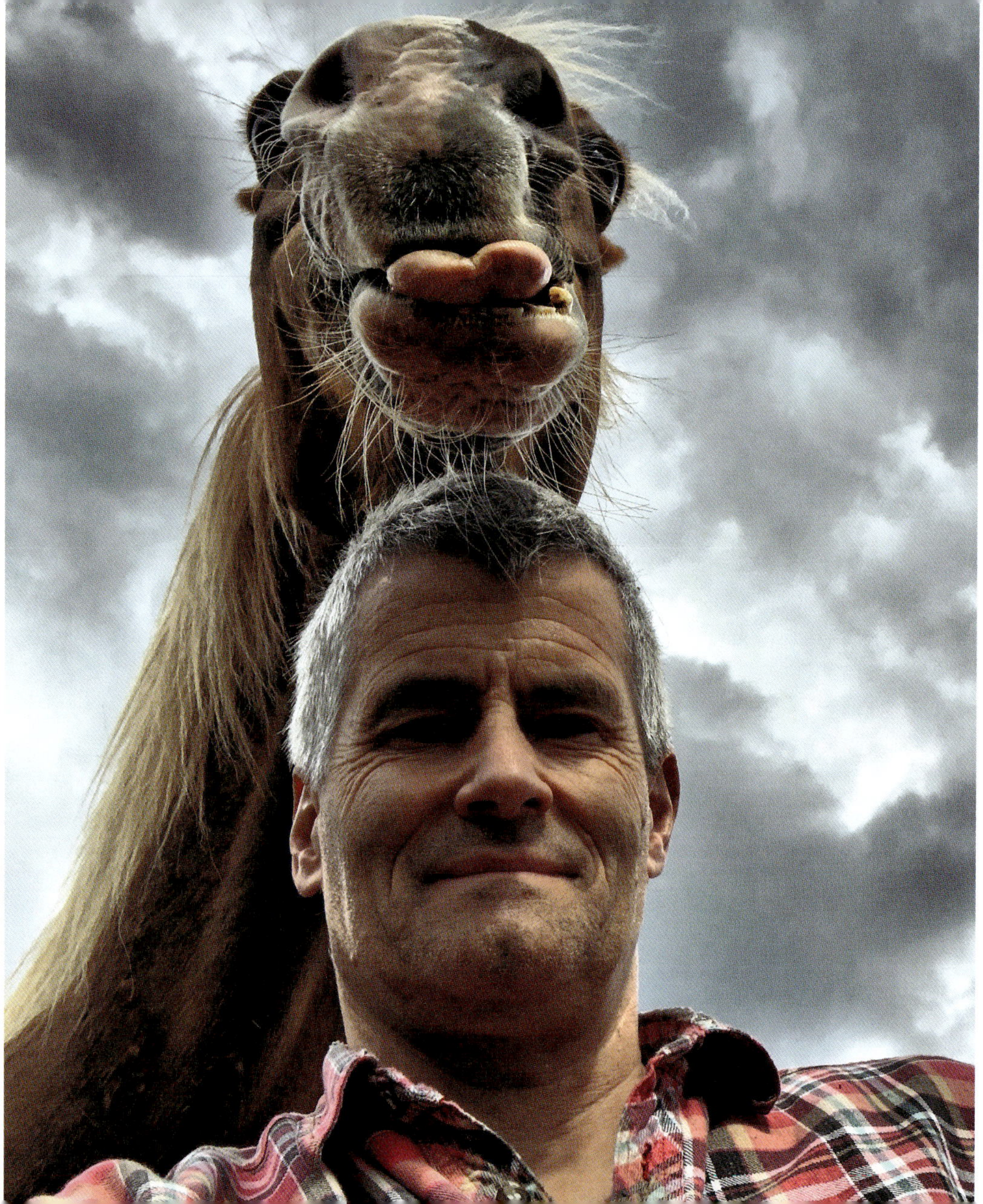

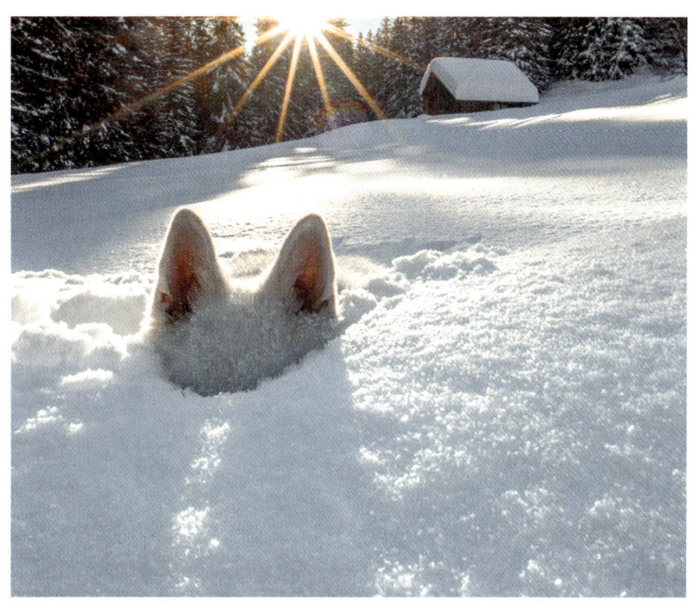

LOCATION: SWITZERLAND

That's going to give you one hell of a brain freeze.

PHOTOGRAPHER: Sylvia Michel

LOCATION: GERMANY

They decided to flip things around for the Grand National
this year, much to this competitor's delight.

PHOTOGRAPHER: Peter von Sheen

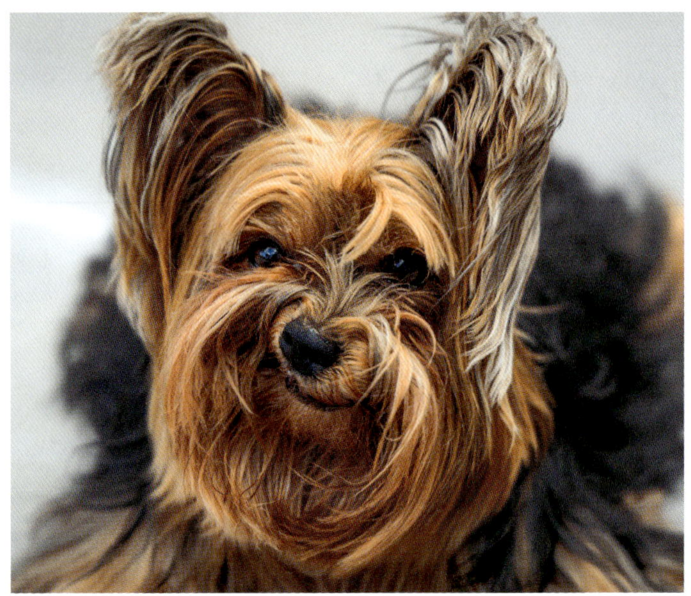

LOCATION: BRAZIL

A dog's nose really does have a life of its own.

PHOTOGRAPHER: Luiza Ribeiro

LOCATION: HEMER, GERMANY

Fido's audition for the hound in *The Hound of the Baskervilles* wasn't going so well.

PHOTOGRAPHER: Annett Mirsberger

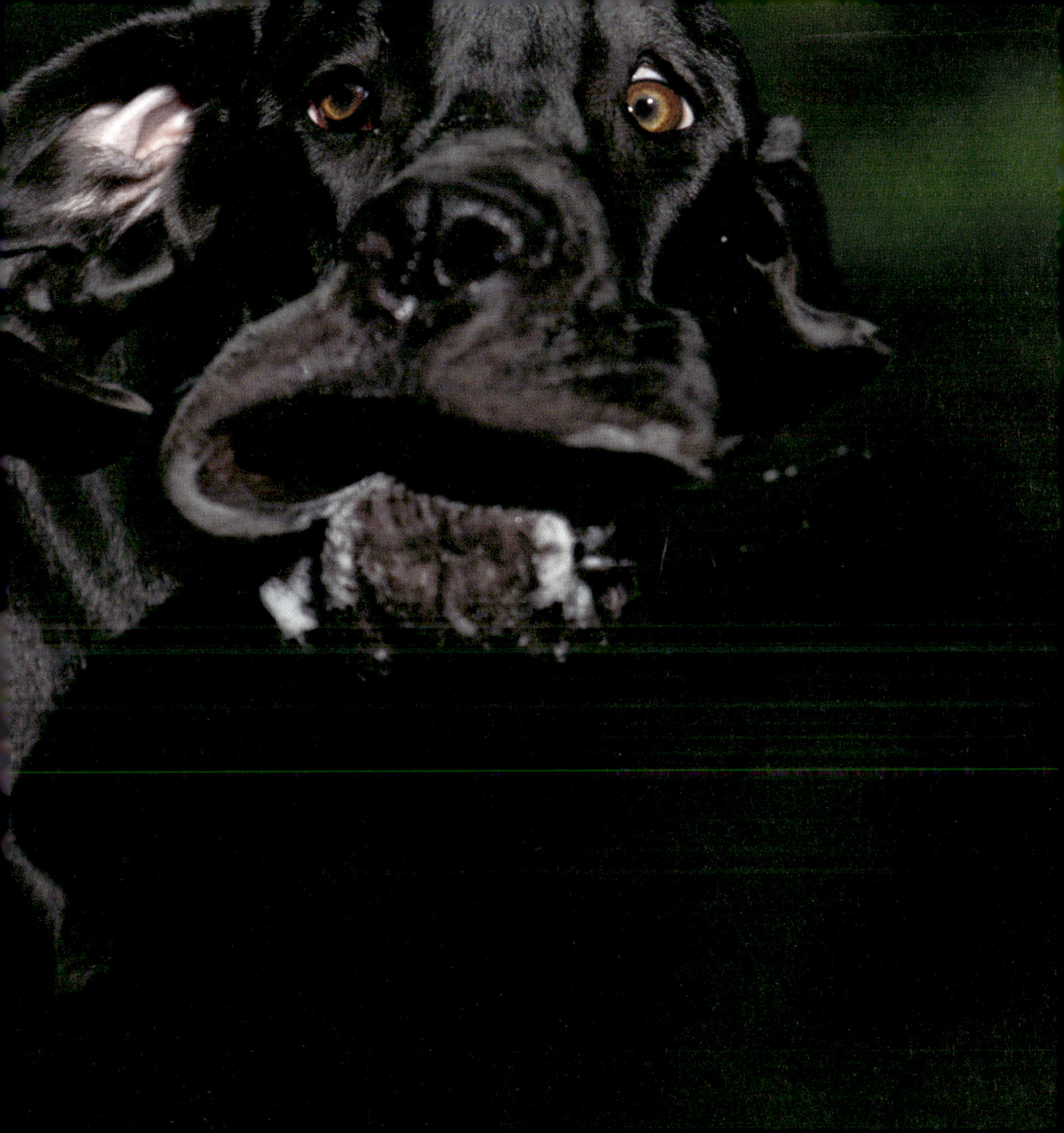

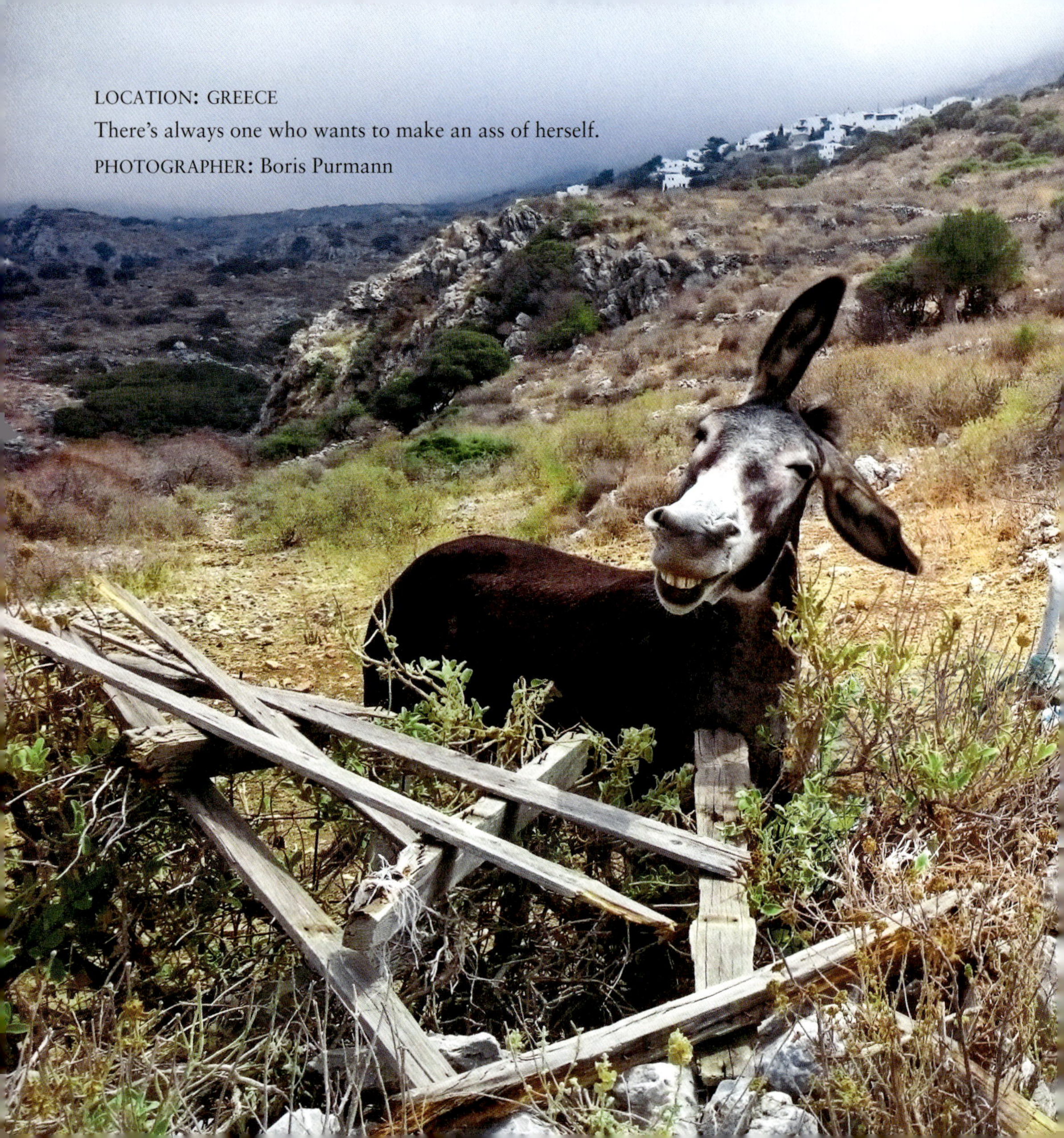

LOCATION: GREECE
There's always one who wants to make an ass of herself.
PHOTOGRAPHER: Boris Purmann

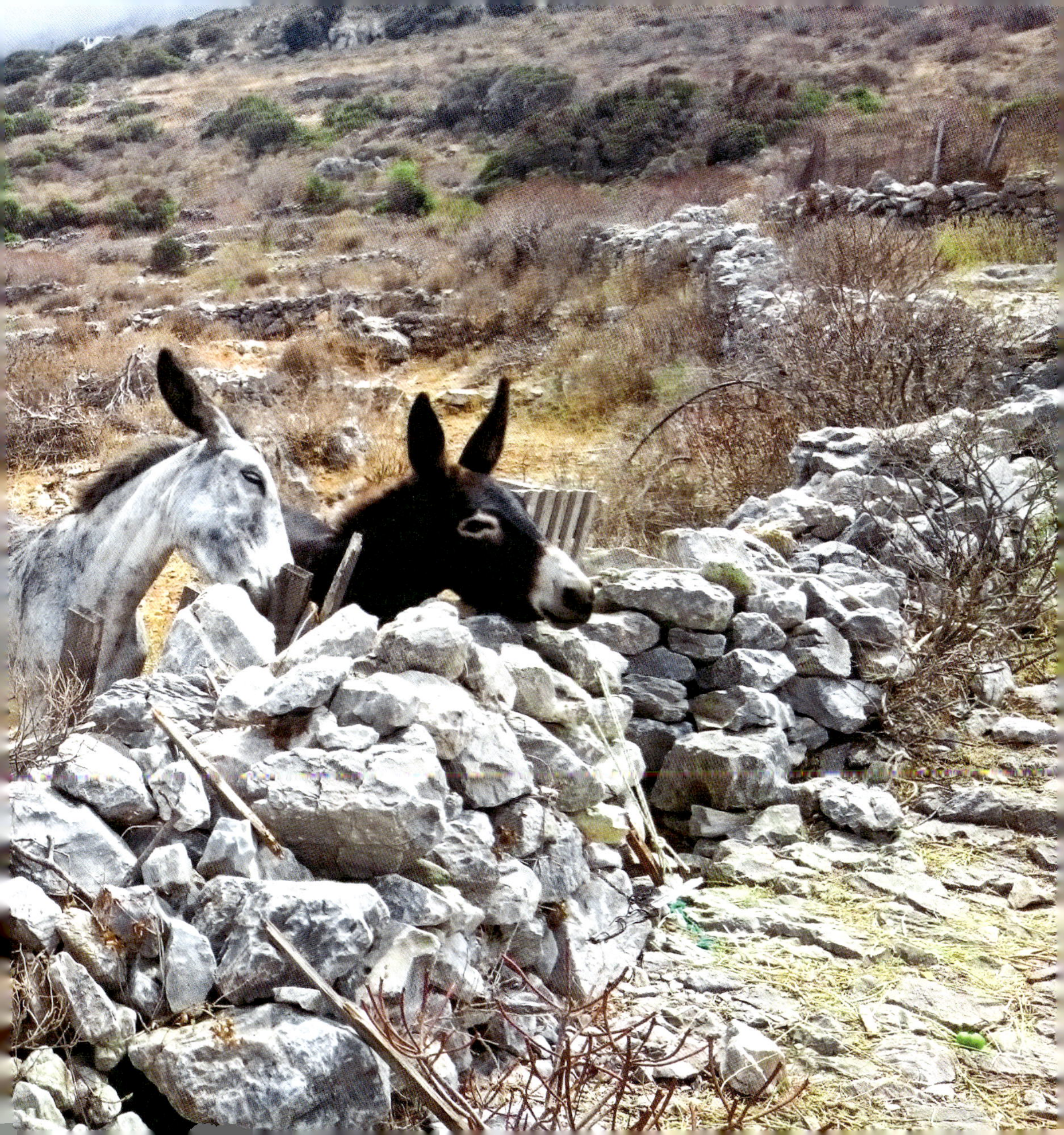

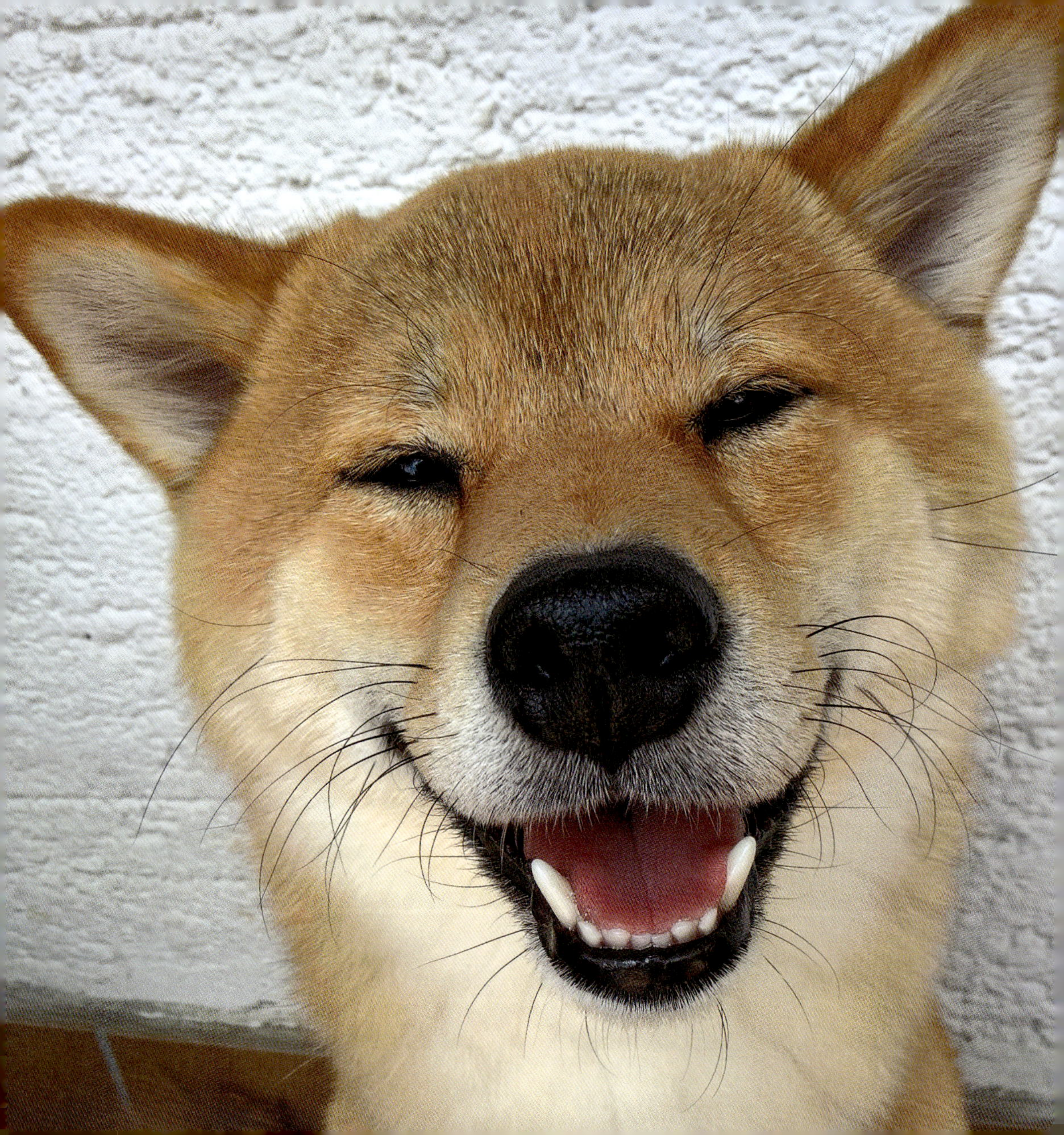

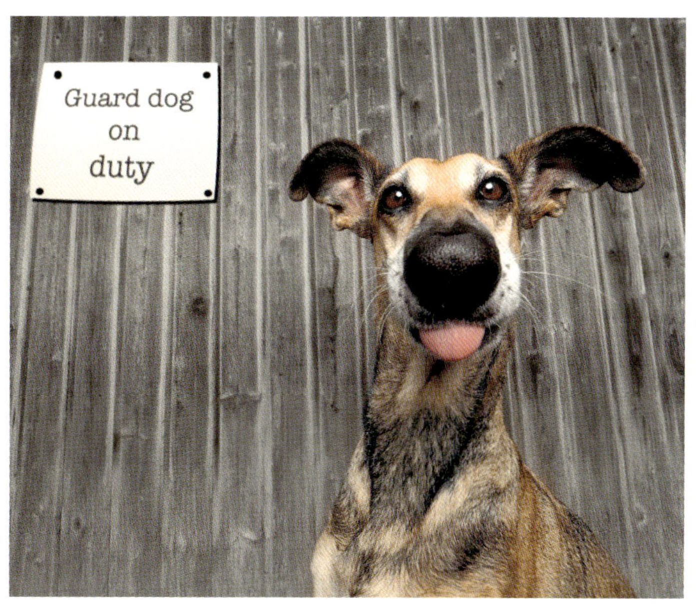

LOCATION: GERMANY

Caught off guard.

PHOTOGRAPHER: Elke Vogelsang

LOCATION: GERMANY

Chheeeeeesssssseee.

PHOTOGRAPHER: Jasmine Hæcker

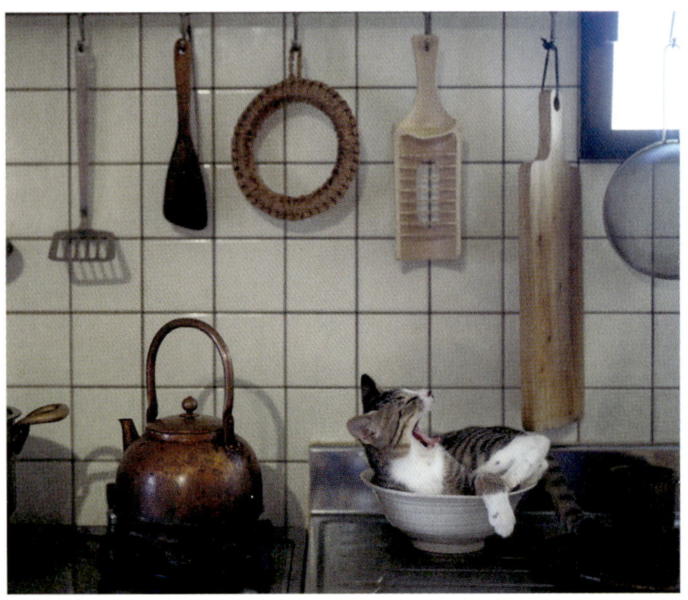

LOCATION: UNITED KINGOM
To be fair, that is a funny name for a boat.
PHOTOGRAPHER: Dean Pollard

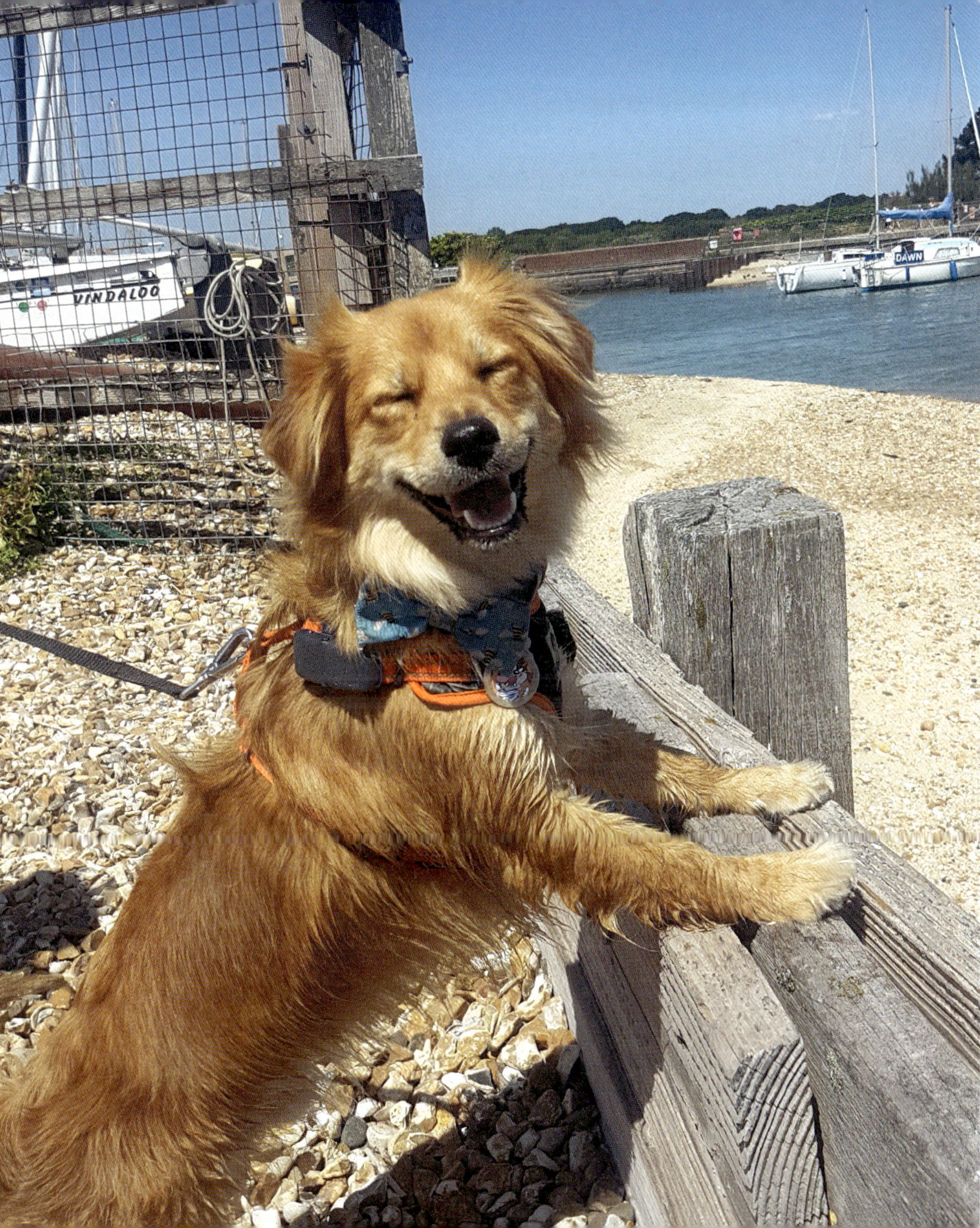

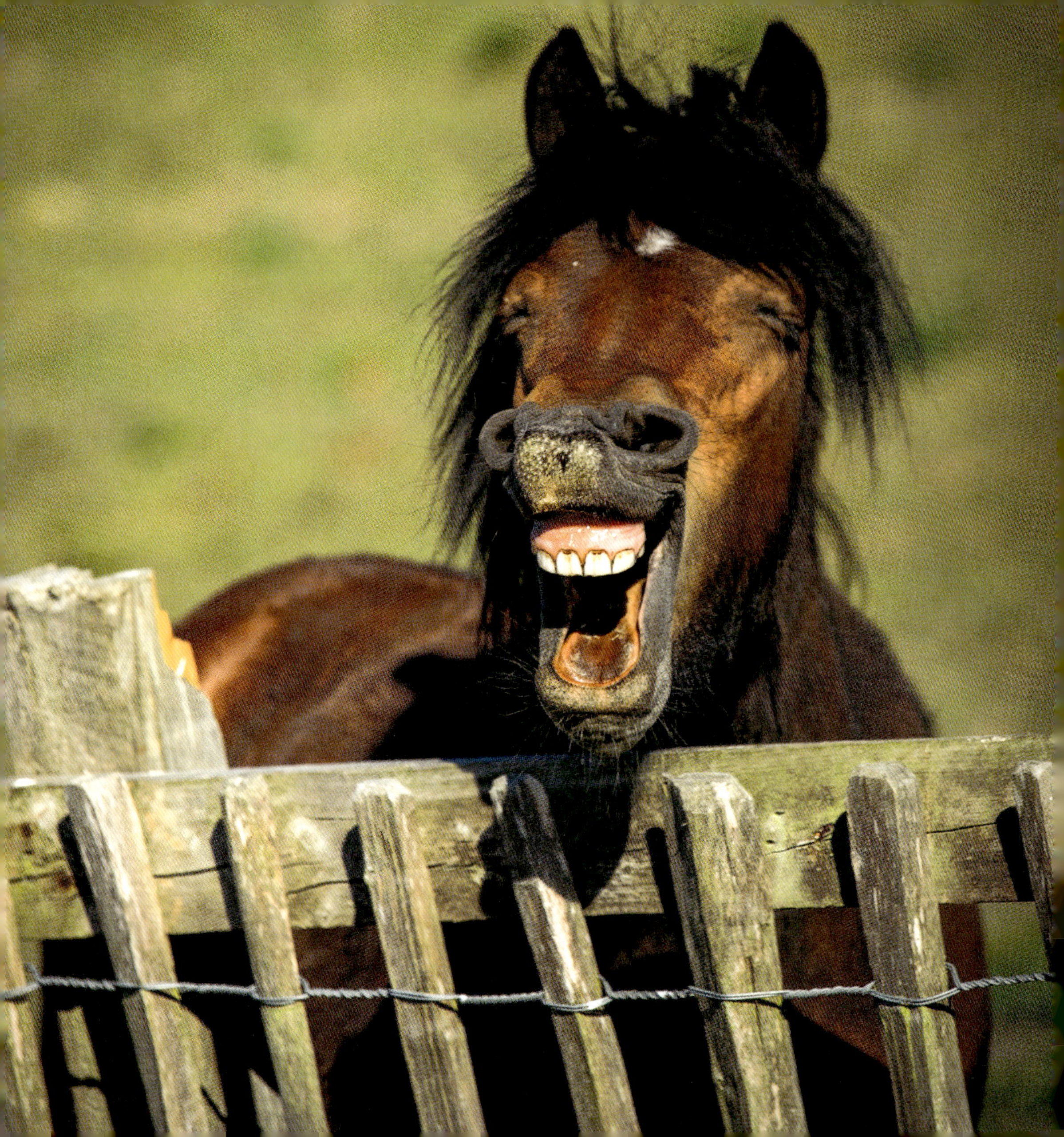

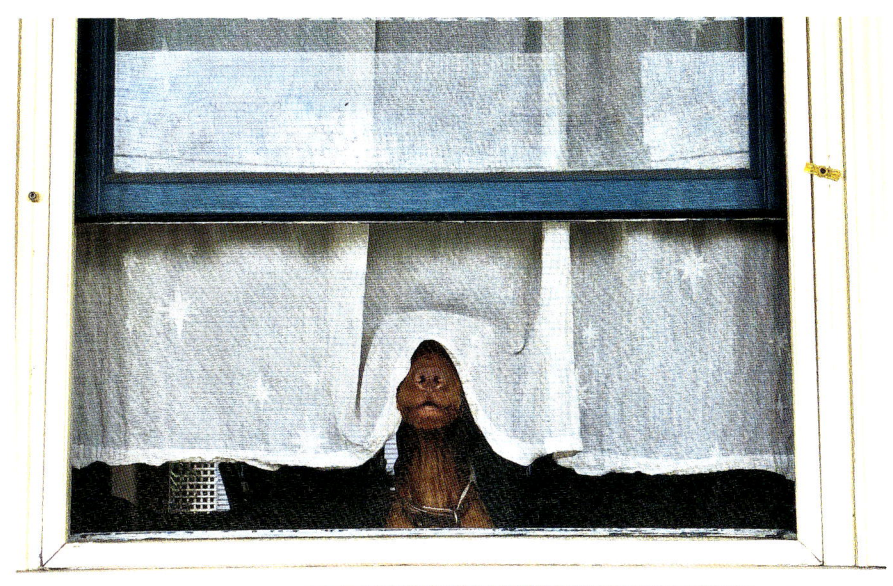

LOCATION: MELBOURNE, AUSTRALIA
Rover didn't quite get the hang of the Covid face covering.
PHOTOGRAPHER: Ilana Rose

LOCATION: UNITED KINGDOM
Unafraid to make a foal of himself.
PHOTOGRAPHER: Daniel Szumilas

LOCATION: AUSTRIA
They call me Stoop Dogg.
PHOTOGRAPHER: Kerstin Ordelt

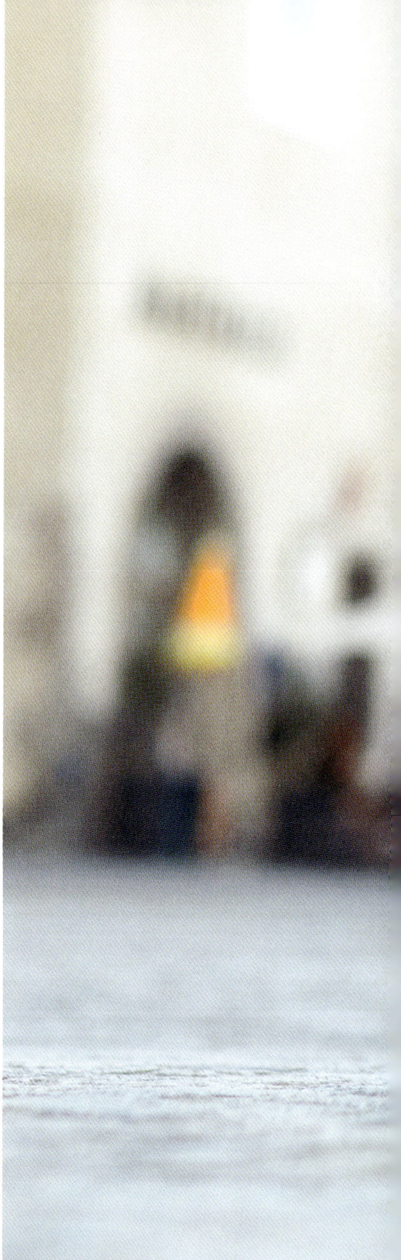

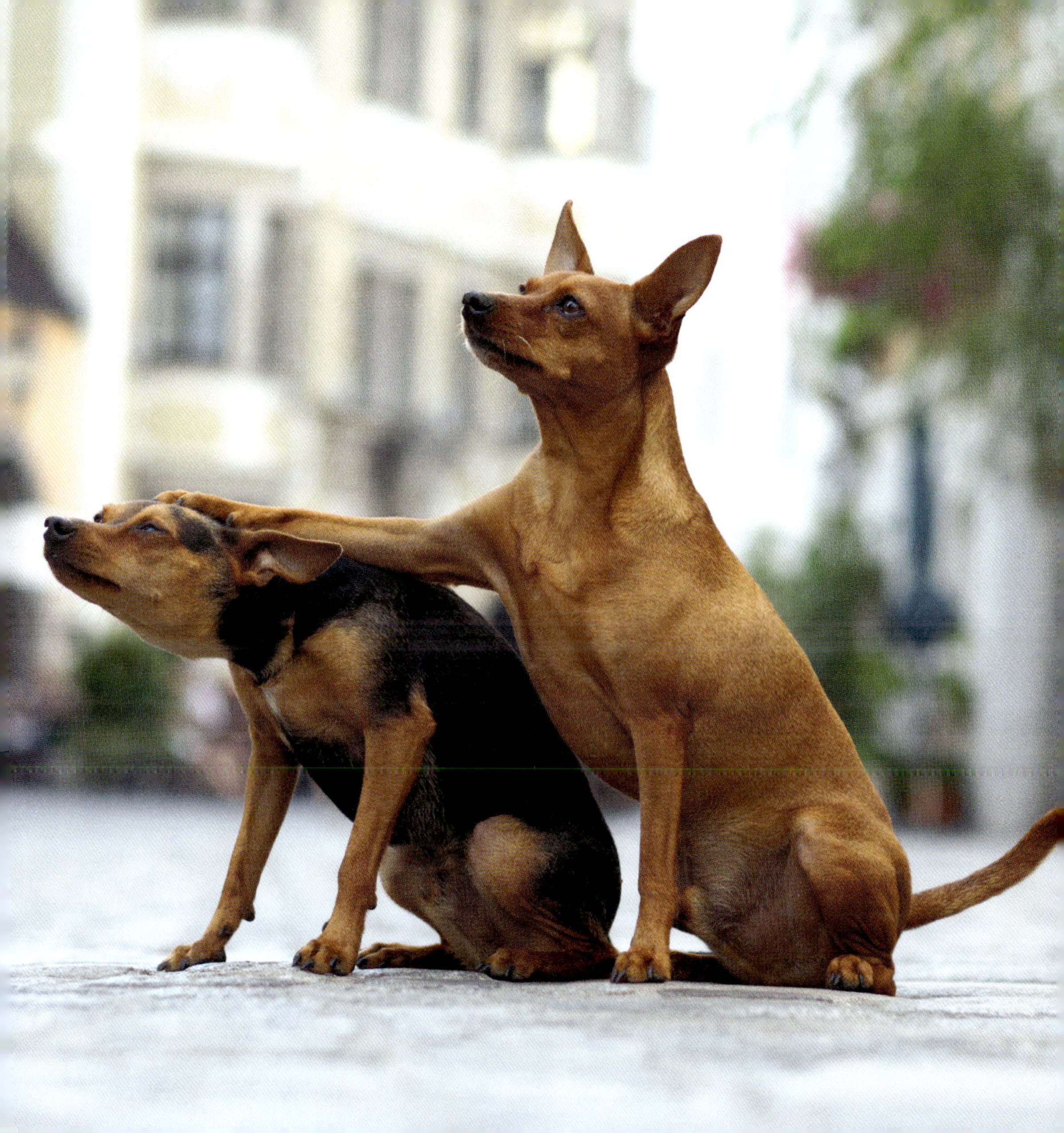

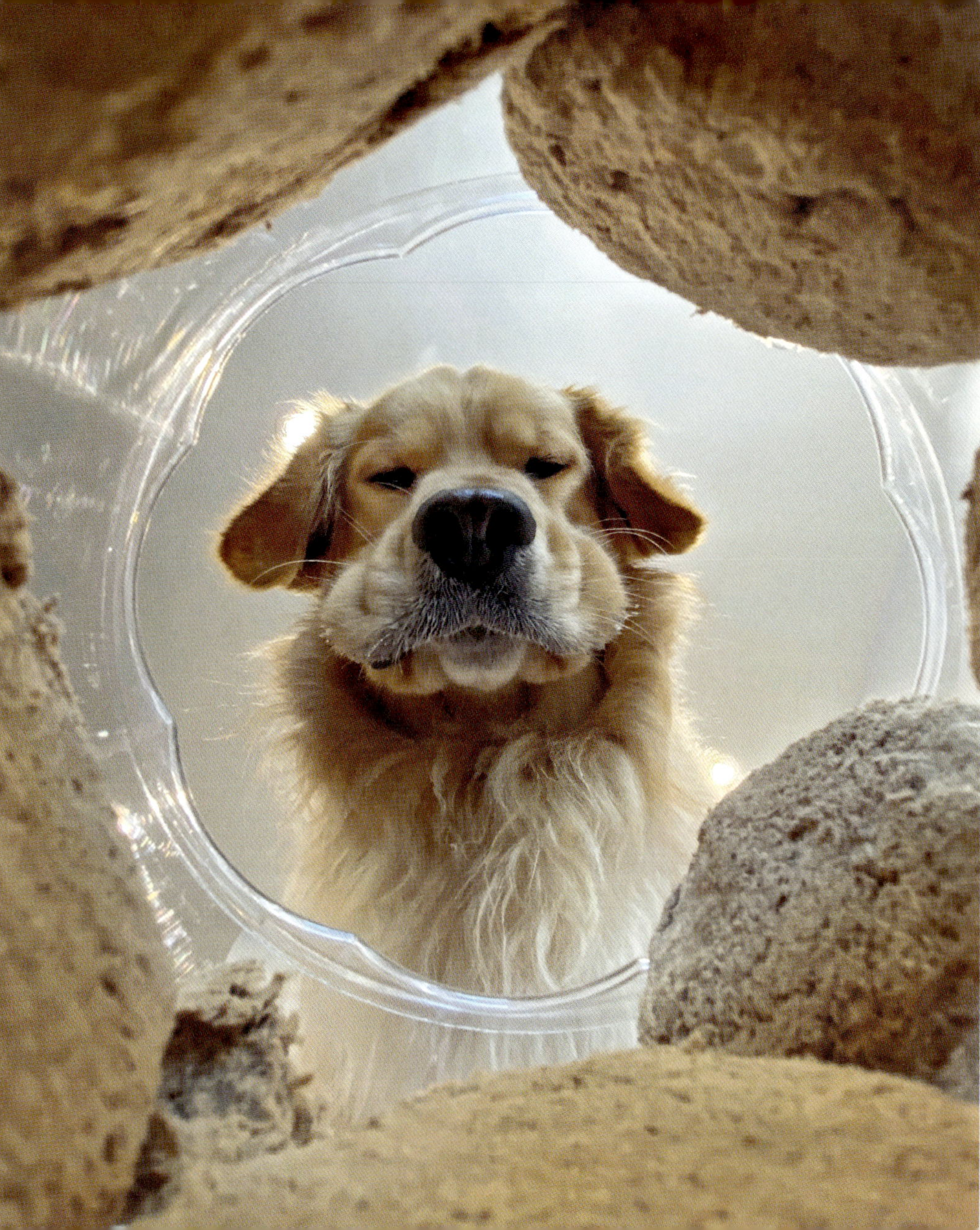

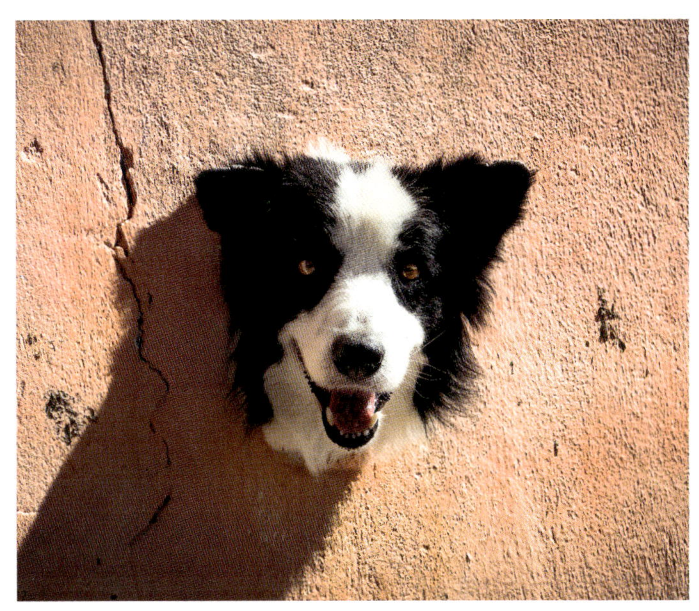

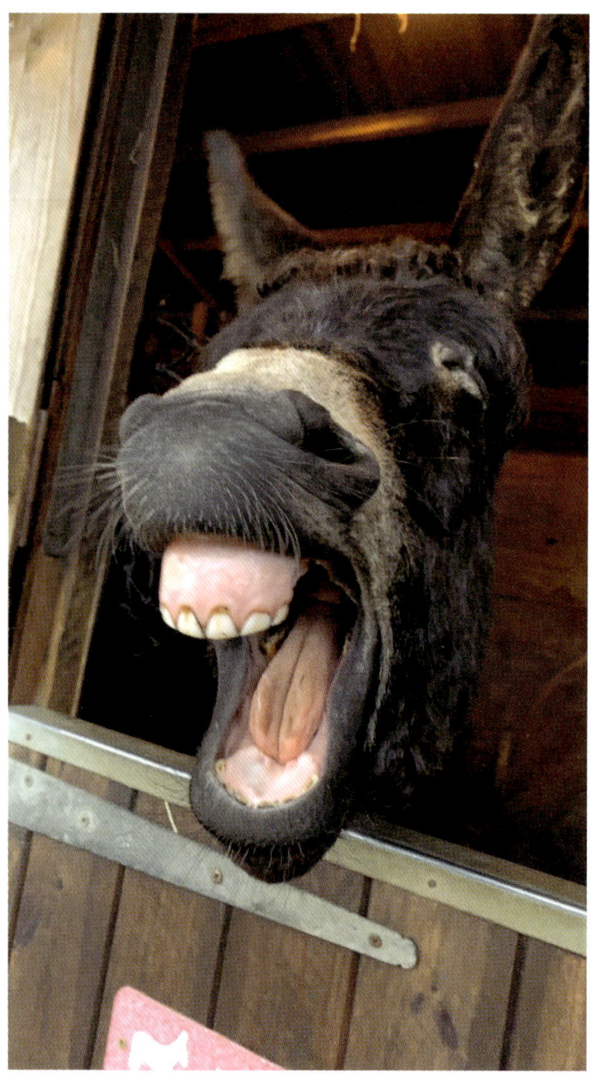

LOCATION: UNITED KINGDOM

And he said, 'to assume is to make an ASS out of U and ME'.

PHOTOGRAPHER: Charlotte Kitchen

LOCATION: WALES

And she nails the dismount!

PHOTOGRAPHER: Iain McConnell

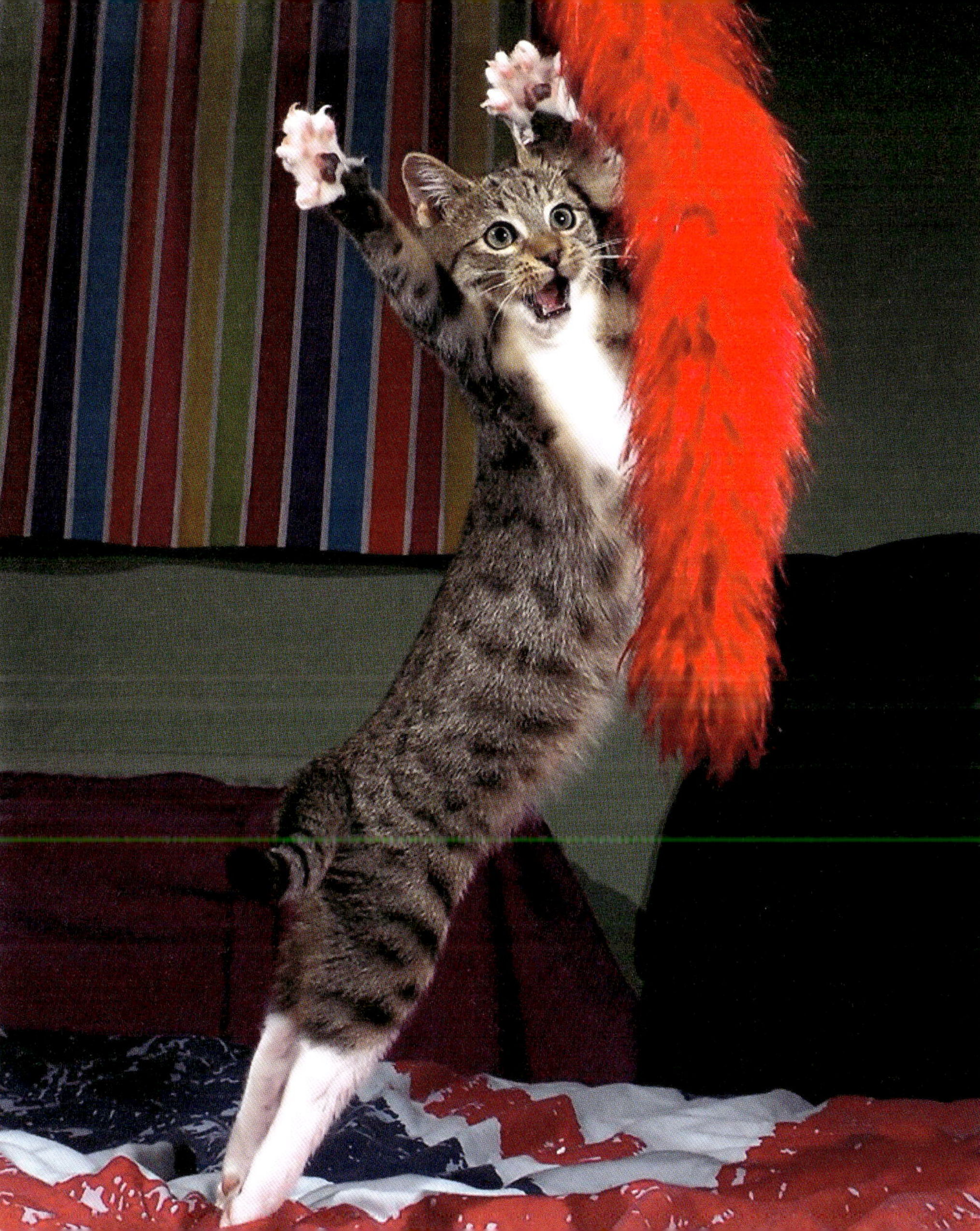

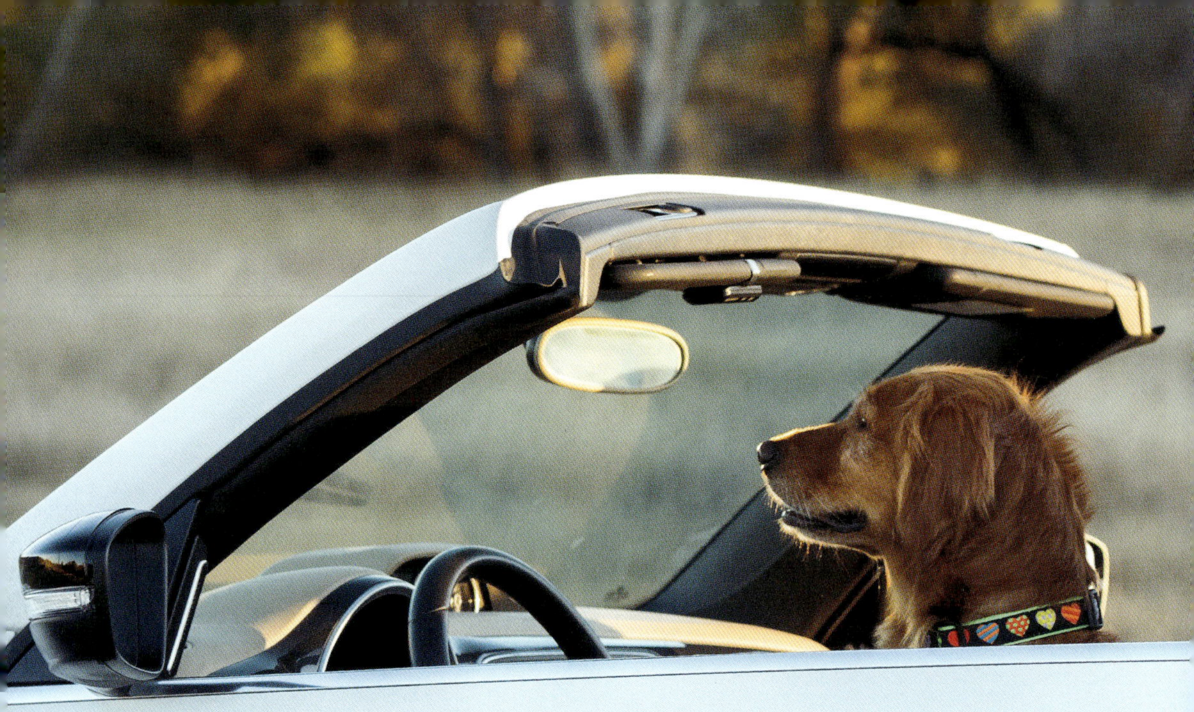

LOCATION: UNITED STATES
Better buckle up – this might be a ruff ride.
PHOTOGRAPHER: Karen Hoglund

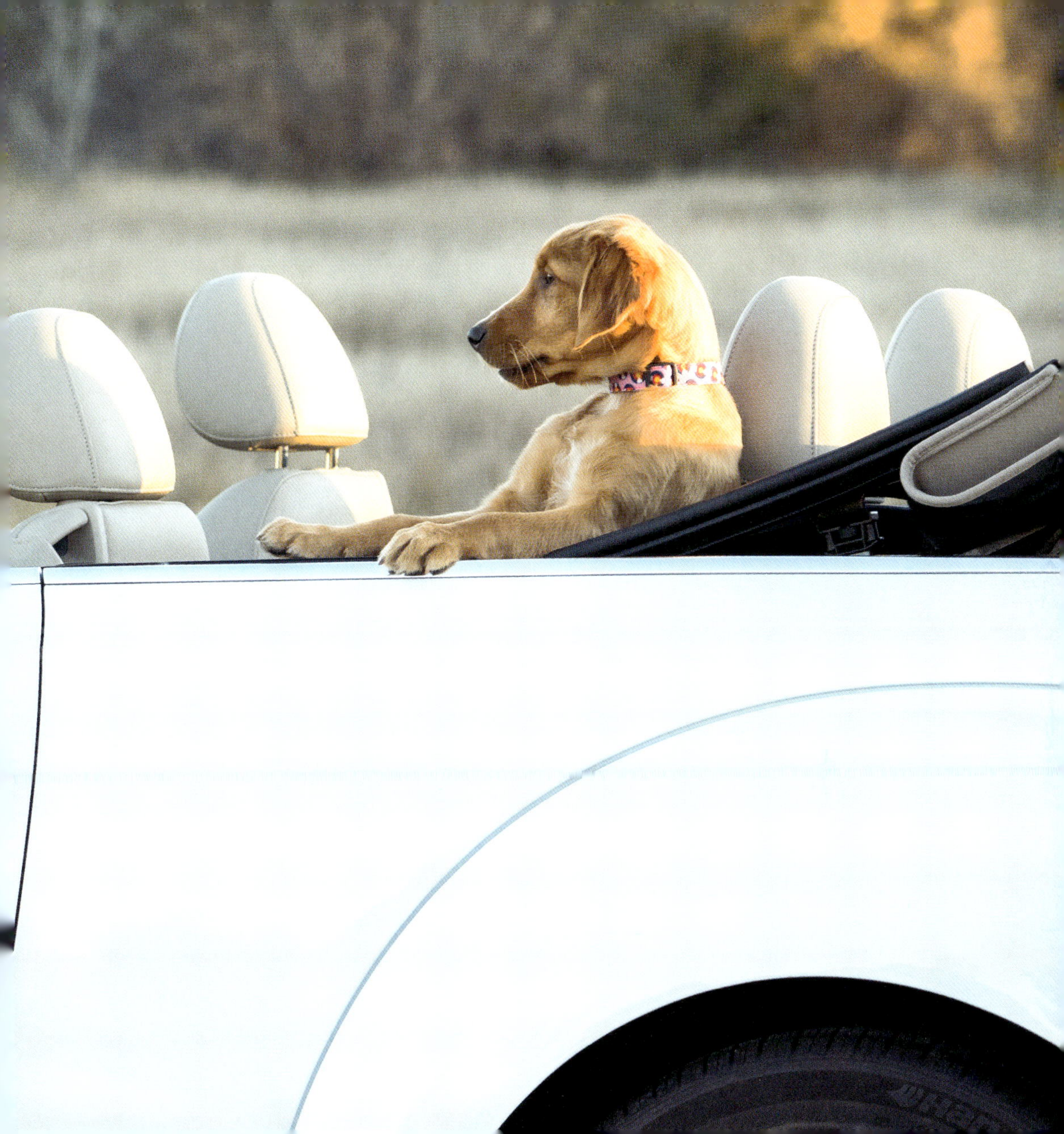

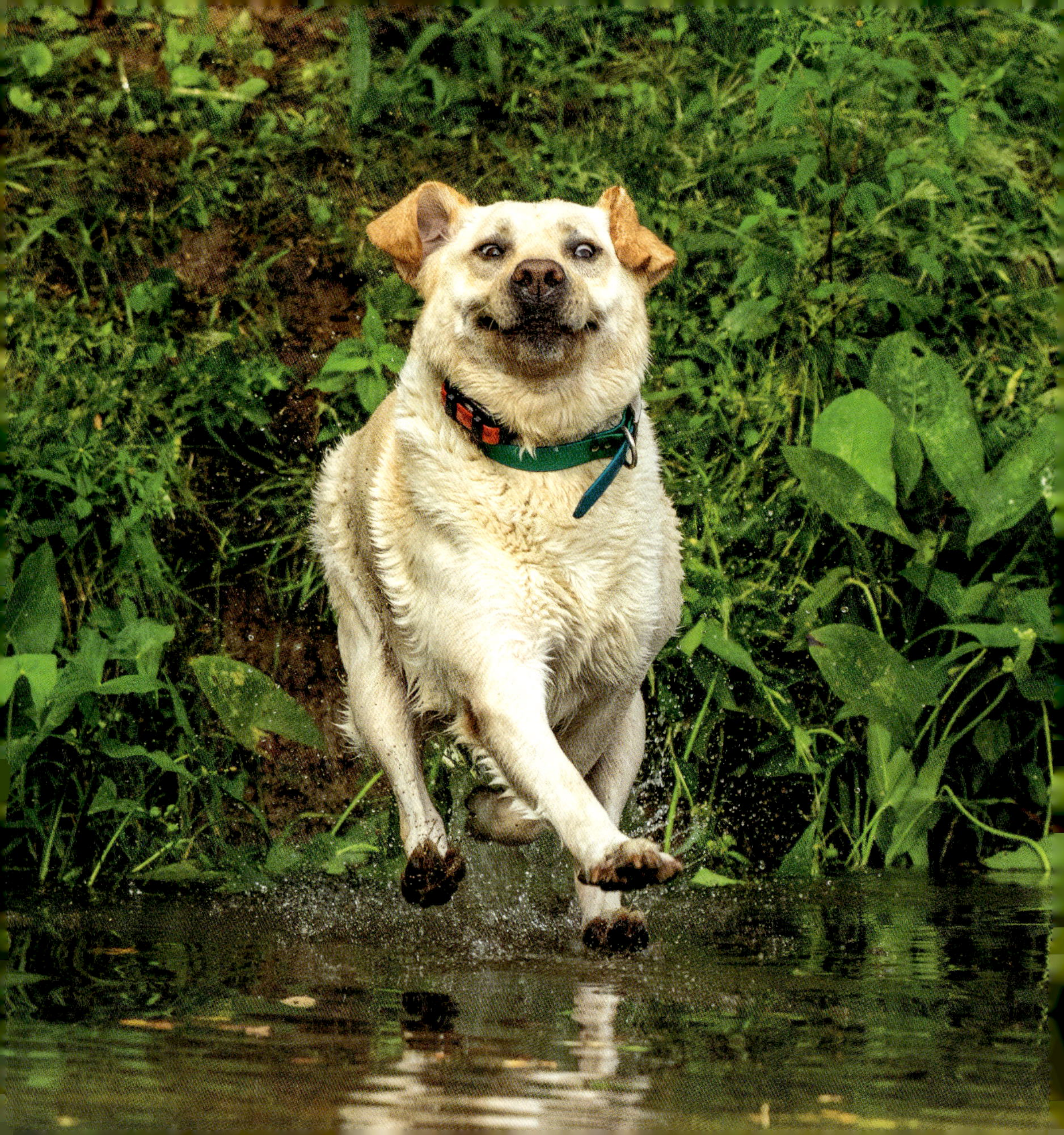

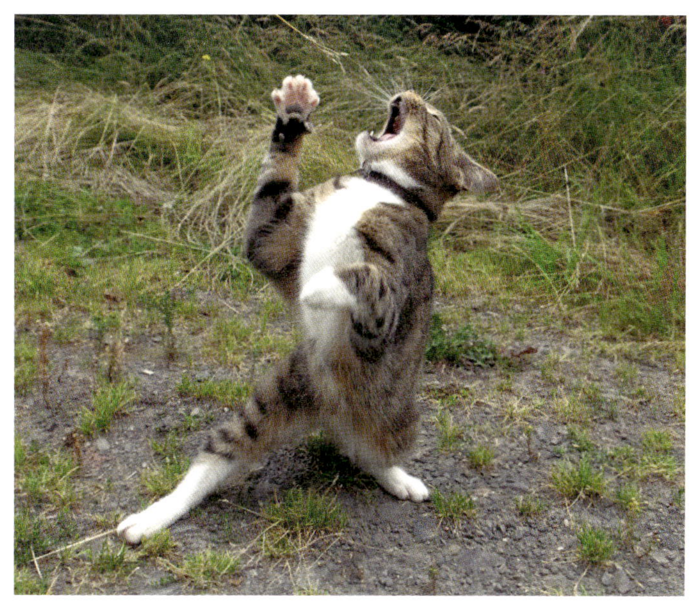

LOCATION: WALES

'I can't get no catisfaction'.

PHOTOGRAPHER: Iain McConnell

LOCATION: UNITED STATES

I'm as surprised as you are!

PHOTOGRAPHER: John Carelli

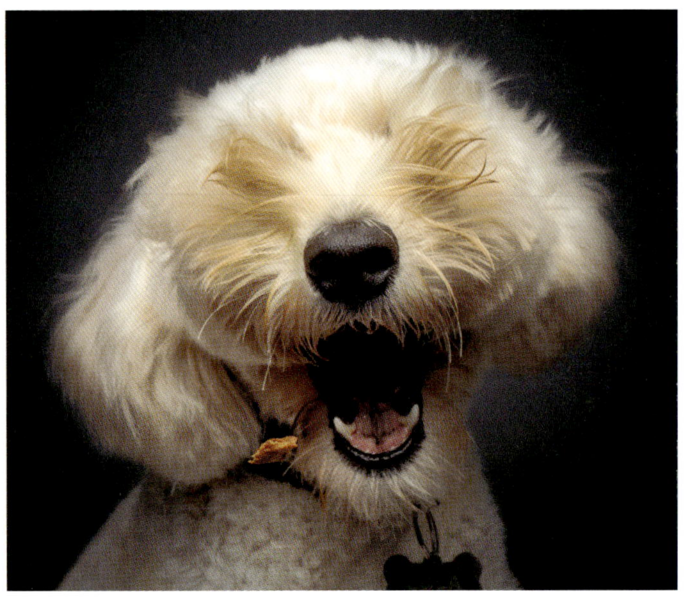

LOCATION: SINGAPORE

When a treat's sailing through the air, not being able
to see won't make any difference.

PHOTOGRAPHER: Bernard Sim

LOCATION: UNITED KINGDOM

This Cockapoo is cock-a-hoop about basketball.

PHOTOGRAPHER: Darren Hall

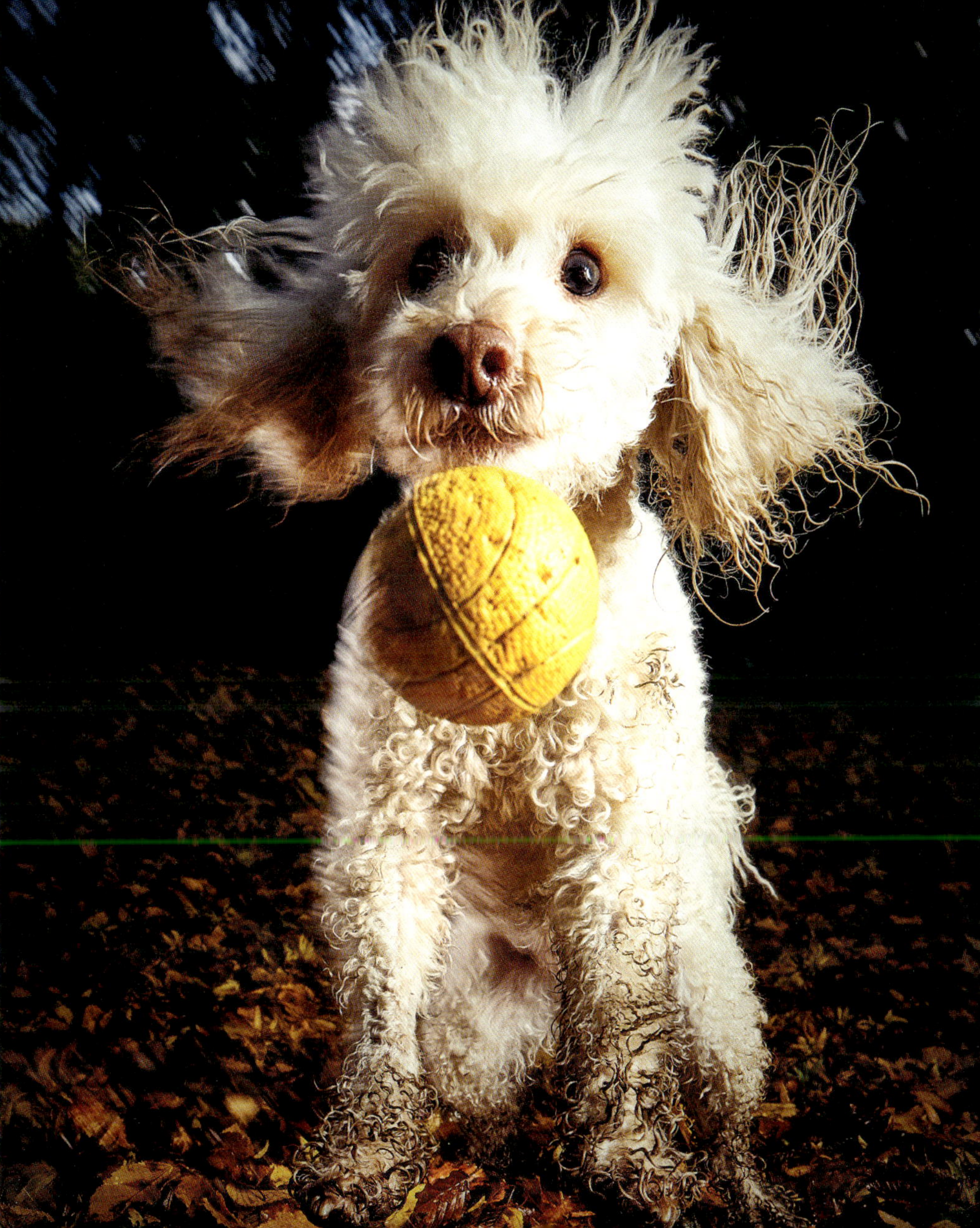

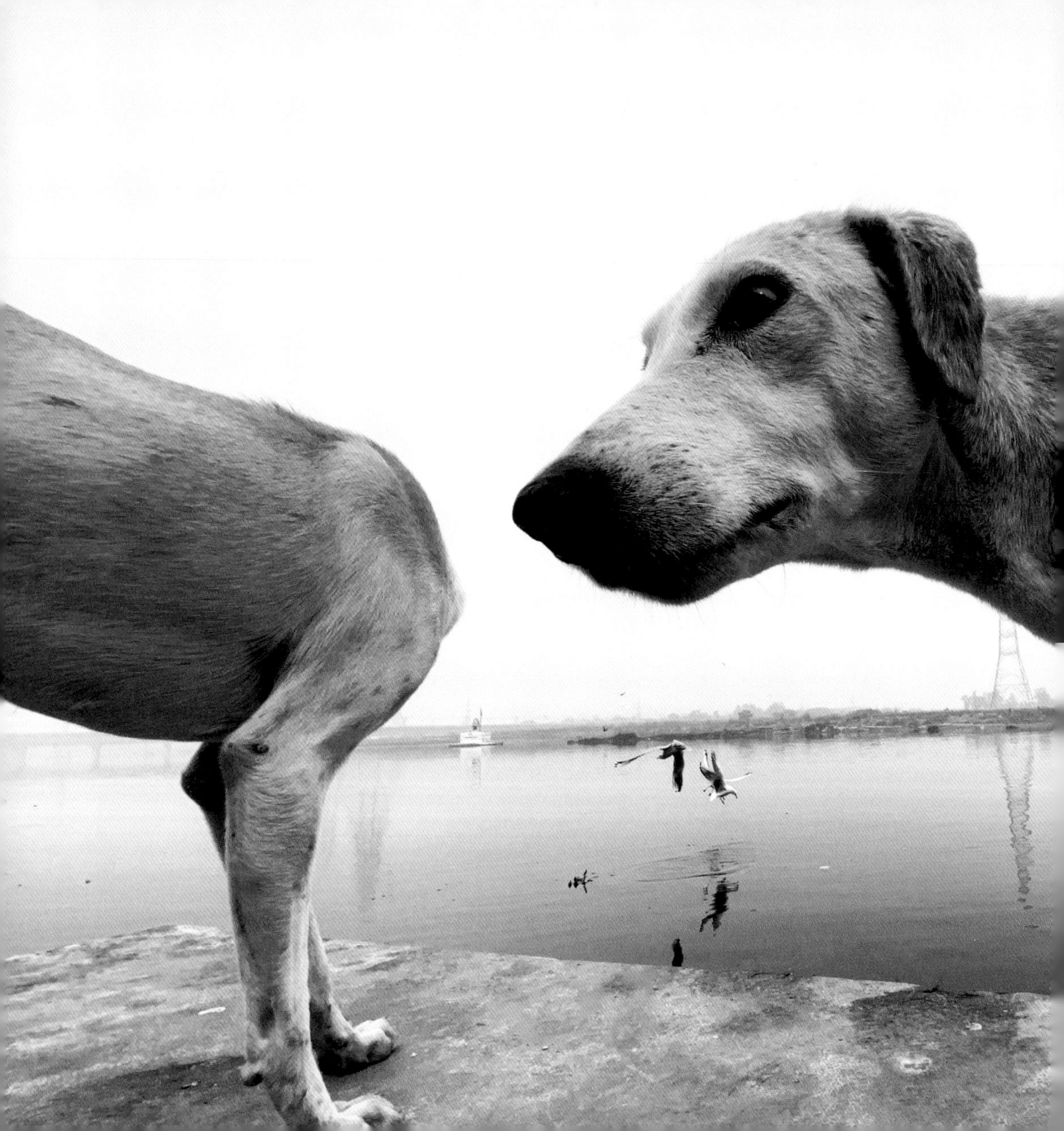

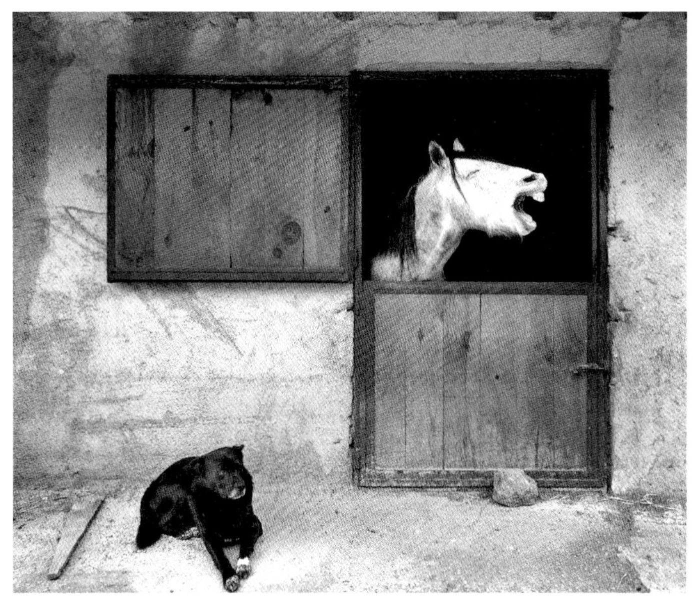

LOCATION: INDIA

We can't make head or tail of this one.

PHOTOGRAPHER: Dimpy Bhalotia

LOCATION: PADERBORN, GERMANY

Autumn: nature's neverending game of catch.

PHOTOGRAPHER: Diana Jill Mehner

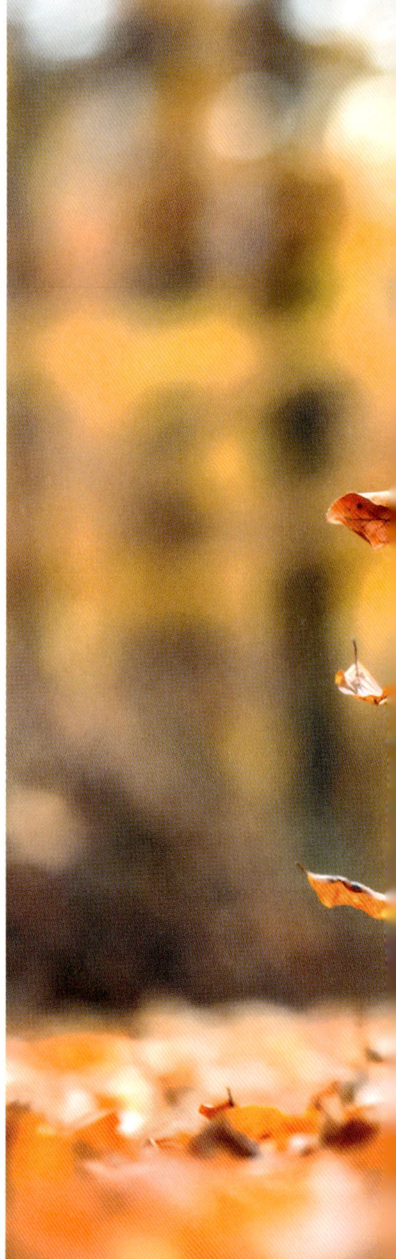

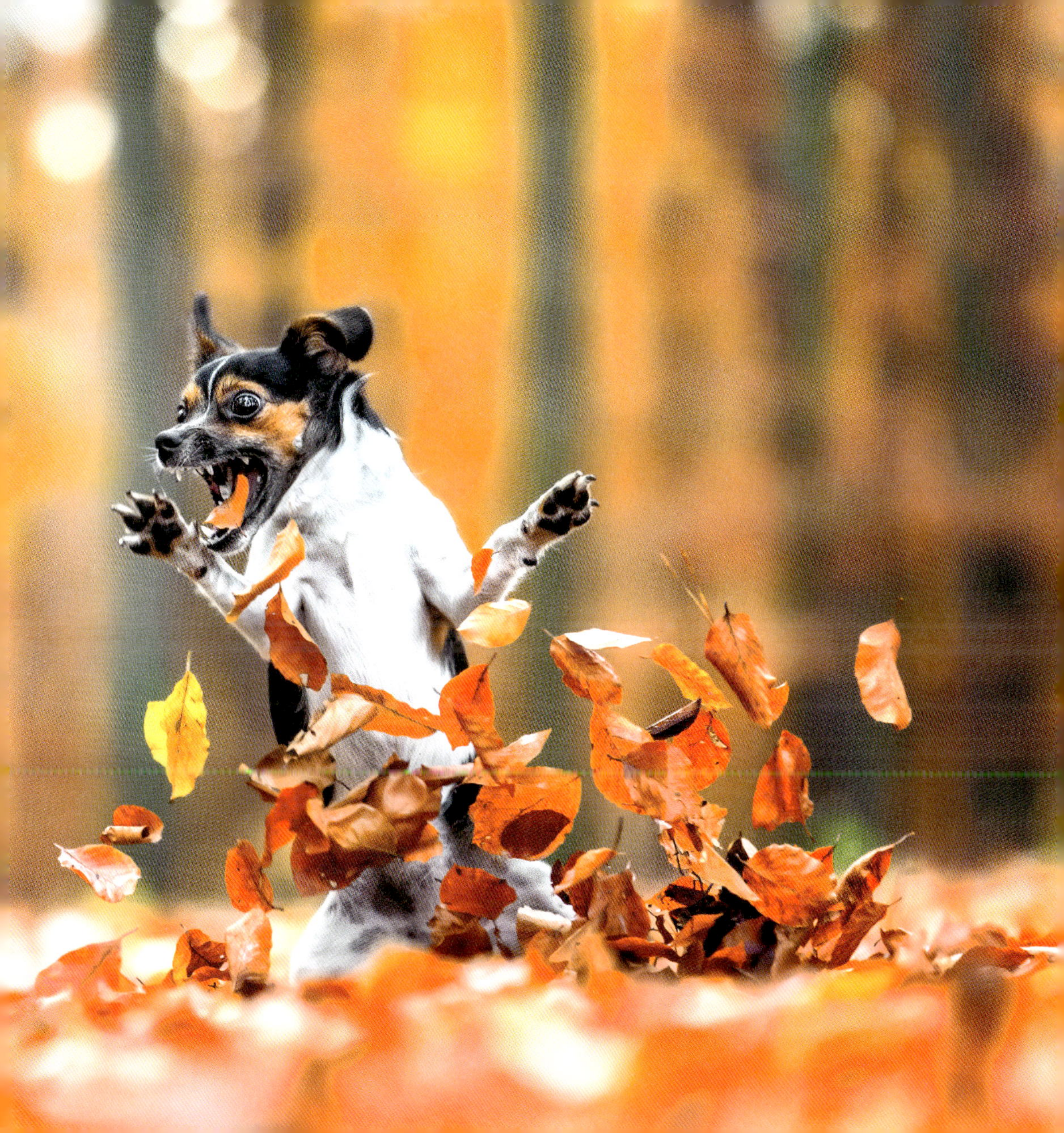

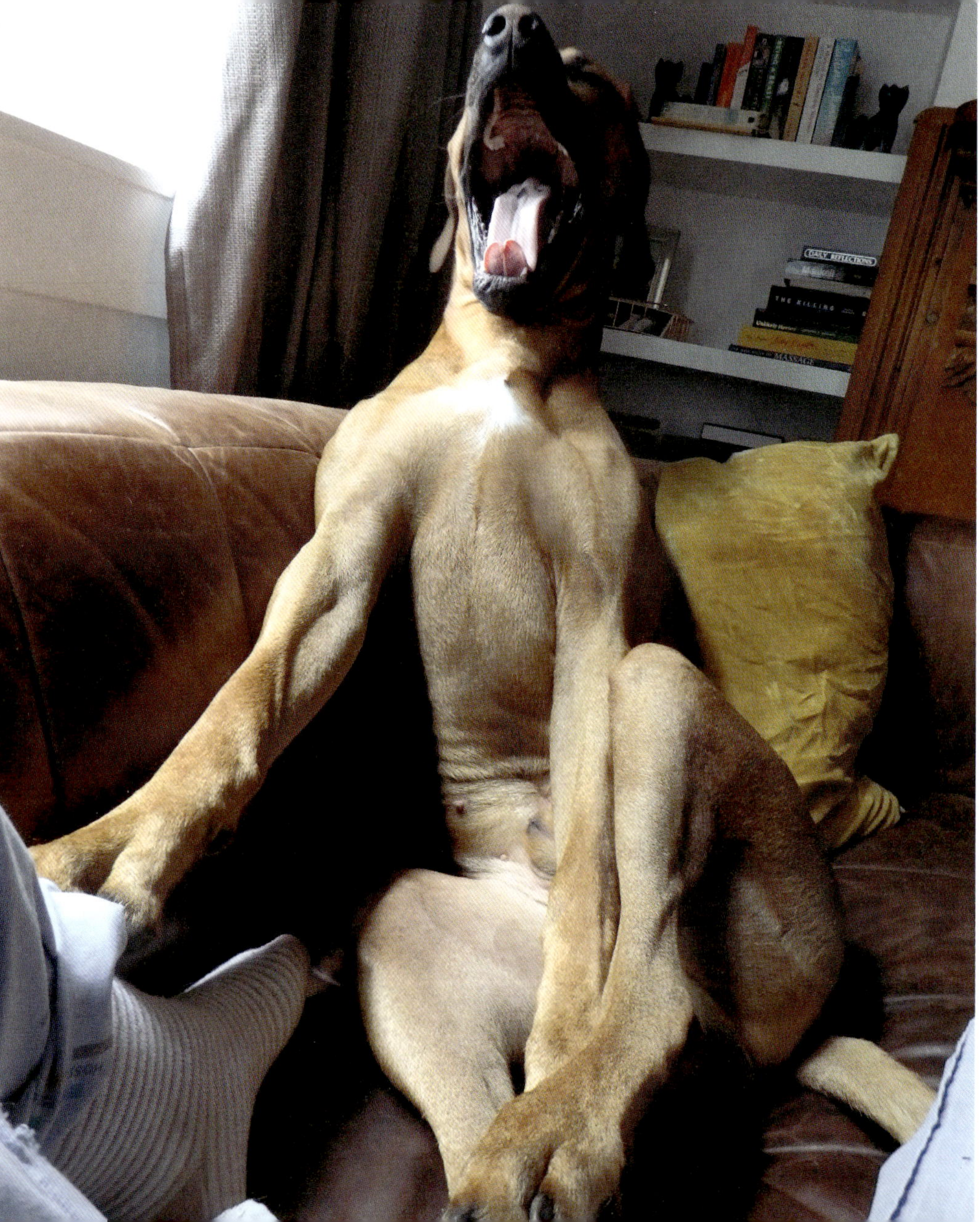

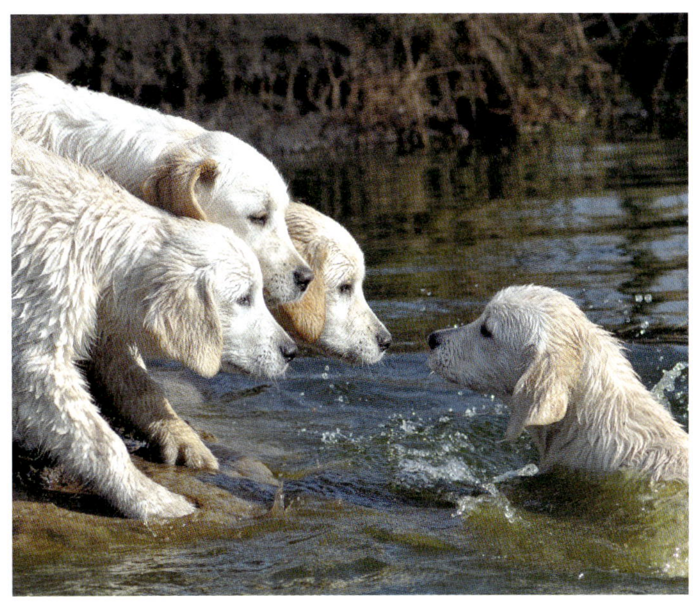

LOCATION: NETHERLANDS

Labrador lifeguards.

PHOTOGRAPHER: Alice van Kempen

LOCATION: NEW ZEALAND

Next up in the upper body workout is the nose curl.

PHOTOGRAPHER: Carol Delaney

LOCATION: UNITED KINGDOM
Talk about nosy neighbours!
PHOTOGRAPHER: Emma Beardsmore

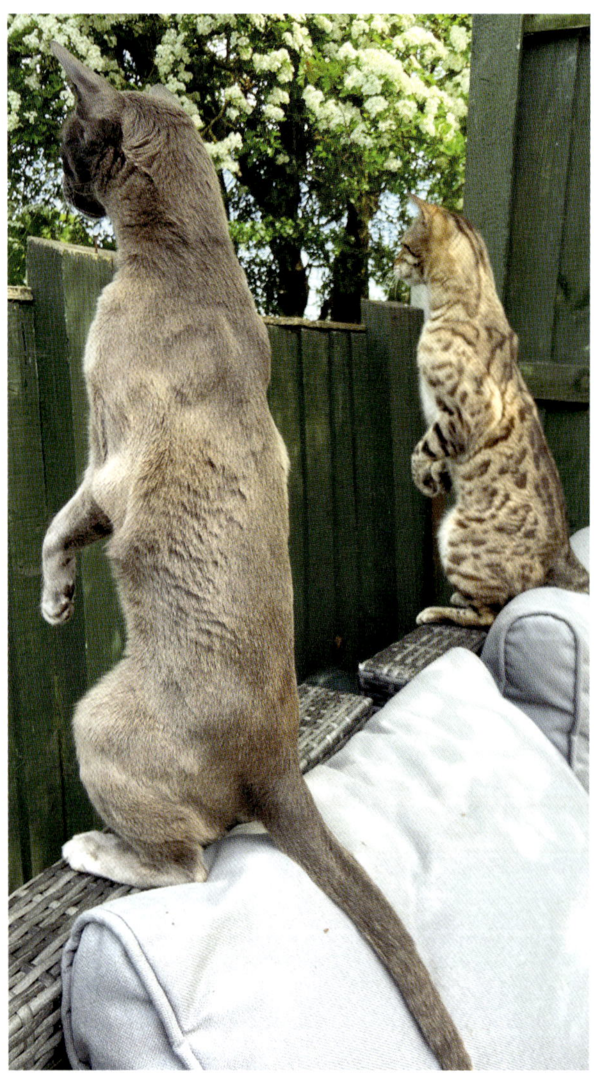

LOCATION: SINGAPORE
The inspiration for my bedroom colour?
Dog-tongue pink of course!
PHOTOGRAPHER: Bernard Sim

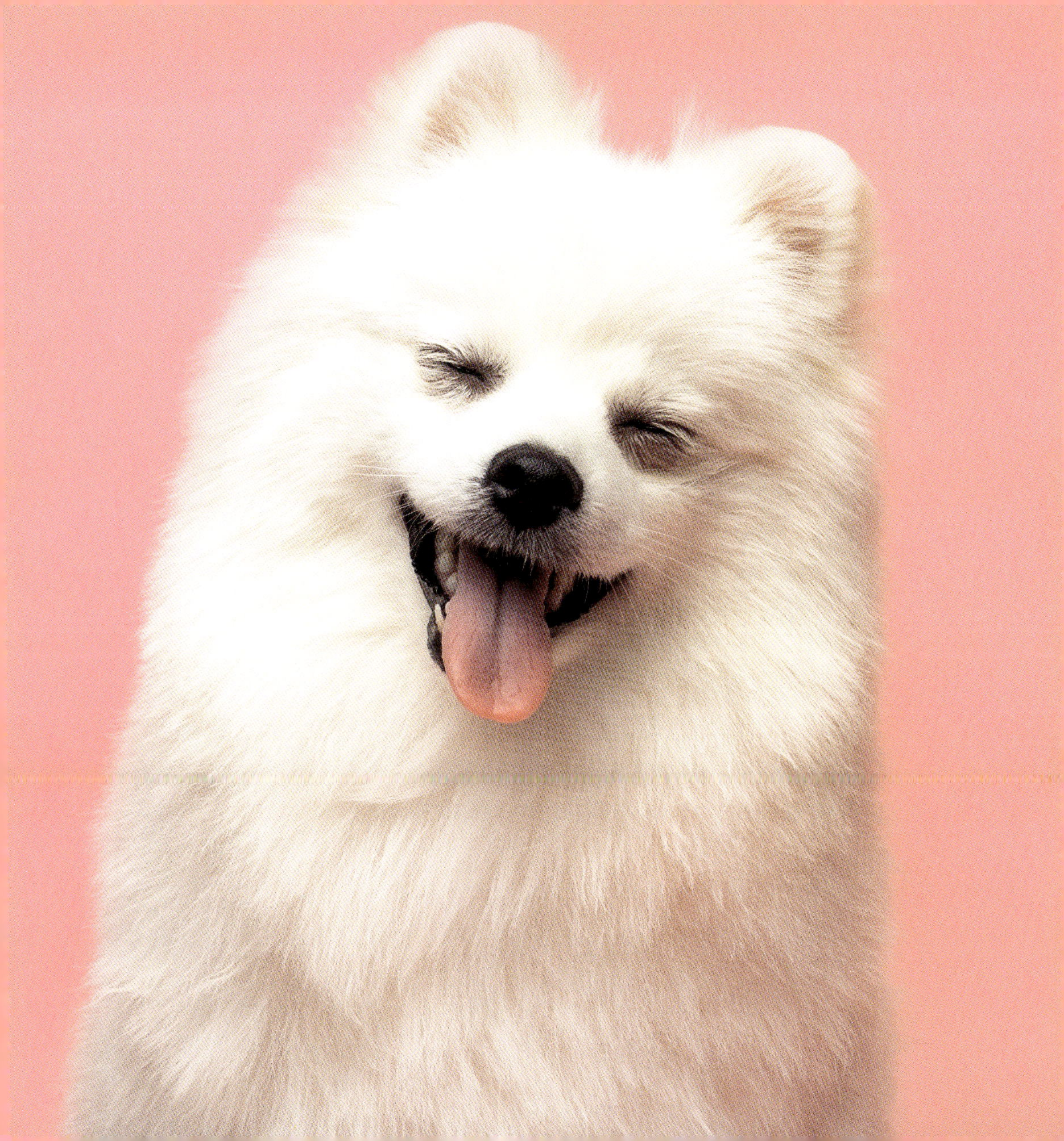

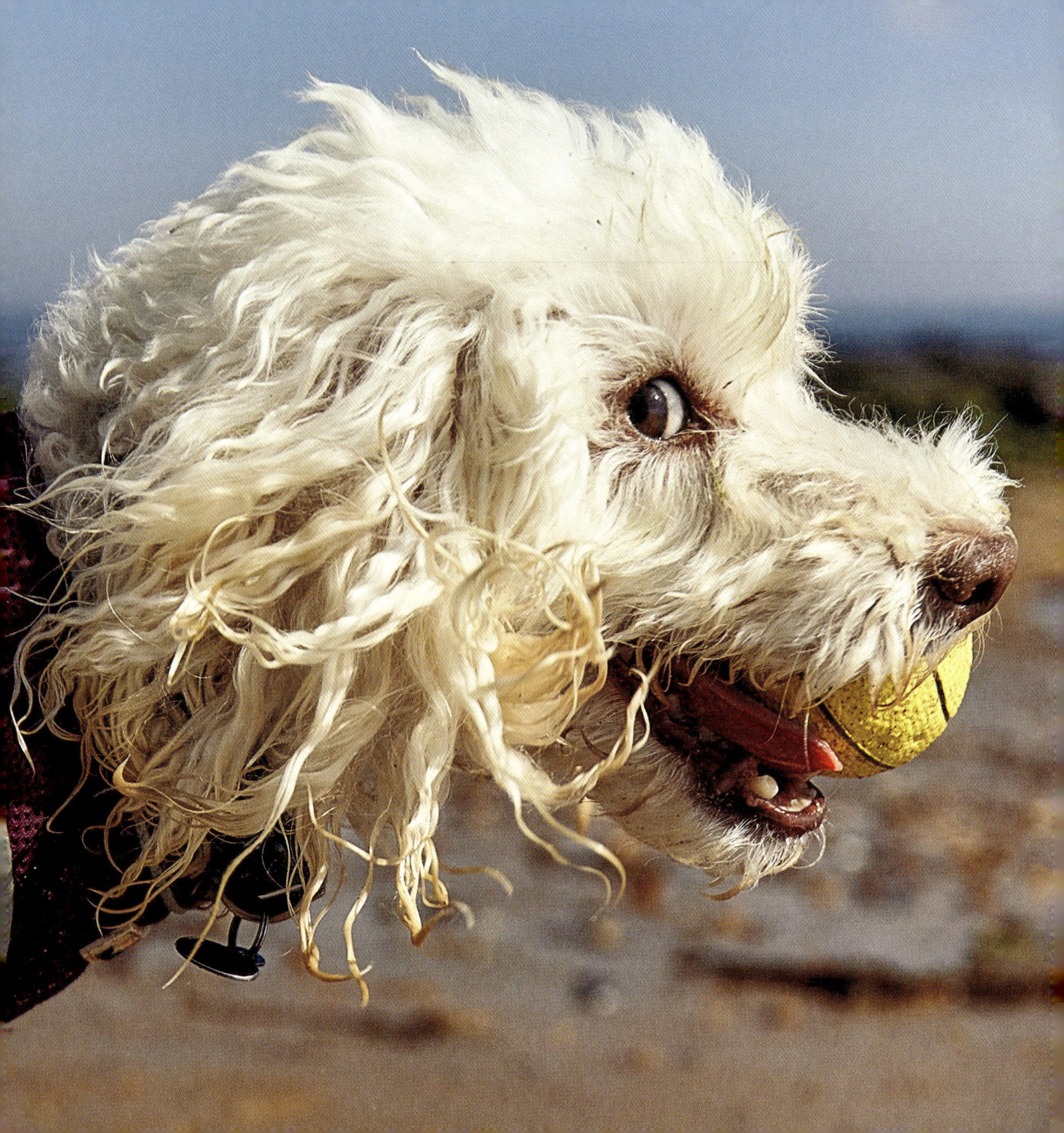

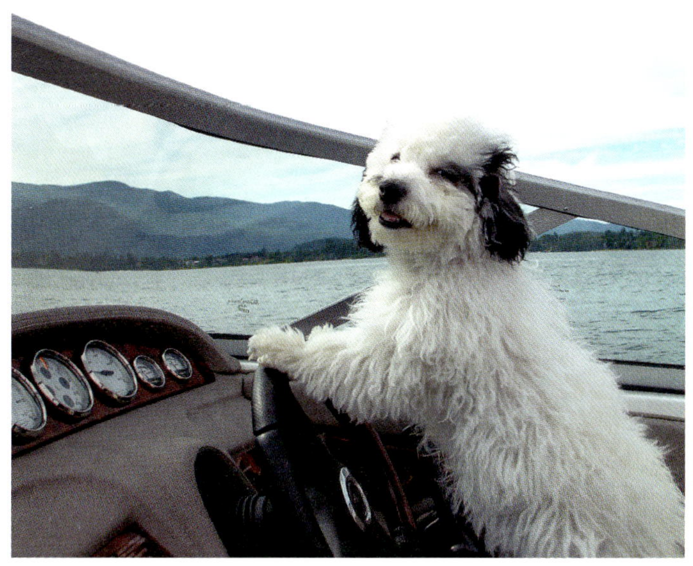

LOCATION: IDAHO, UNITED STATES
Nice ride – wait til you hear the sub-woofer.
PHOTOGRAPHER: Donna Deshon

LOCATION: WHITLEY BAY, UNITED KINGDOM
Er, is my body still behind me?
PHOTOGRAPHER: Darren Hall

LOCATION: NORTH CAROLINA, UNITED STATES
Jurassic Bark.
PHOTOGRAPHER: Carmen Cromer

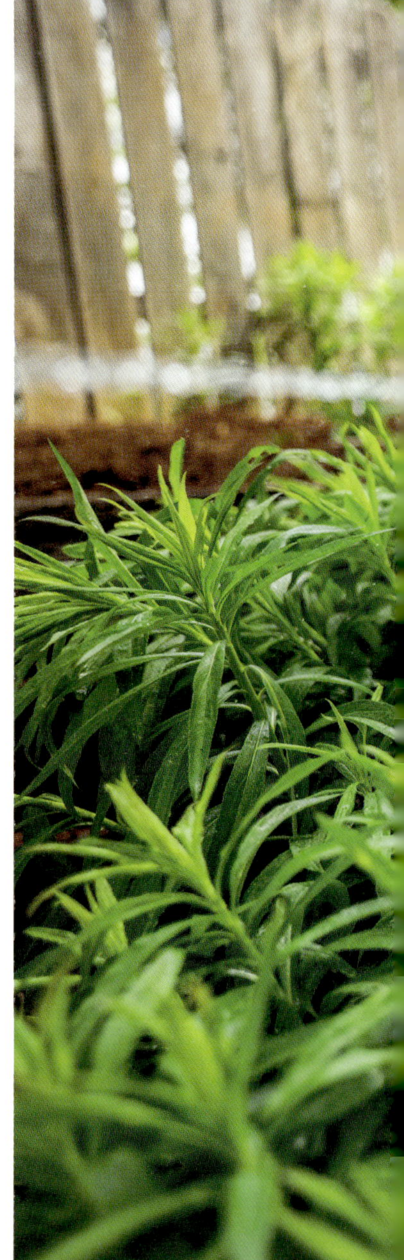

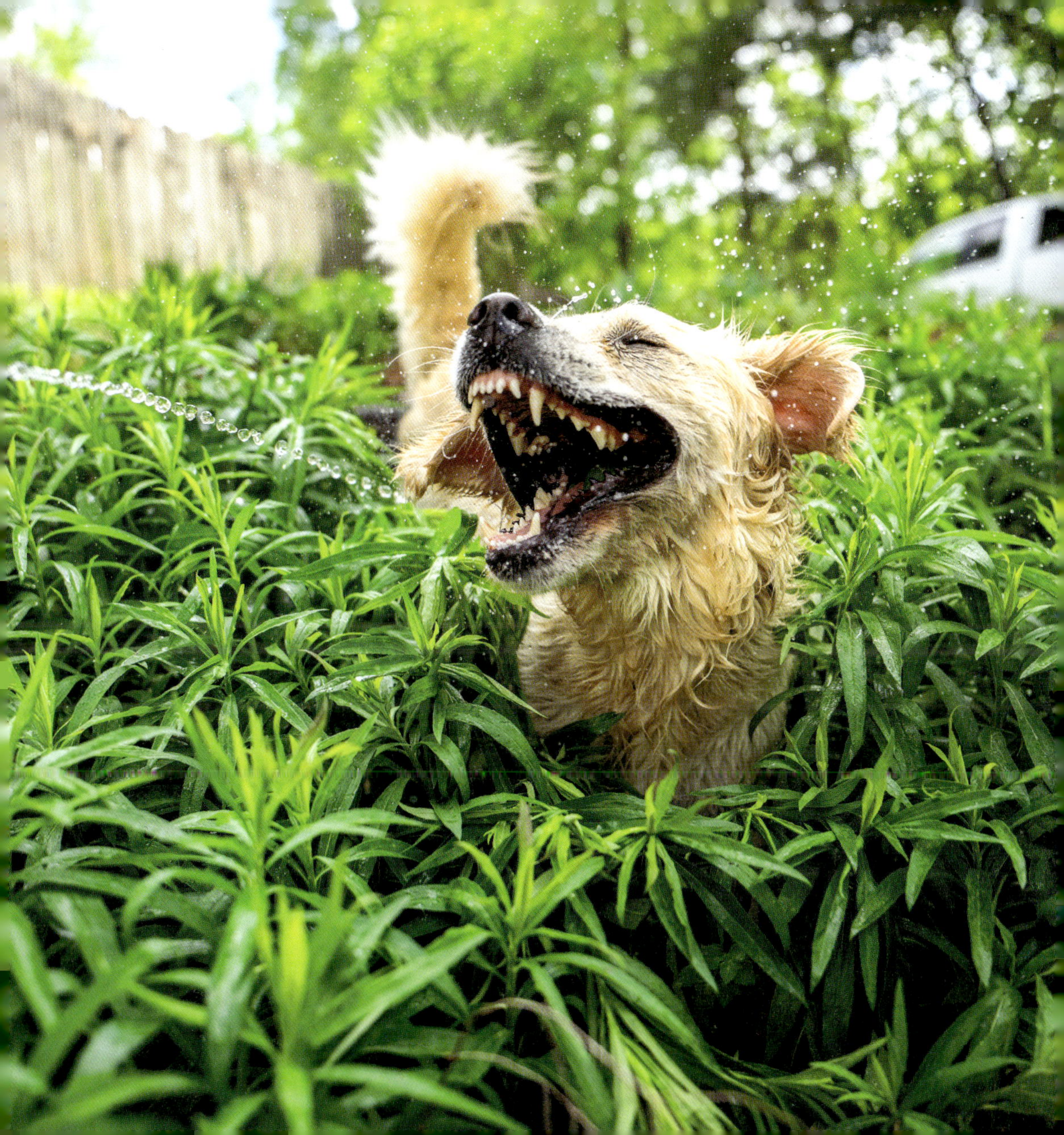

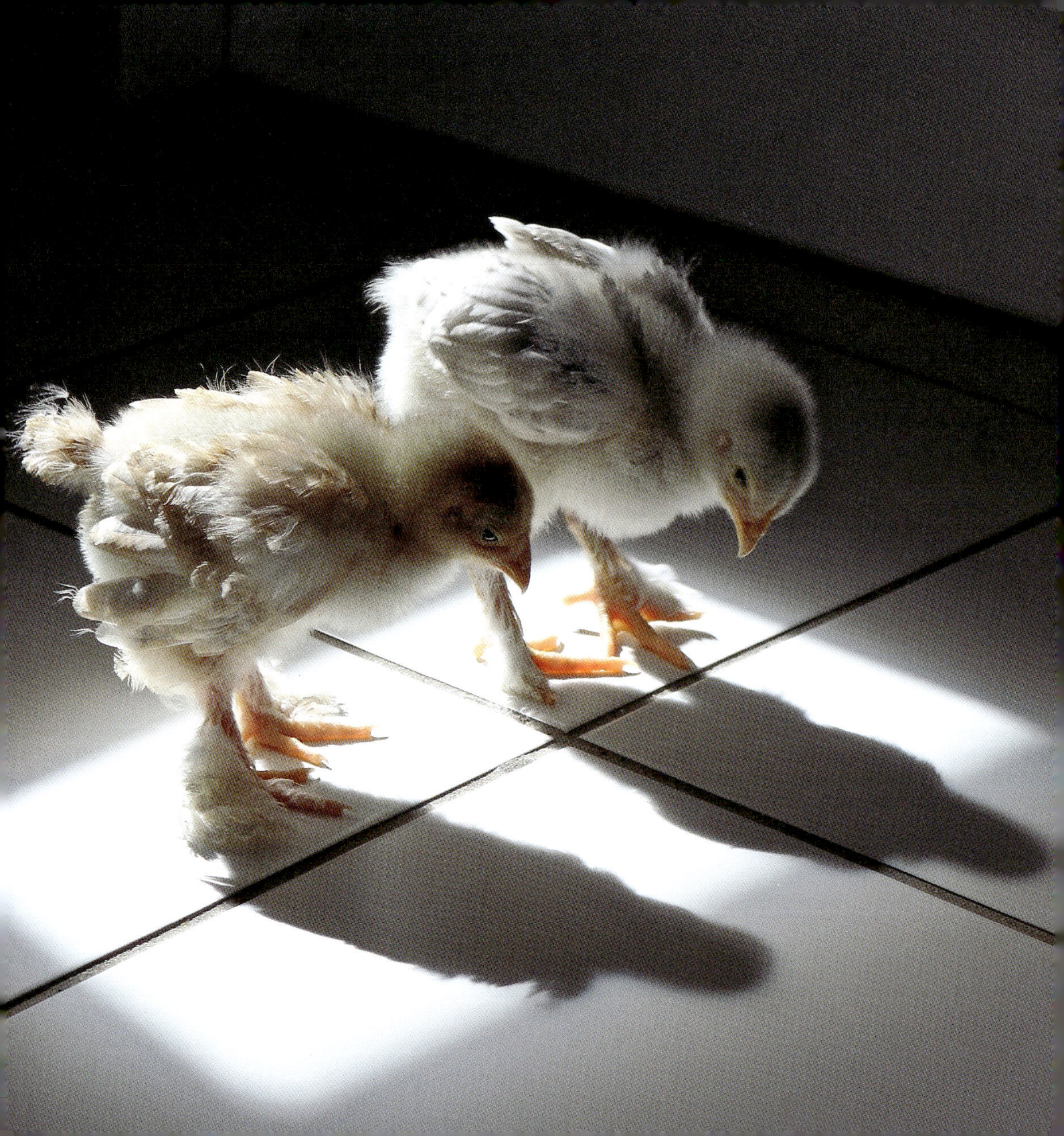

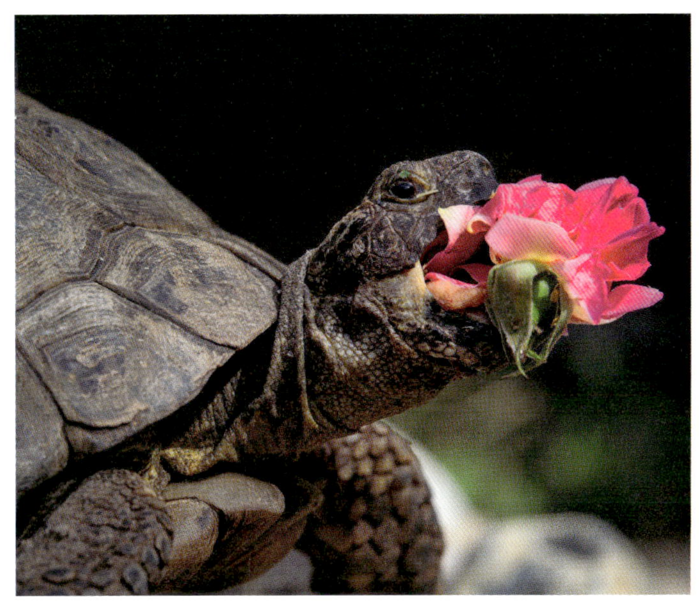

LOCATION: UNITED KINGDOM

Tortoises really pull out all the stops on first dates.

PHOTOGRAPHER: Jonathan Casey

LOCATION: OXFORD, UNITED KINGDOM

Their shadow puppet game needs work.

PHOTOGRAPHER: Sophie Bonnefoi

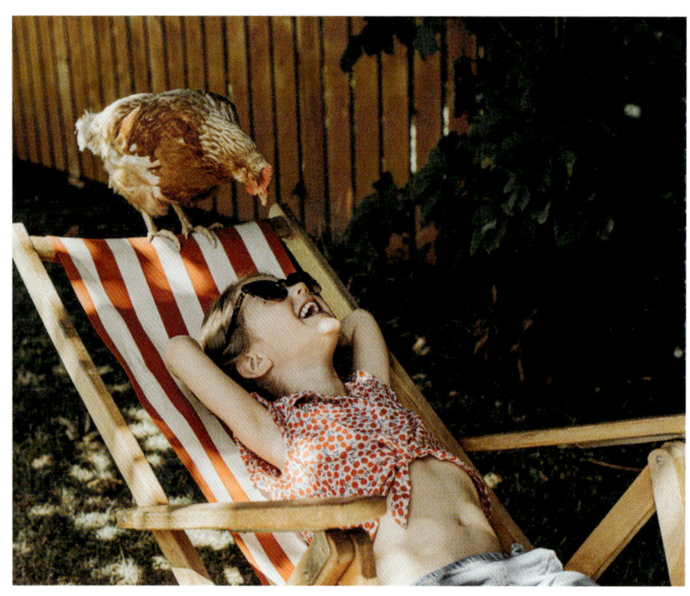

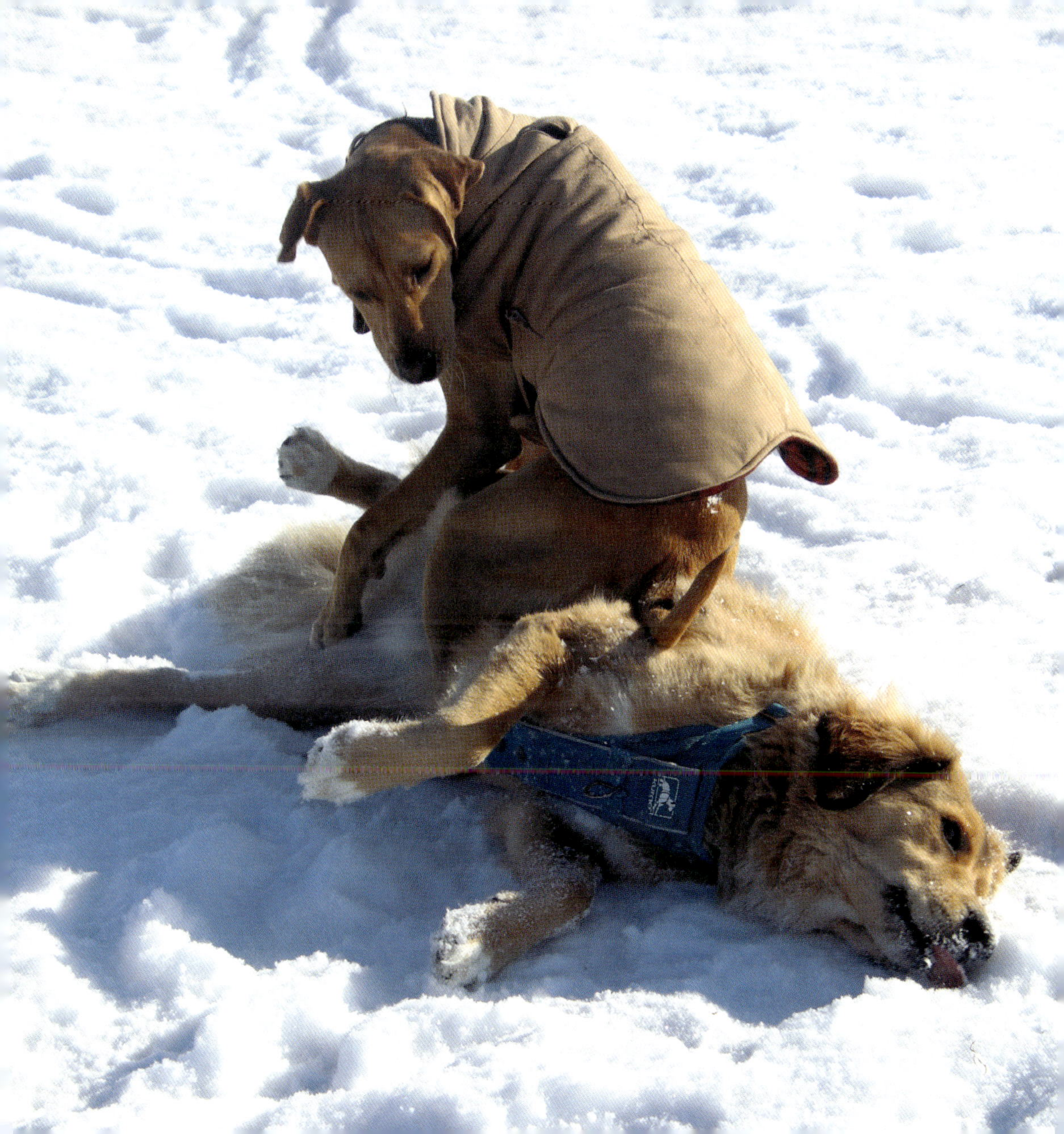

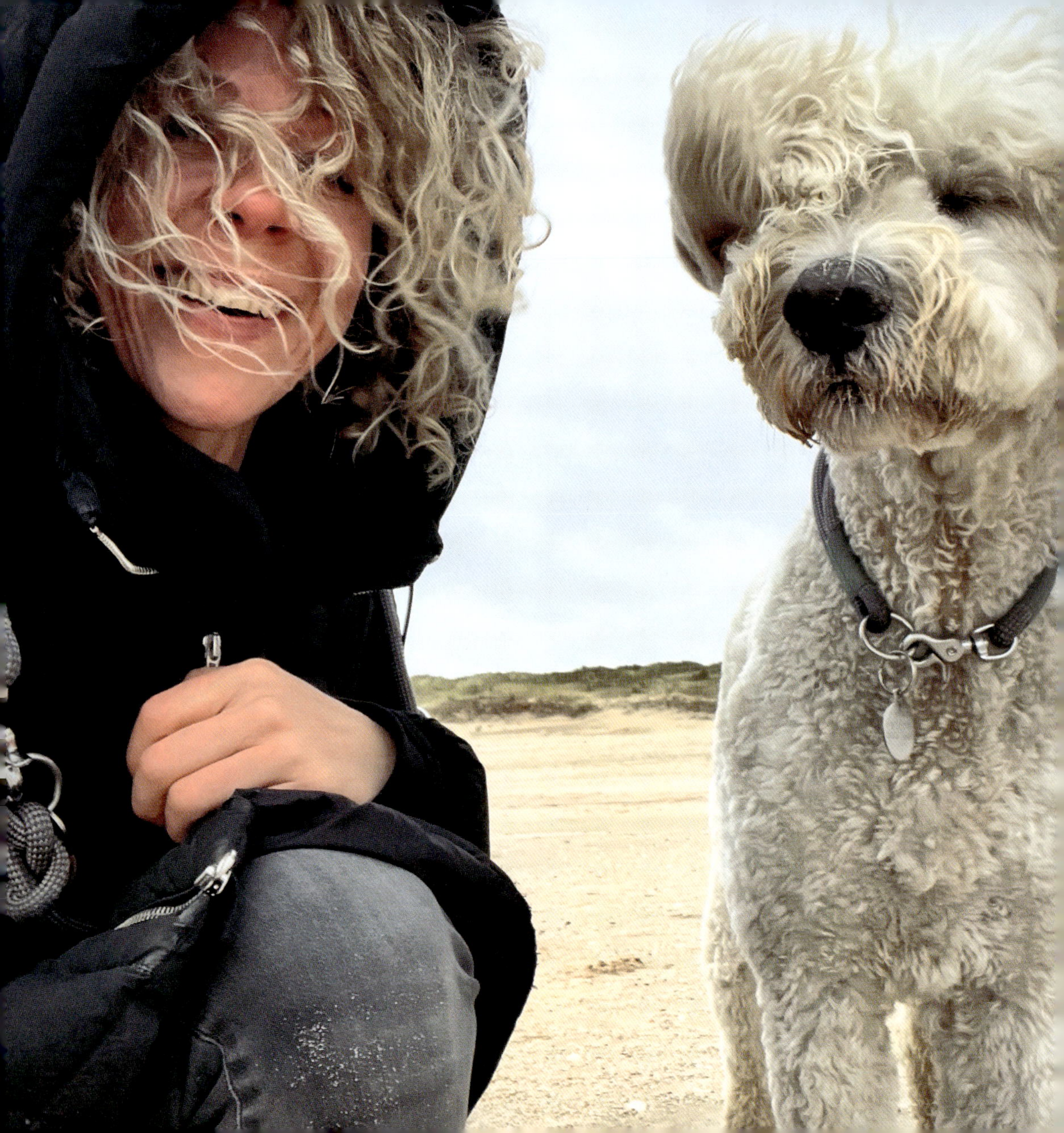

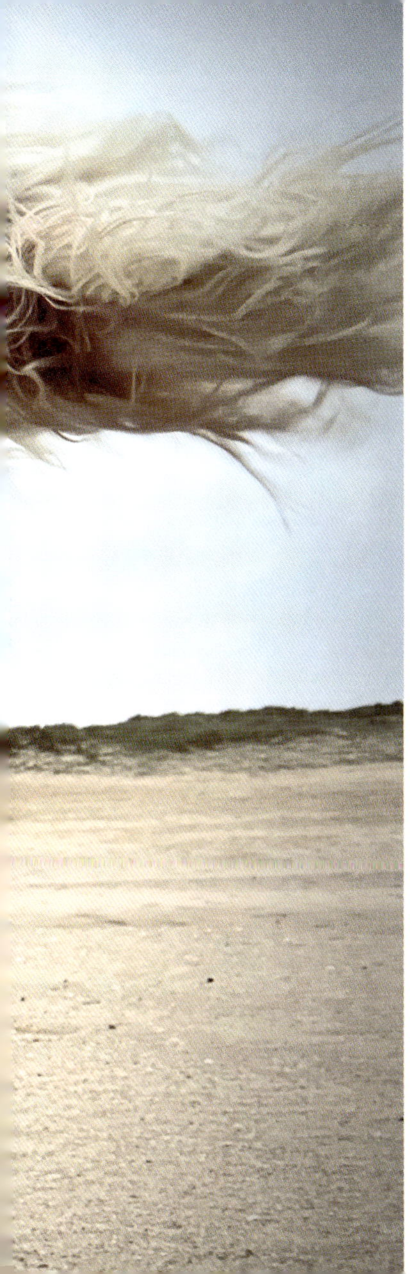

LOCATION: GERMANY

Nothing more invigorating than a dash through the dunes.

PHOTOGRAPHER: Julia Illig

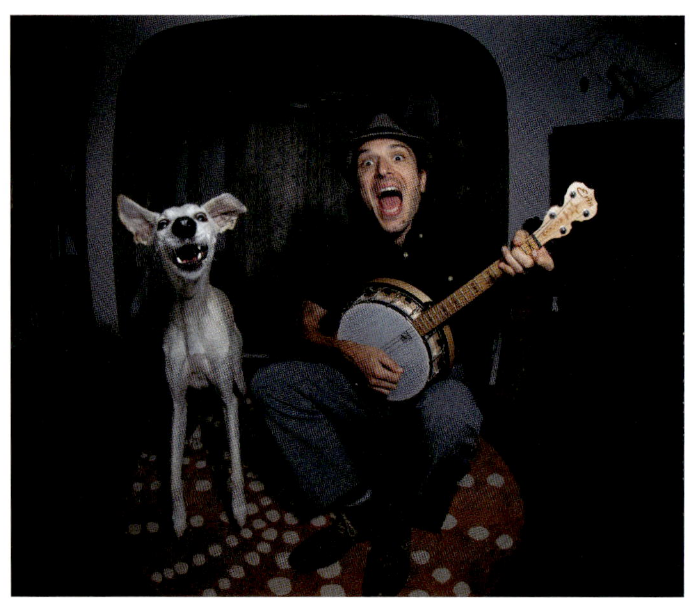

LOCATION: COVENTRY, UNITED KINGDOM
Muttford and chum.
PHOTOGRAPHER: Luke O'Brien

LOCATION: CHINA
She's really brought her A-game for the stare-out,
but there's only going to be one winner here!
PHOTOGRAPHER: Silvia Jiang

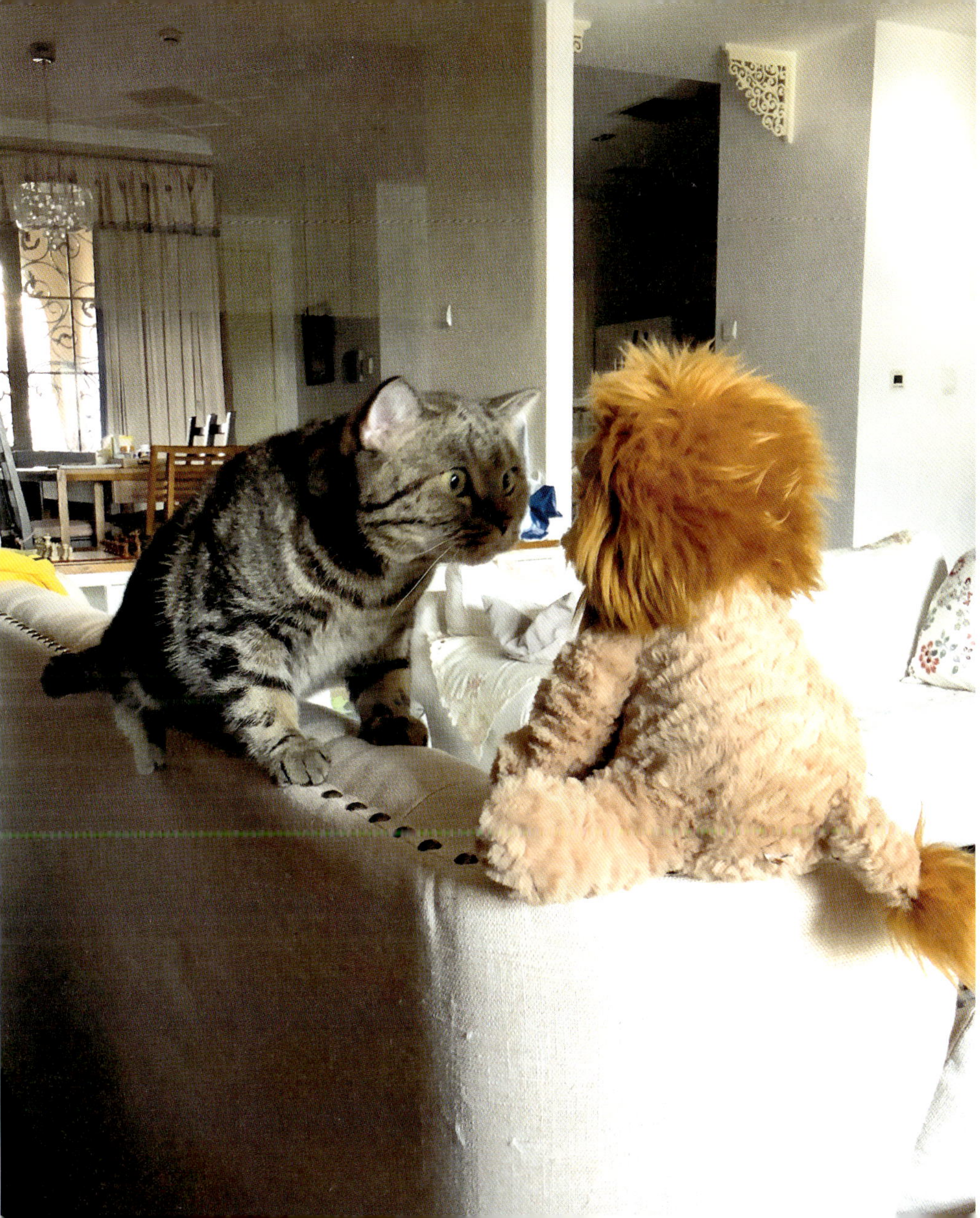

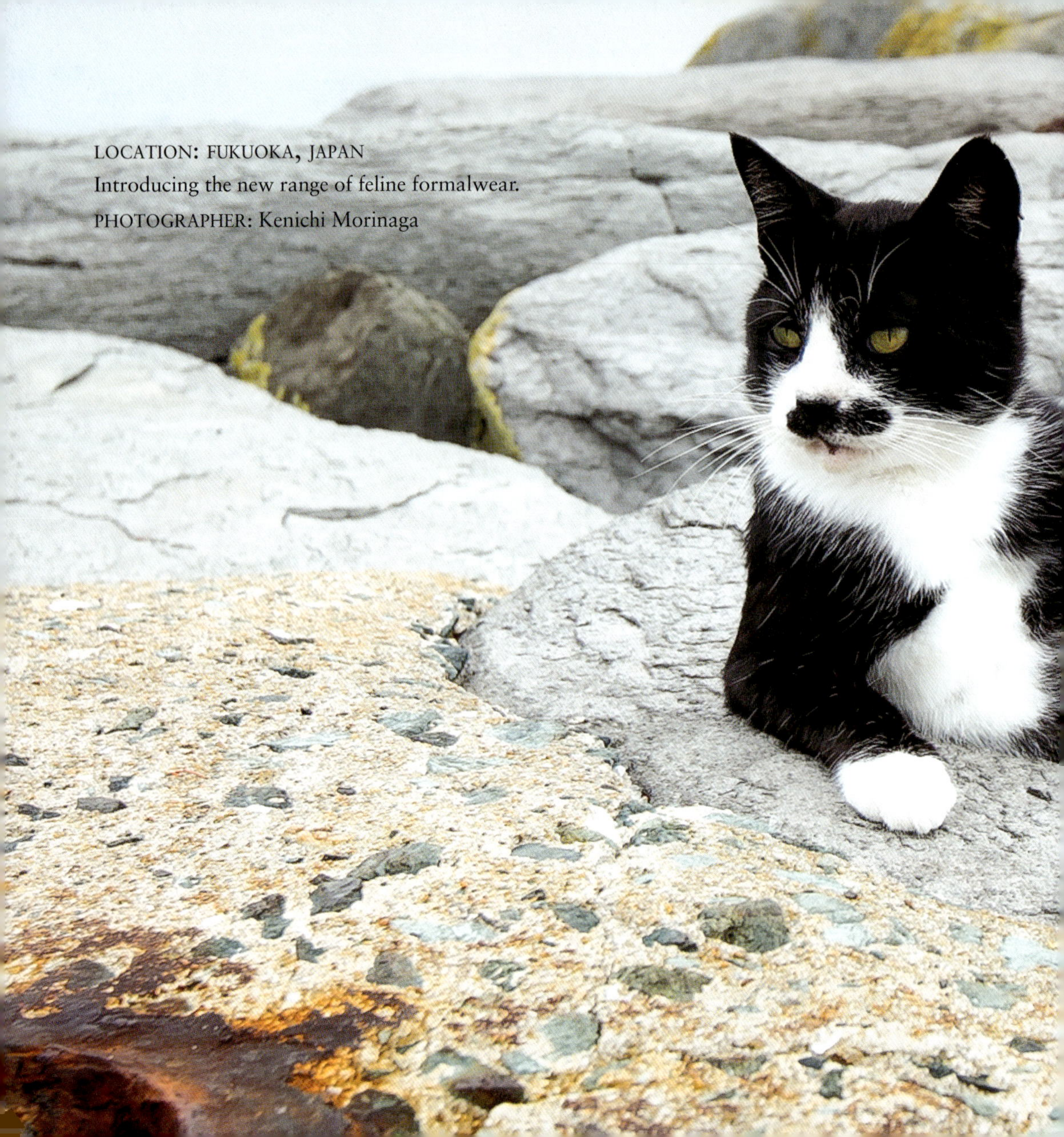

LOCATION: FUKUOKA, JAPAN
Introducing the new range of feline formalwear.
PHOTOGRAPHER: Kenichi Morinaga

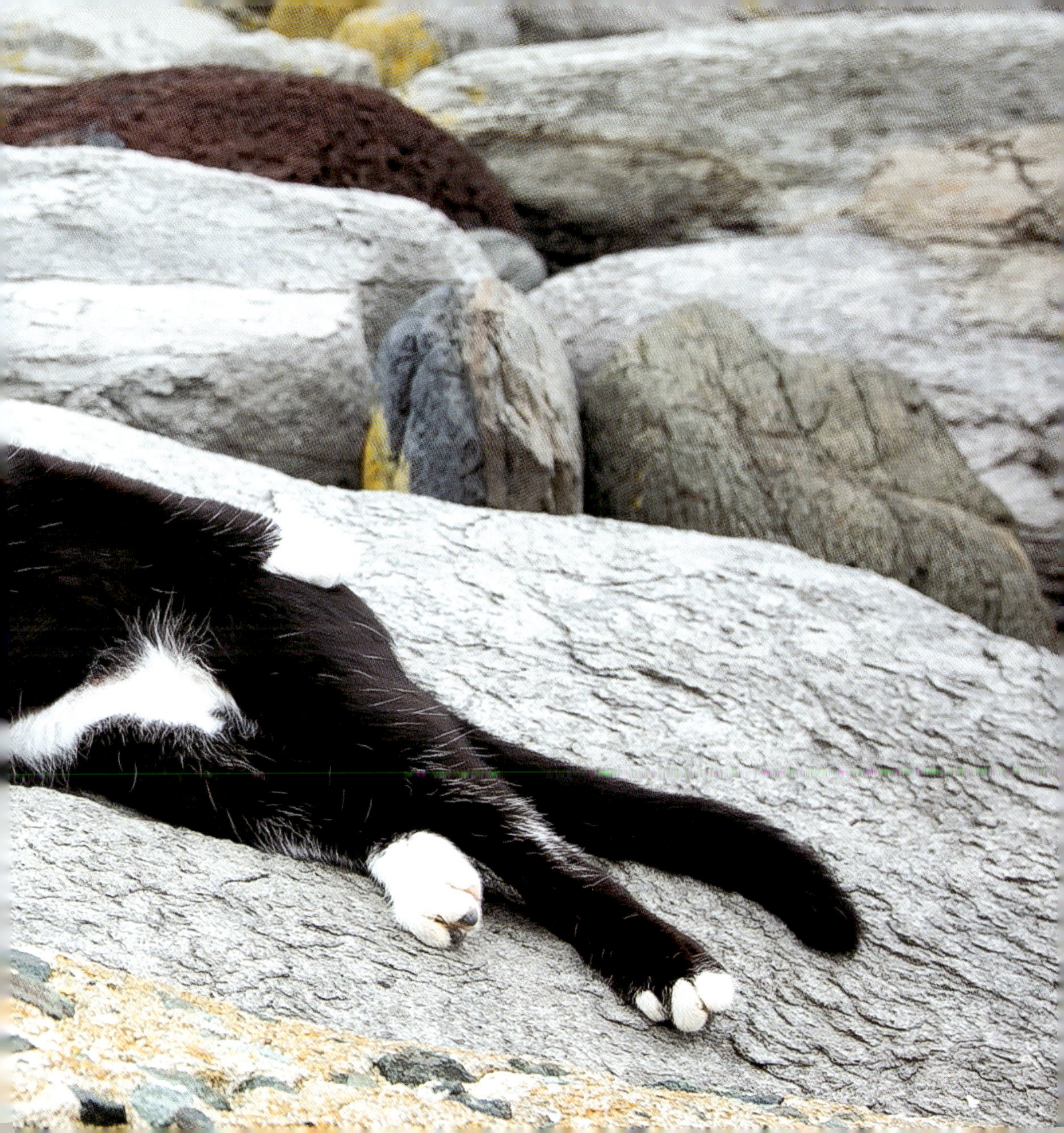

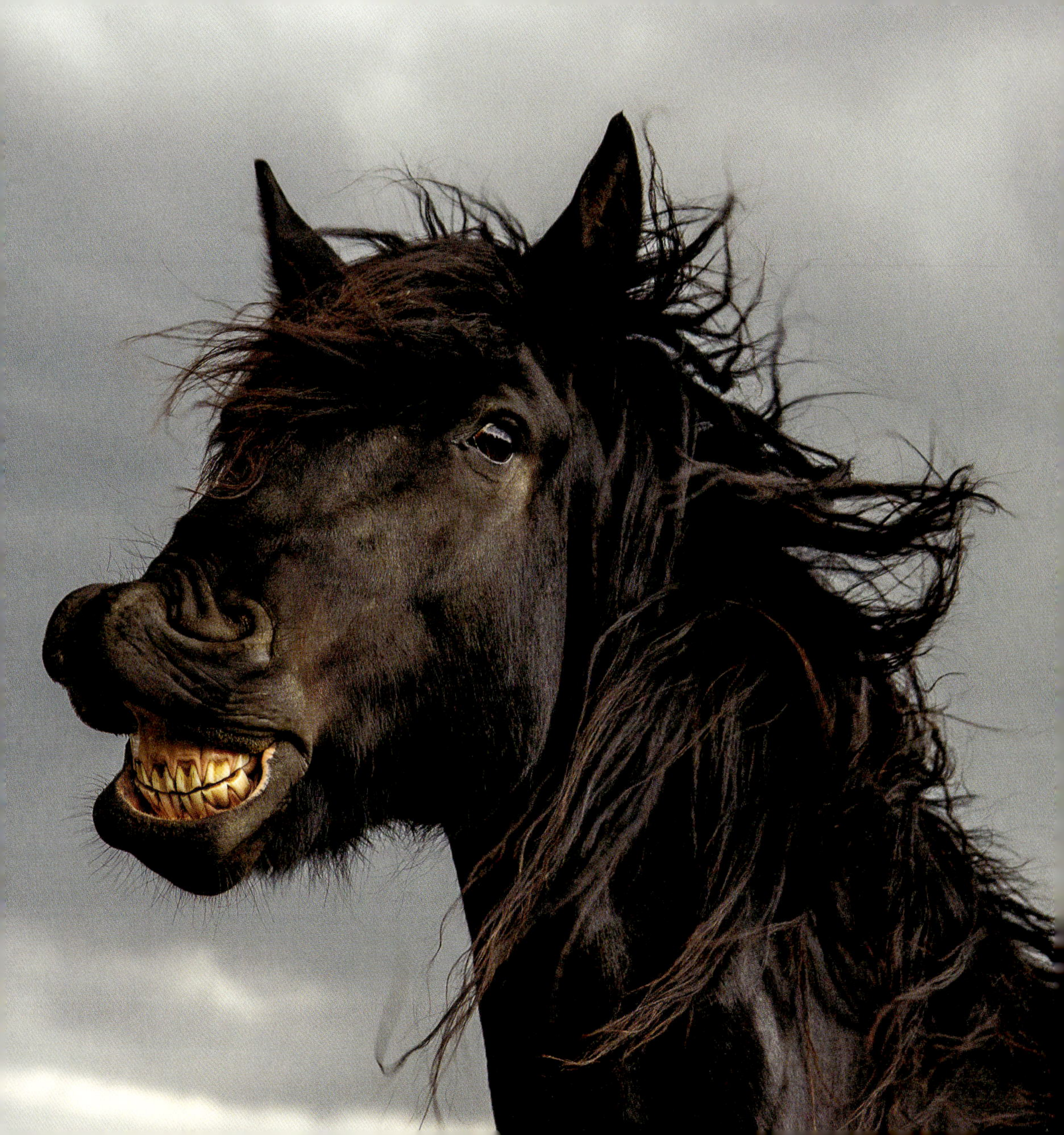

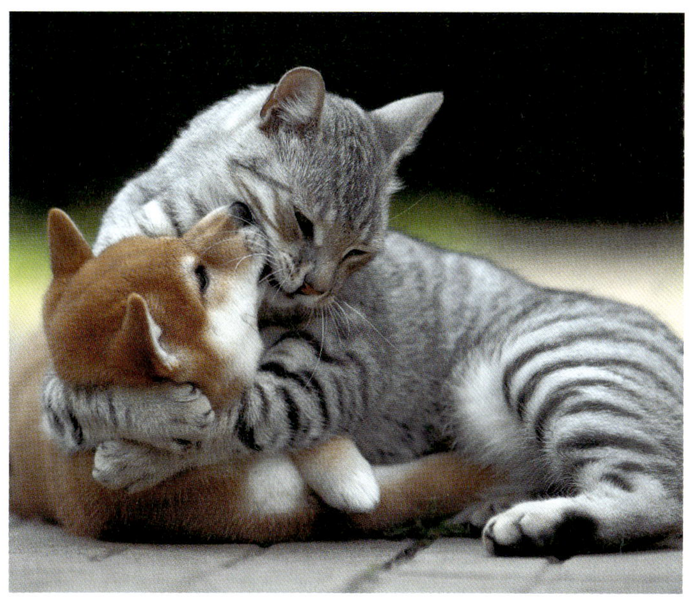

LOCATION: RUSSIA

BFFS (best fur-ends forever).

PHOTOGRAPHER: Svetlana Pisareva

LOCATION: FRANCE

This guy just can't help but horse around.

PHOTOGRAPHER: David Poznanter

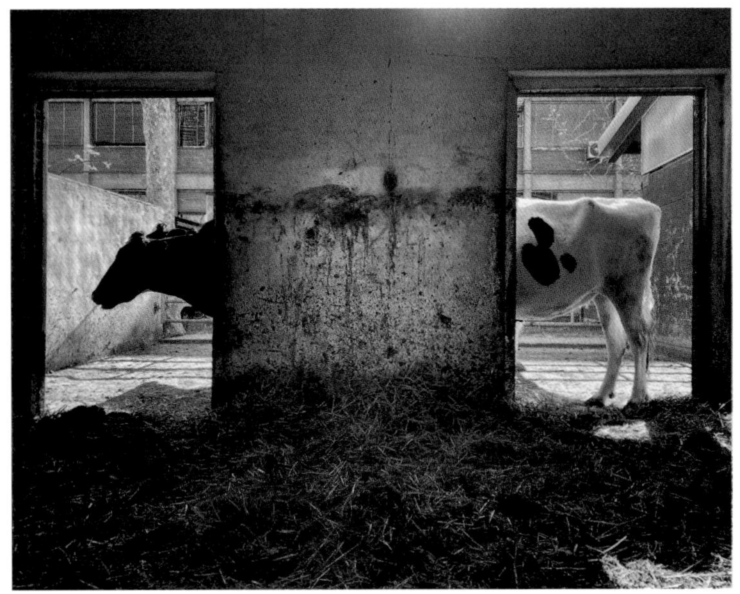

LOCATION: FIDENZA, ITALY
Stretch limooo.
PHOTOGRAPHER: Pier Luigi Dodi

LOCATION: SAN ANTONIO, UNITED STATES
The cruise ship's new pet deck welcomed its first passenger.
PHOTOGRAPHER: Millie Kerr

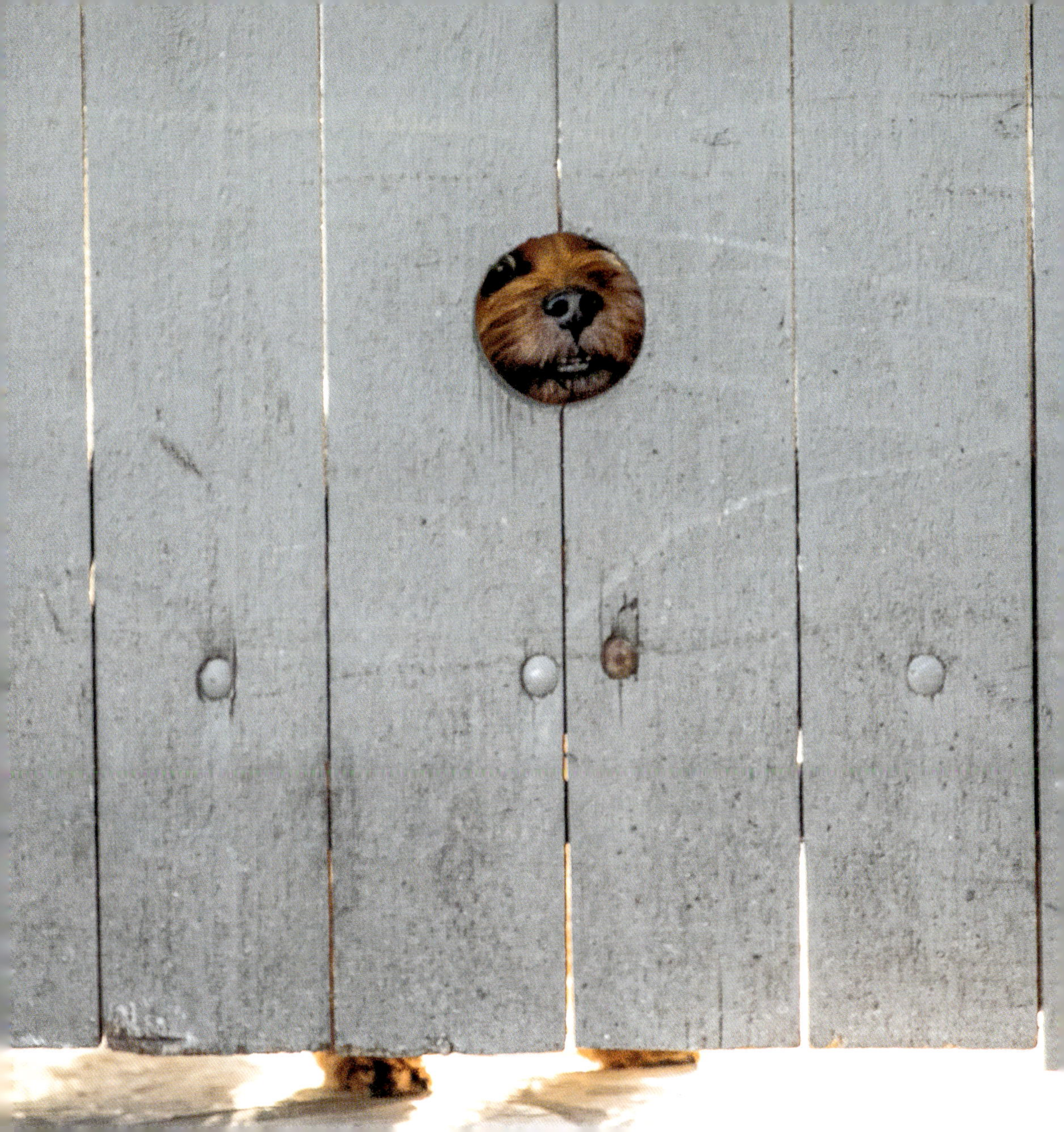

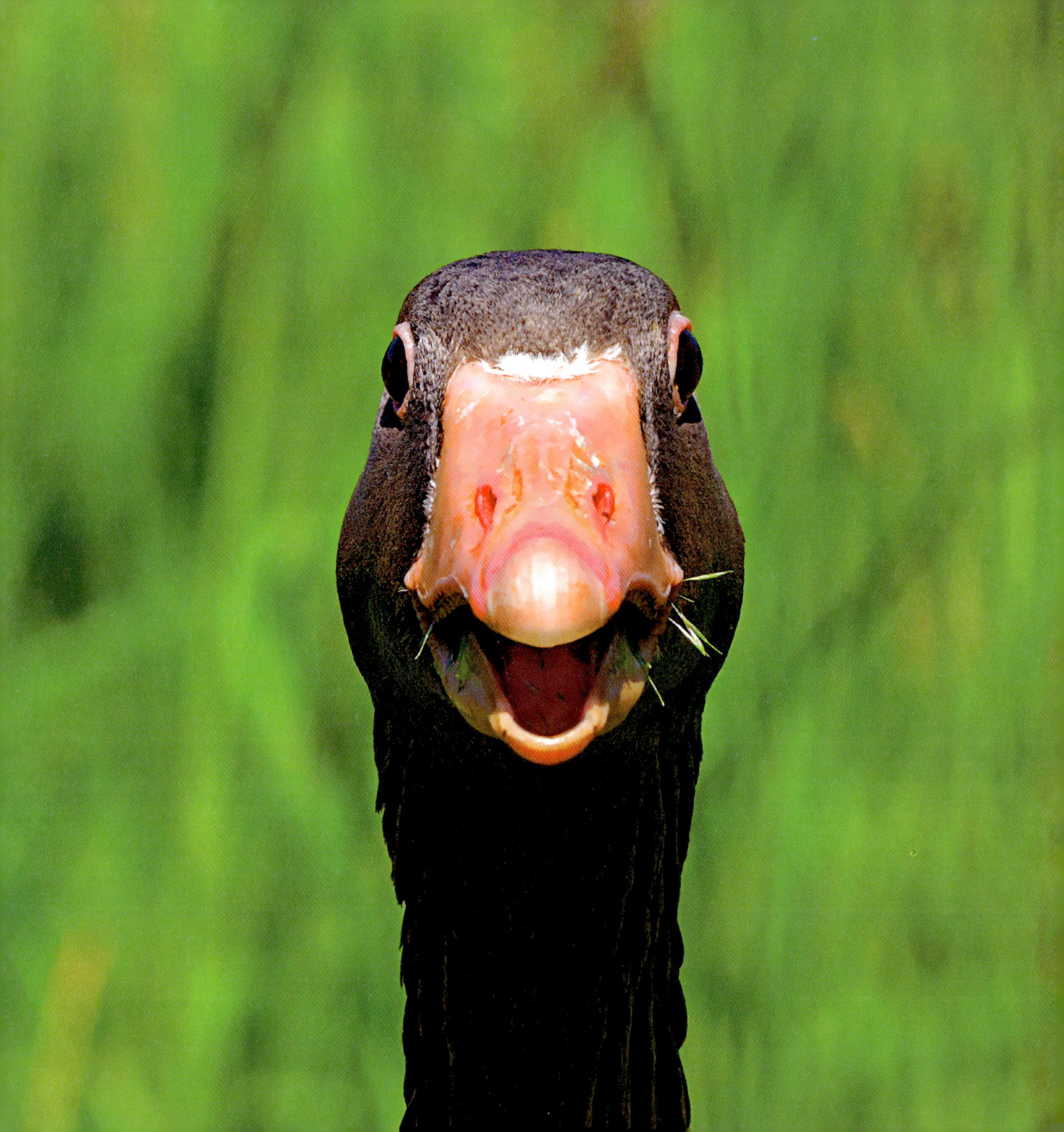

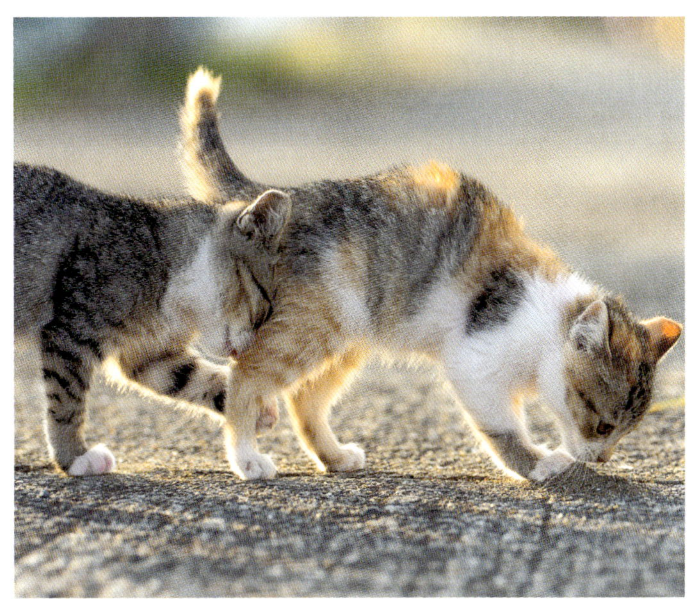

LOCATION: JAPAN

We are not a-mew-sed.

PHOTOGRAPHER: Tomoaki Tanto

LOCATION: GERMANY

Had enough of a gander have you?

PHOTOGRAPHER: Stefan Brusius

LOCATION: WARRINGTON, UNITED KINGDOM
Look before you leap.
PHOTOGRAPHER: Christine Johnson

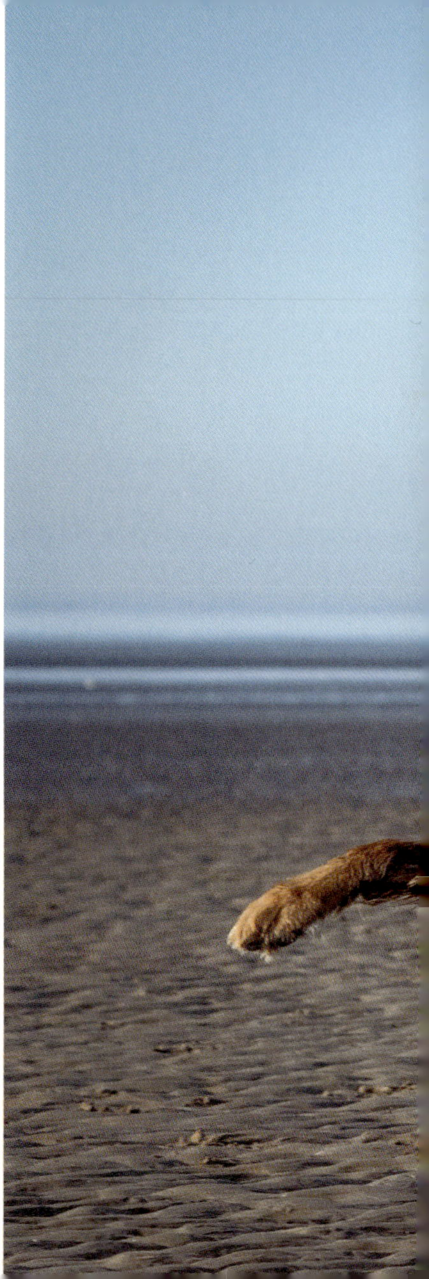

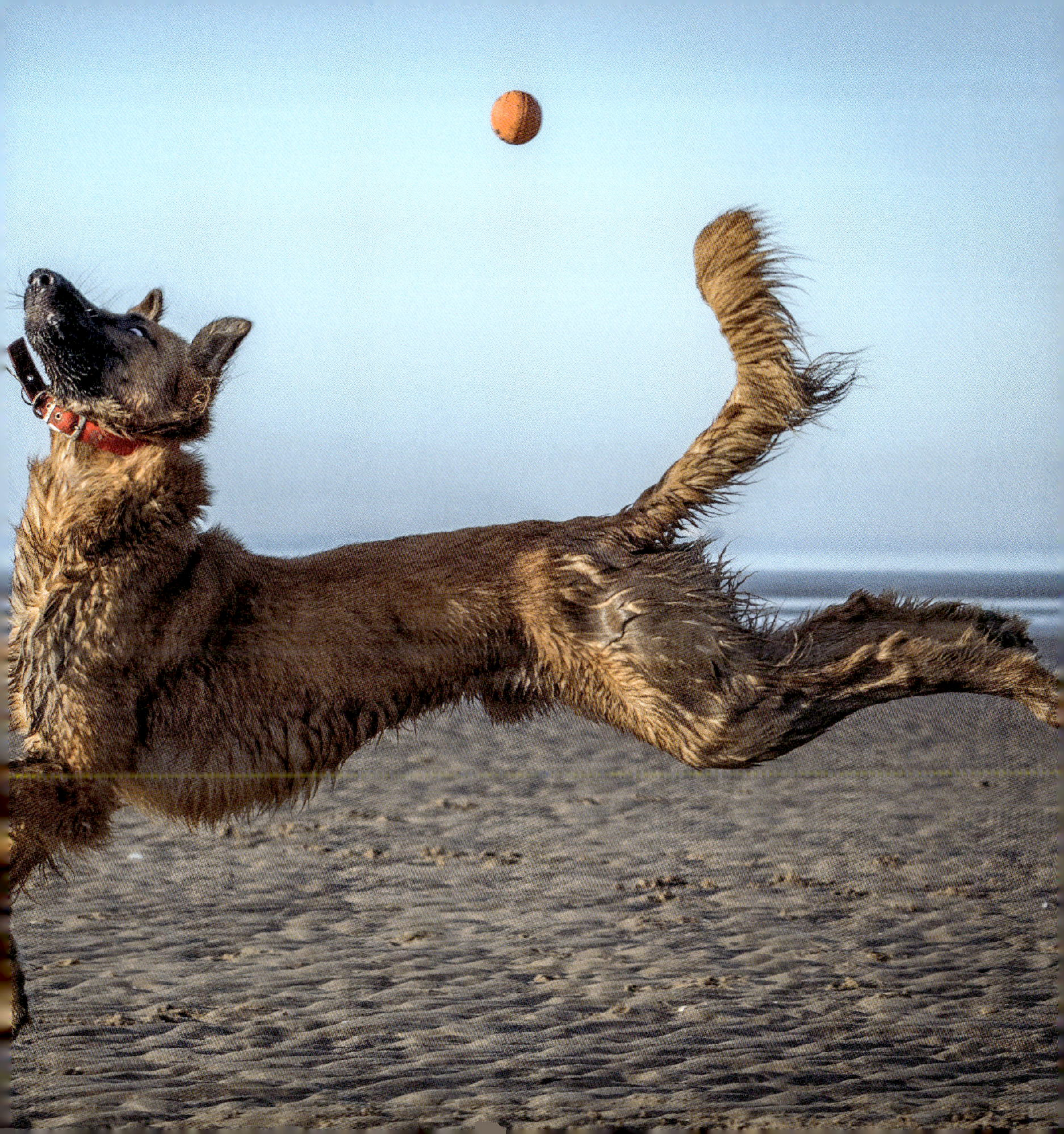

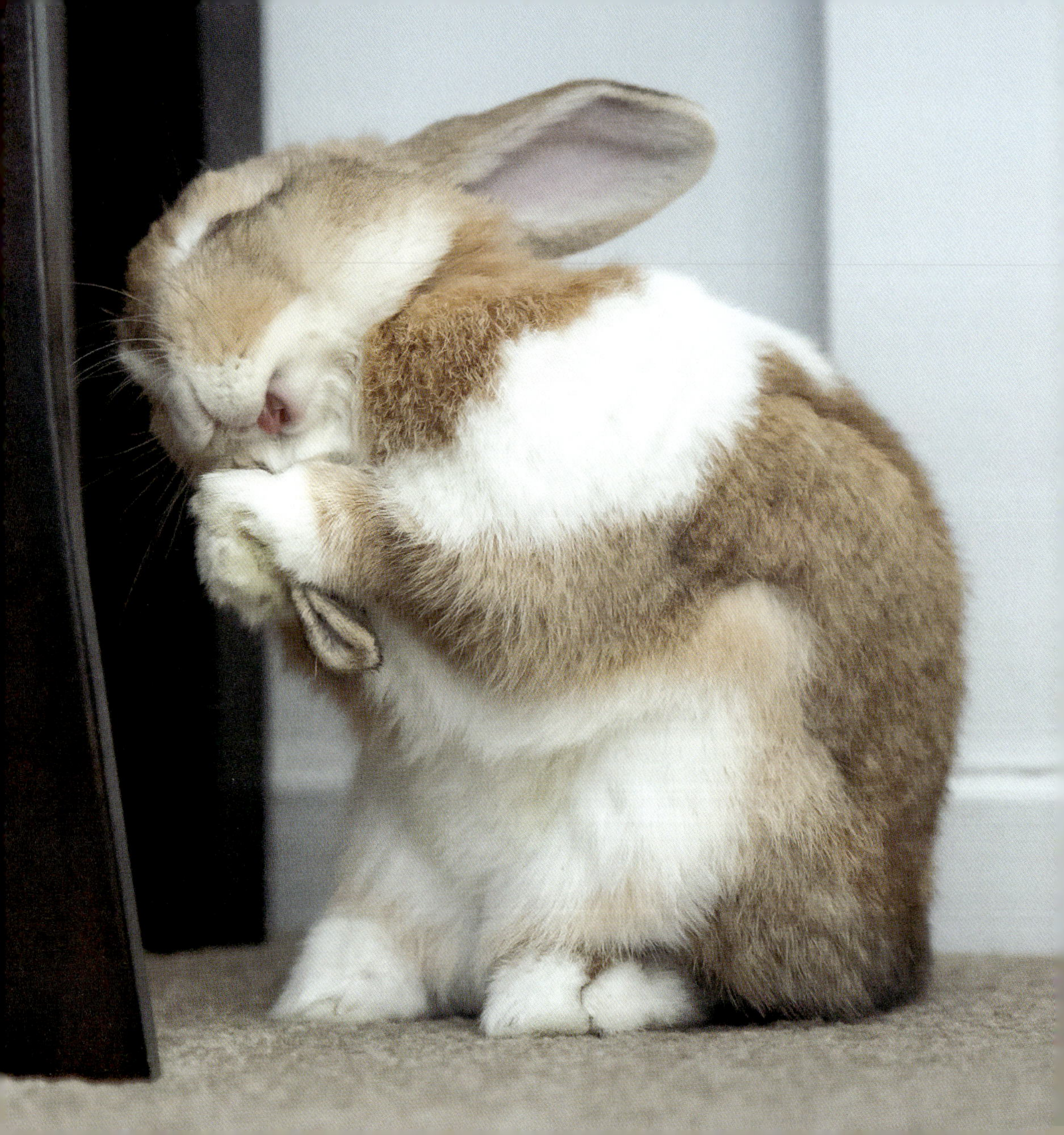

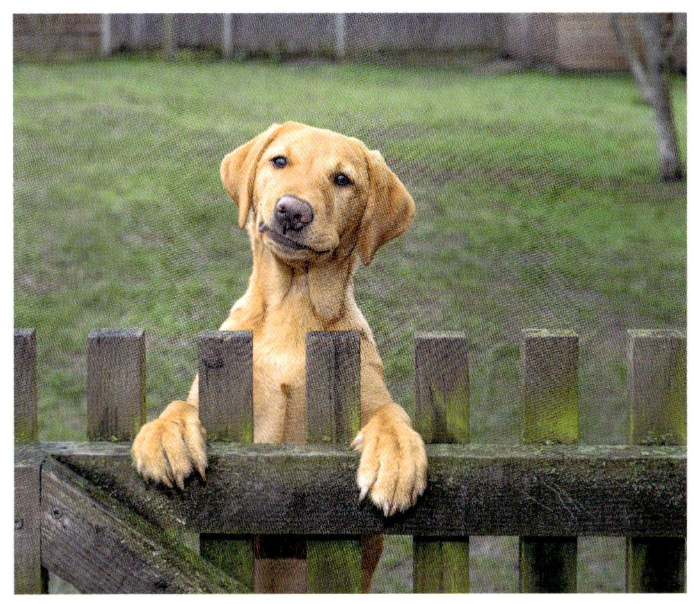

LOCATION: UNITED KINGDOM

Not bad thanks – the lawn's gone to the dogs though.

PHOTOGRAPHER: Holly Stranks

LOCATION: CANADA

Well, mum always said wash behind your ears.

PHOTOGRAPHER: Sarah von Keitz

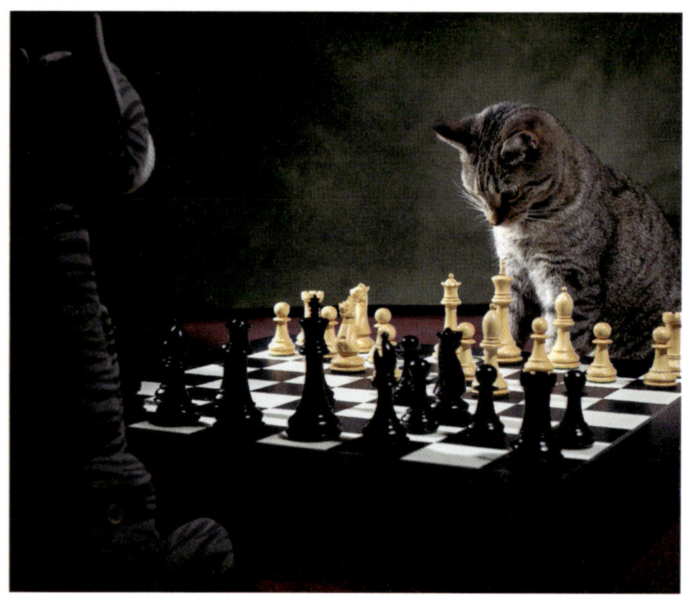

LOCATION: WYMONDHAM, NORFOLK, UNITED KINGDOM
Paws for thought for the Tabby grandmaster.
PHOTOGRAPHER: Jonathan Casey

LOCATION: CZECH REPUBLIC
Cut it out mum, you're so embarrassing!
PHOTOGRAPHER: Radim Filipek

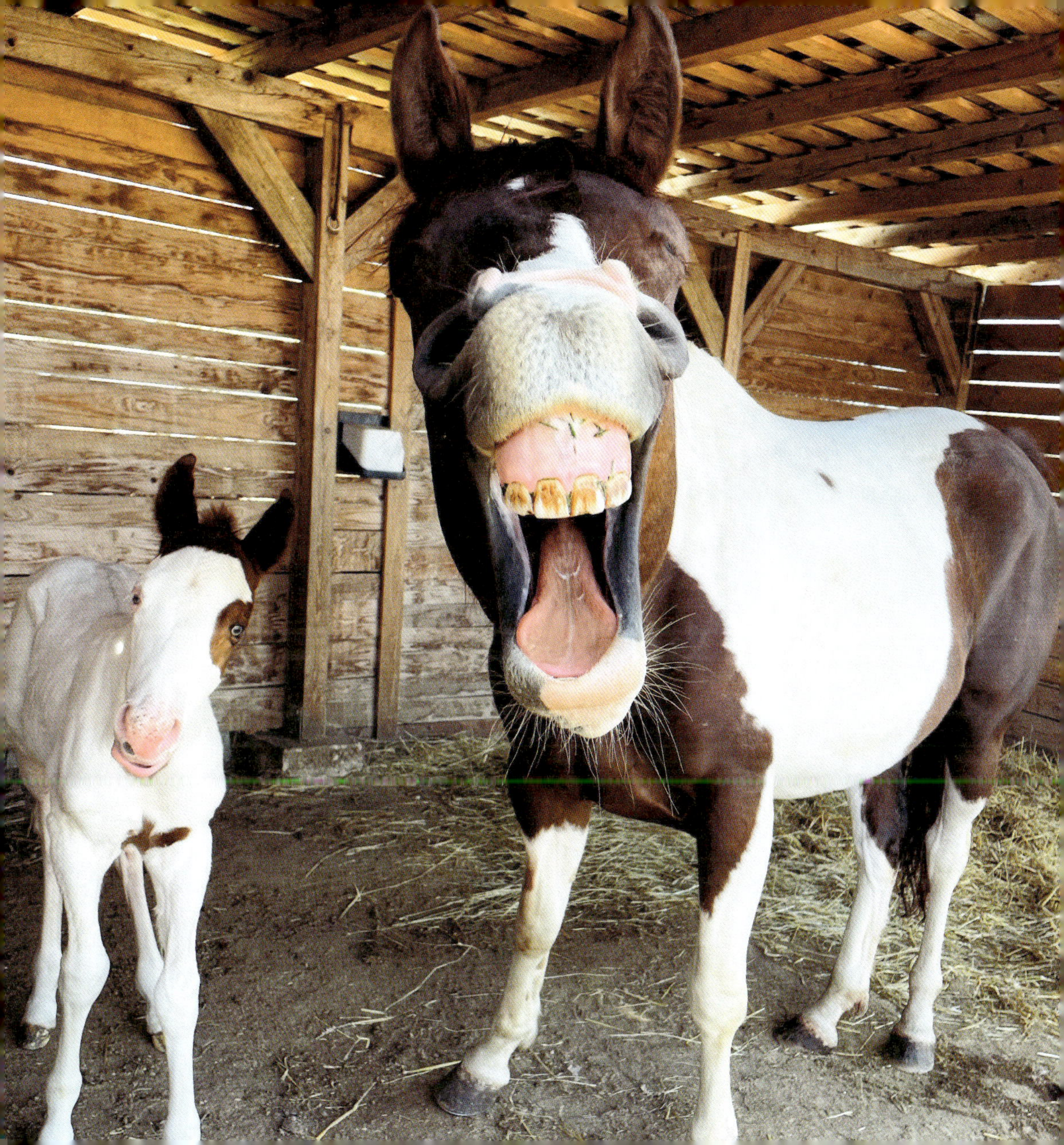

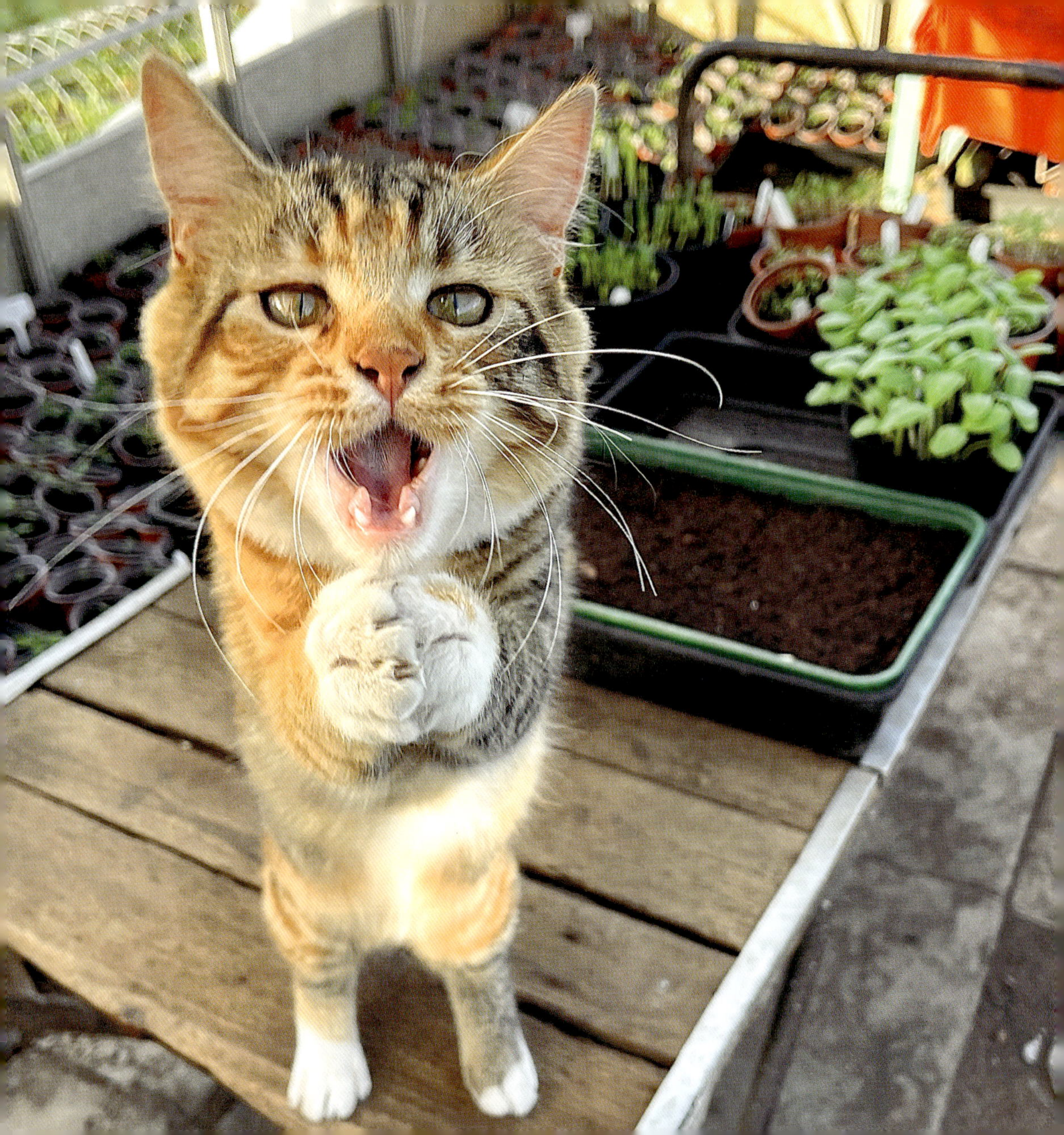

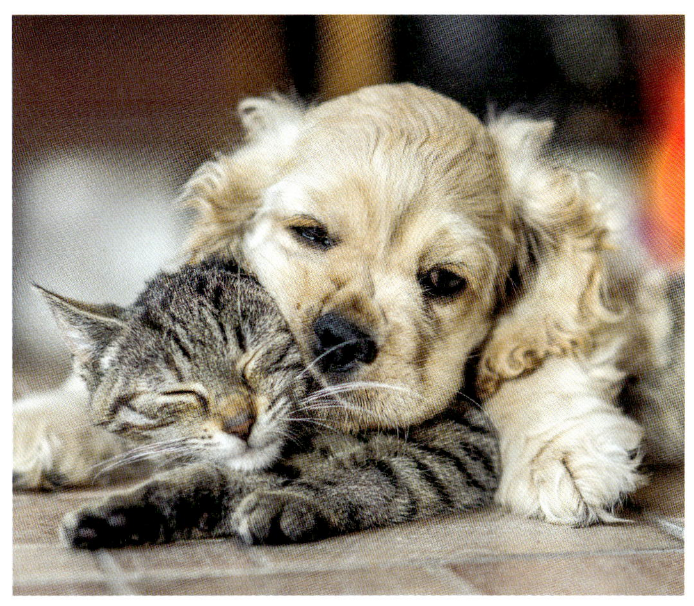

LOCATION: UNITED KINGDOM

I'm begging you – please tell me where you've moved the catnip!

PHOTOGRAPHER: Sarah Fiona Helme

LOCATION: UNITED KINGDOM
Nothing to see here, pal.
PHOTOGRAPHER: Lucy Sellors

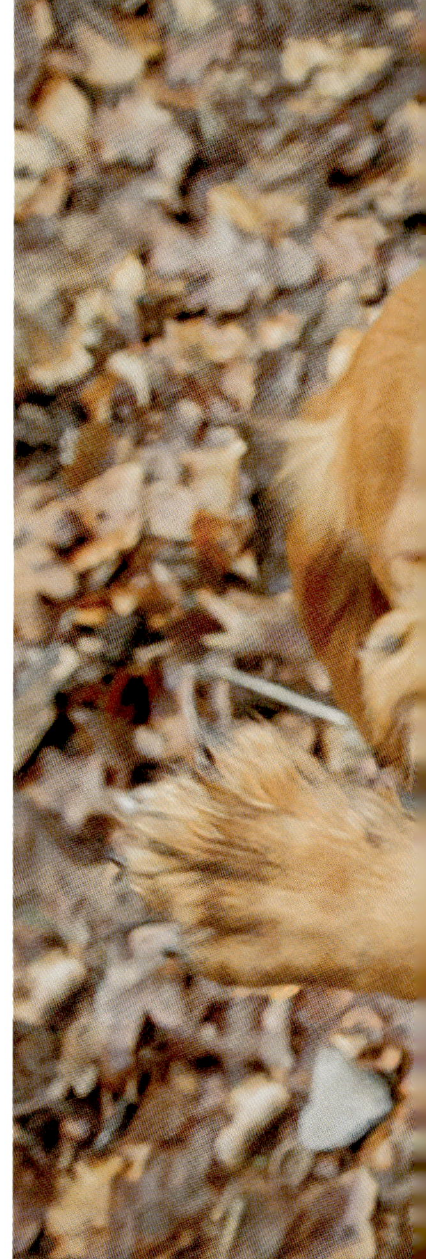

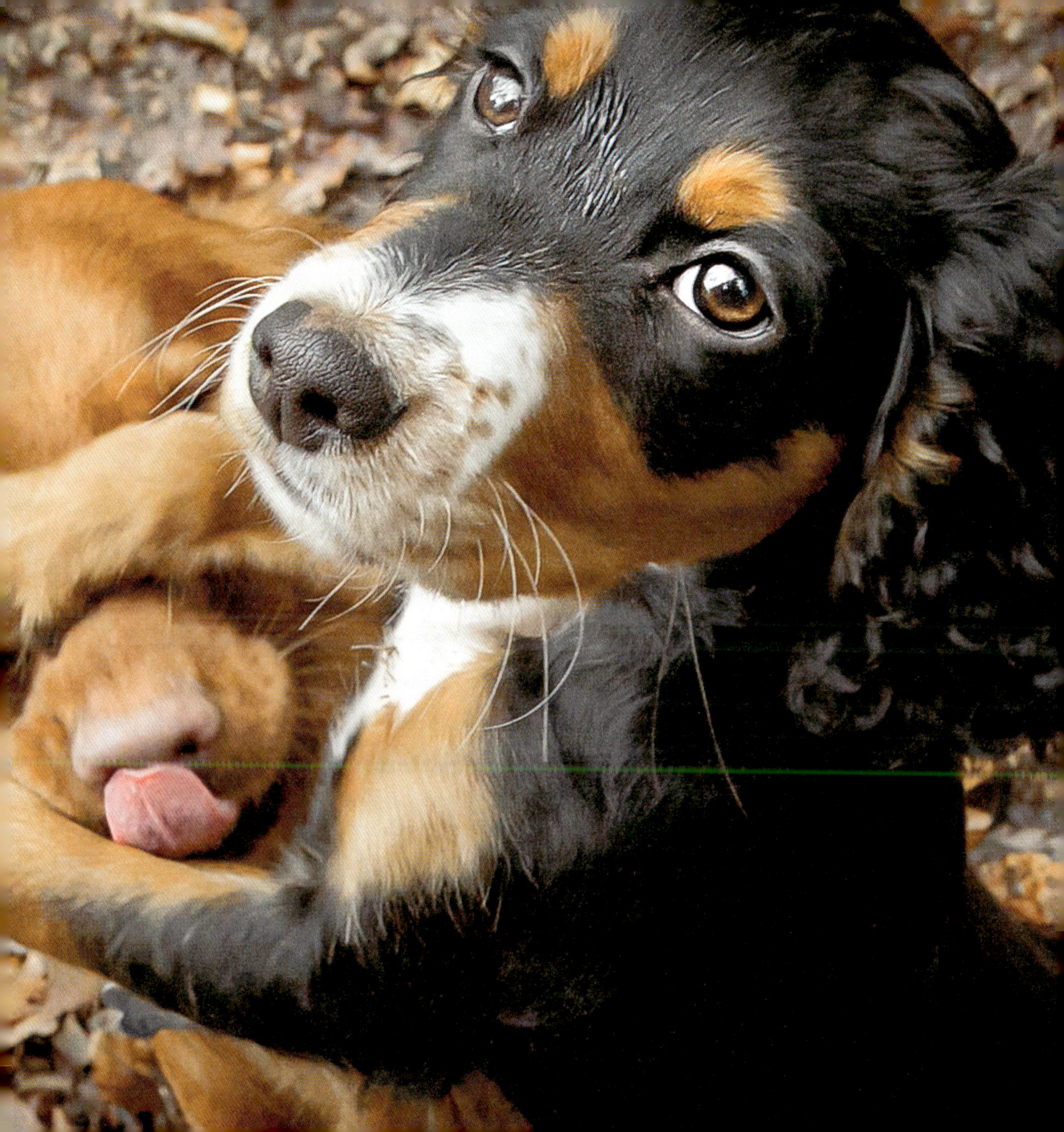

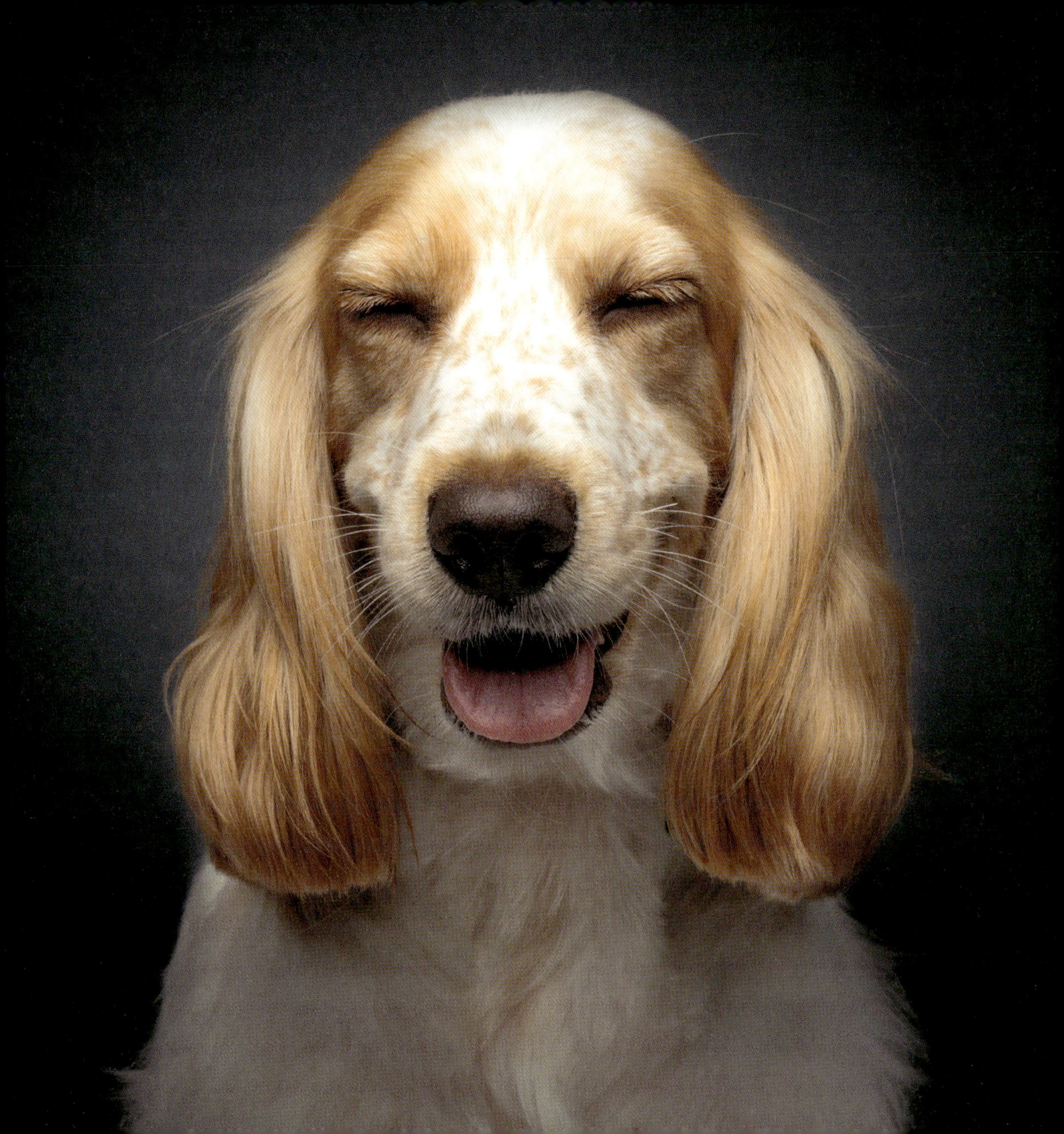

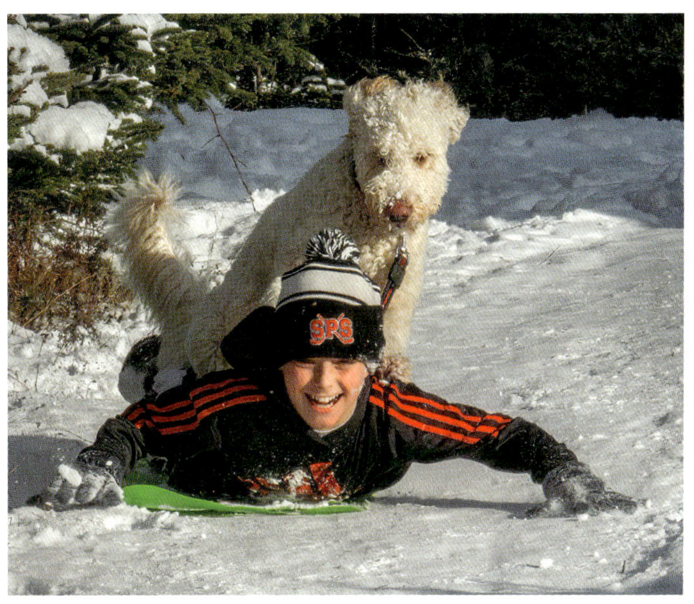

LOCATION: CANADA

Not quite the dog sled I was imagining, but I like it!

PHOTOGRAPHER: Neville Tait

LOCATION: SINGAPORE

They've definitely cleaned up Muttley for the revamp
of *Wacky Races*.

PHOTOGRAPHER: Bernard Sim

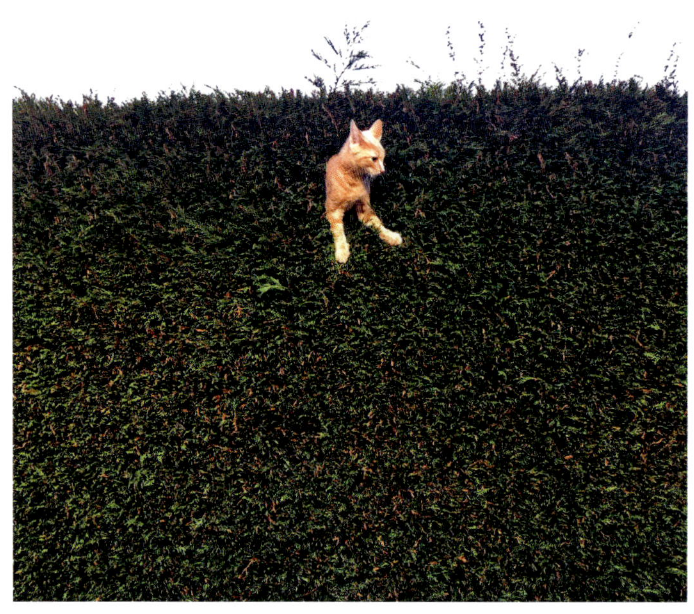

LOCATION: LEICESTERSHIRE, UNITED KINGDOM
Whoever said a bird in the hand is worth two in the bush is right
PHOTOGRAPHER: Freya Sharpe

LOCATION: UNITED STATES
I only have ice for you.
PHOTOGRAPHER: Mark Jovanovic

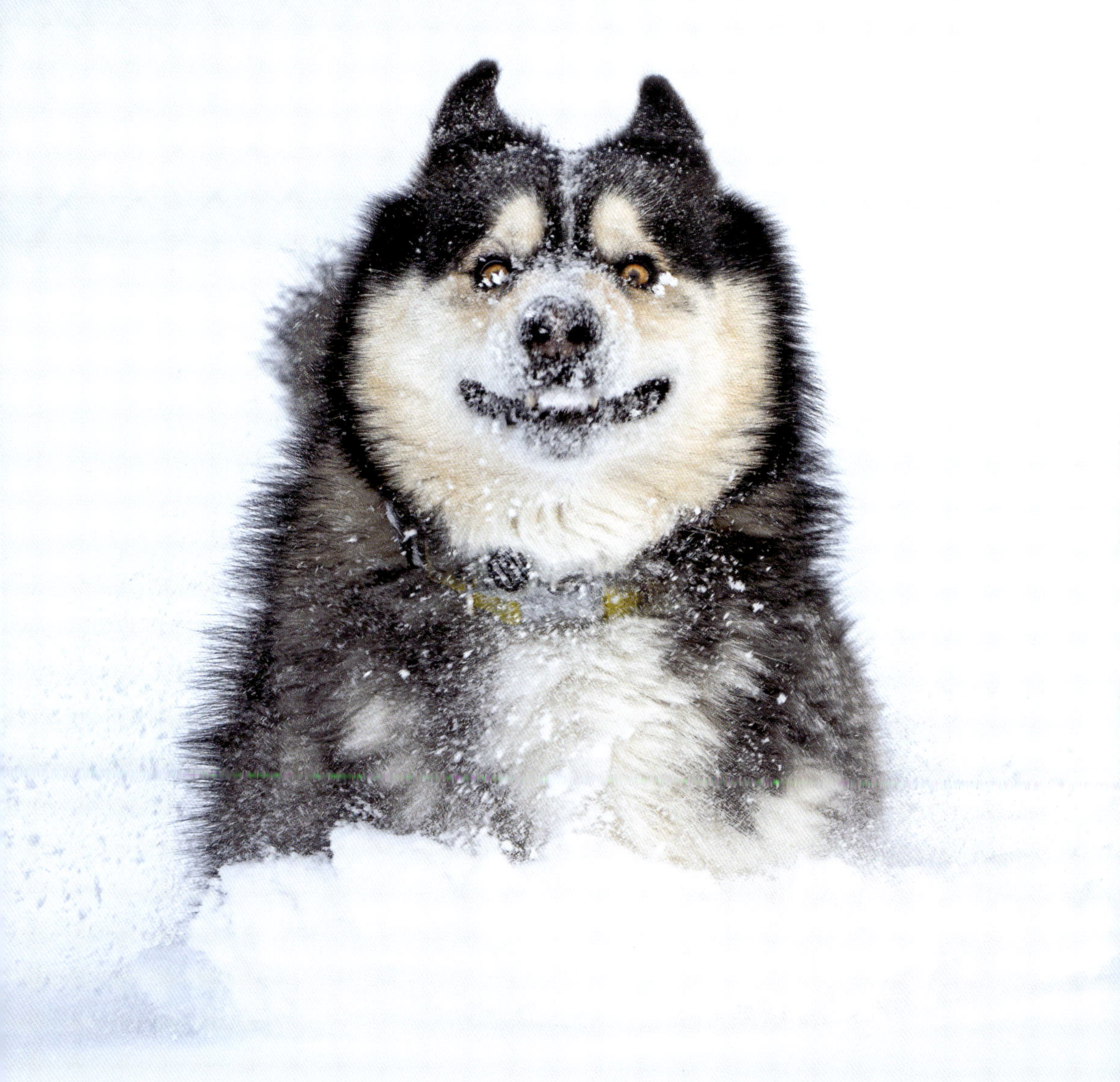

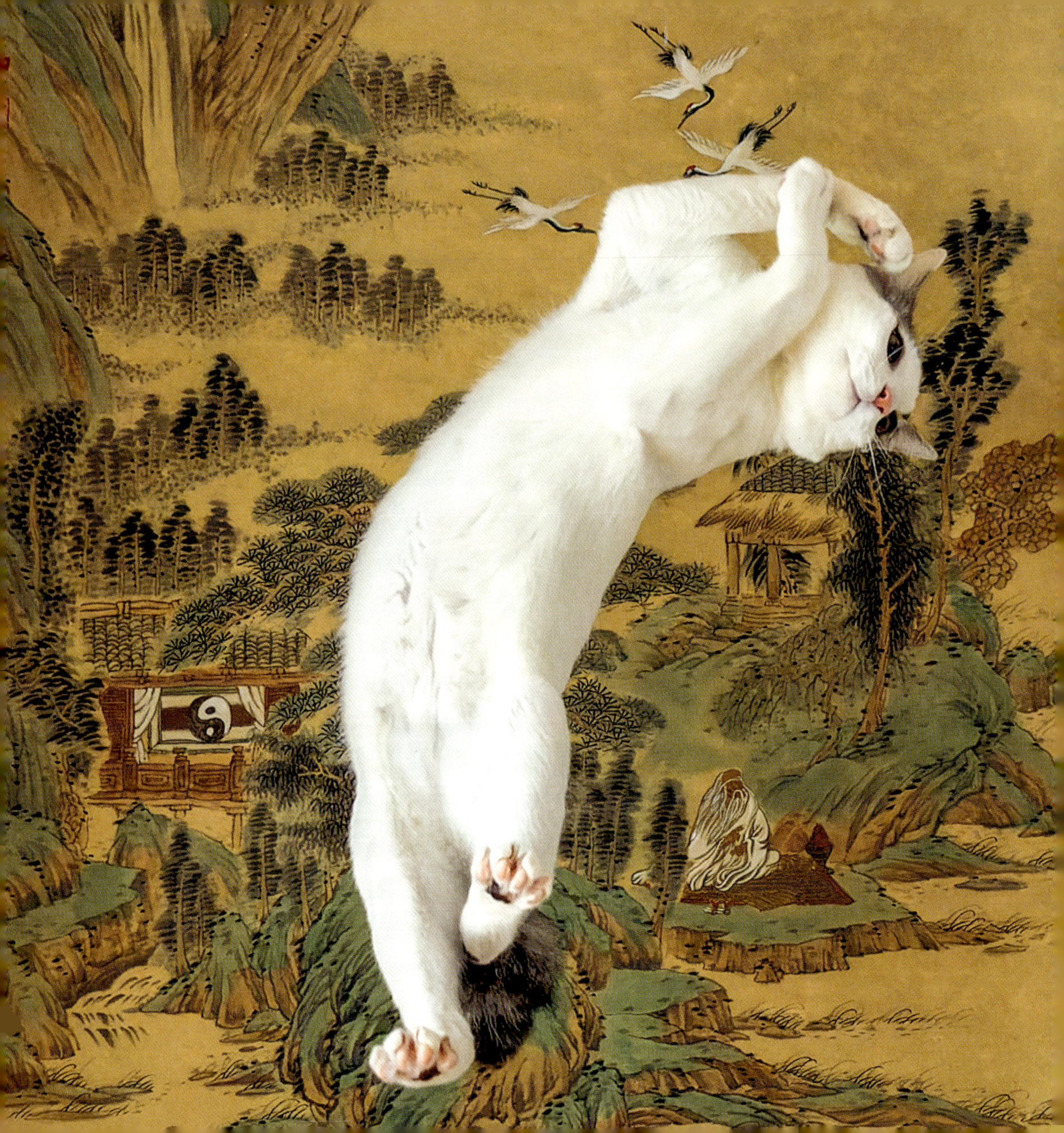

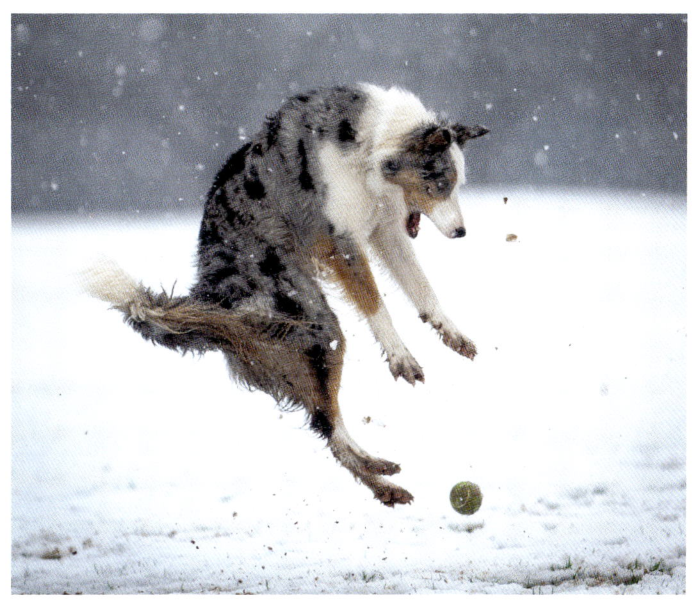

LOCATION: JAPAN

Styling out an aborted pounce on what turned out to be three
painted birds.

PHOTOGRAPHER: Kazutoshi Ono

LOCATION: FUKUOKA, JAPAN
Trust me guys – this is how you need to stand for the free kick.
PHOTOGRAPHER: Kenichi Morinaga

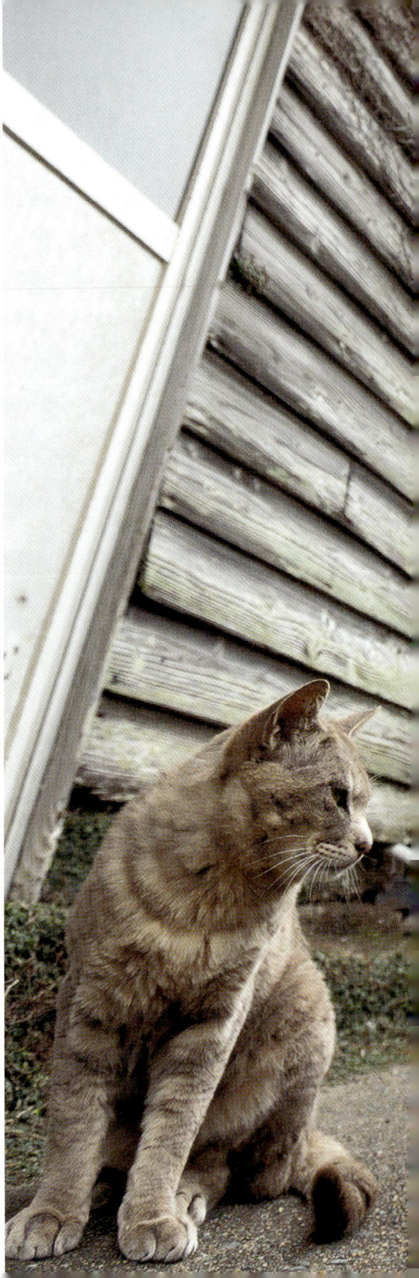

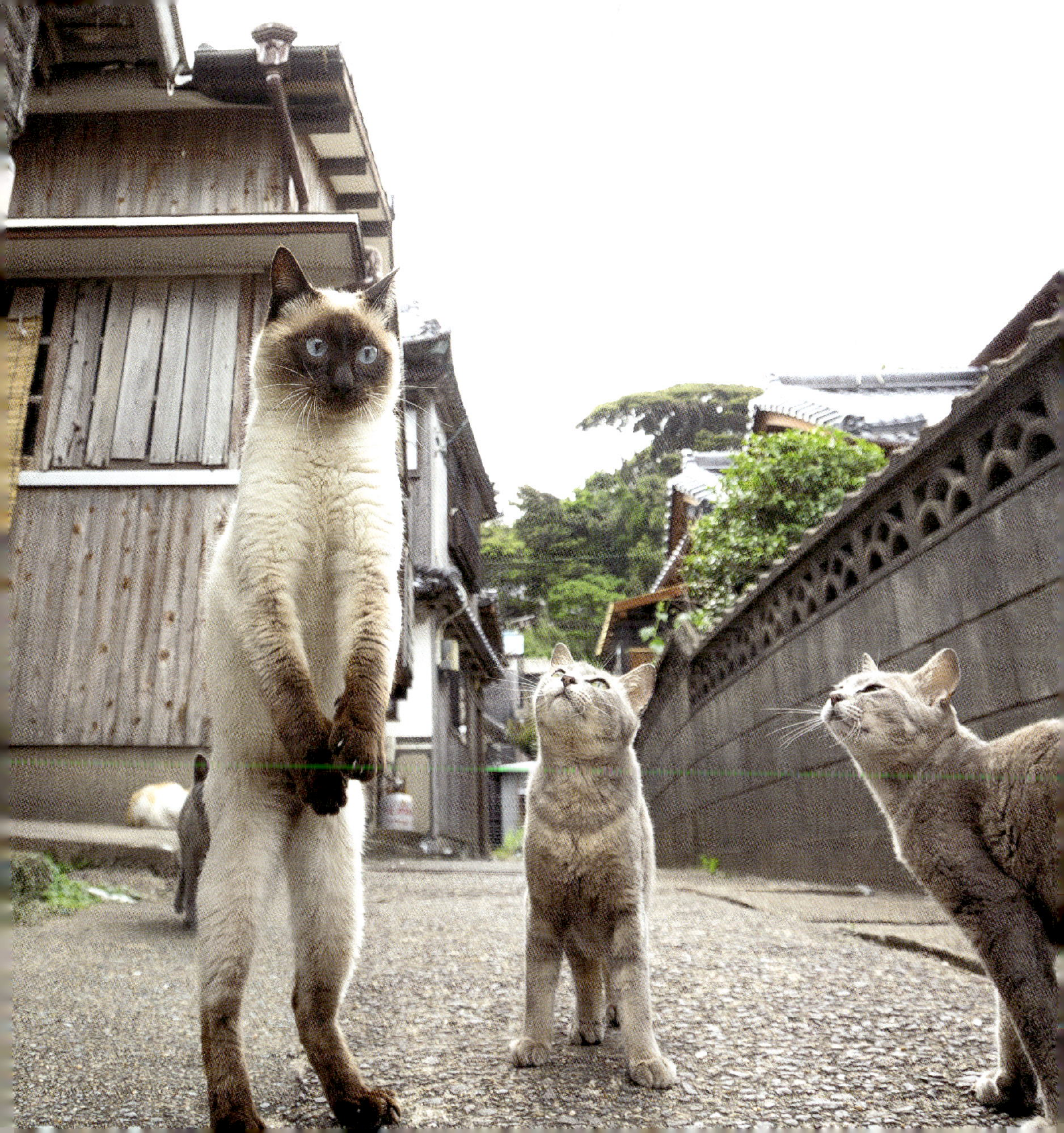

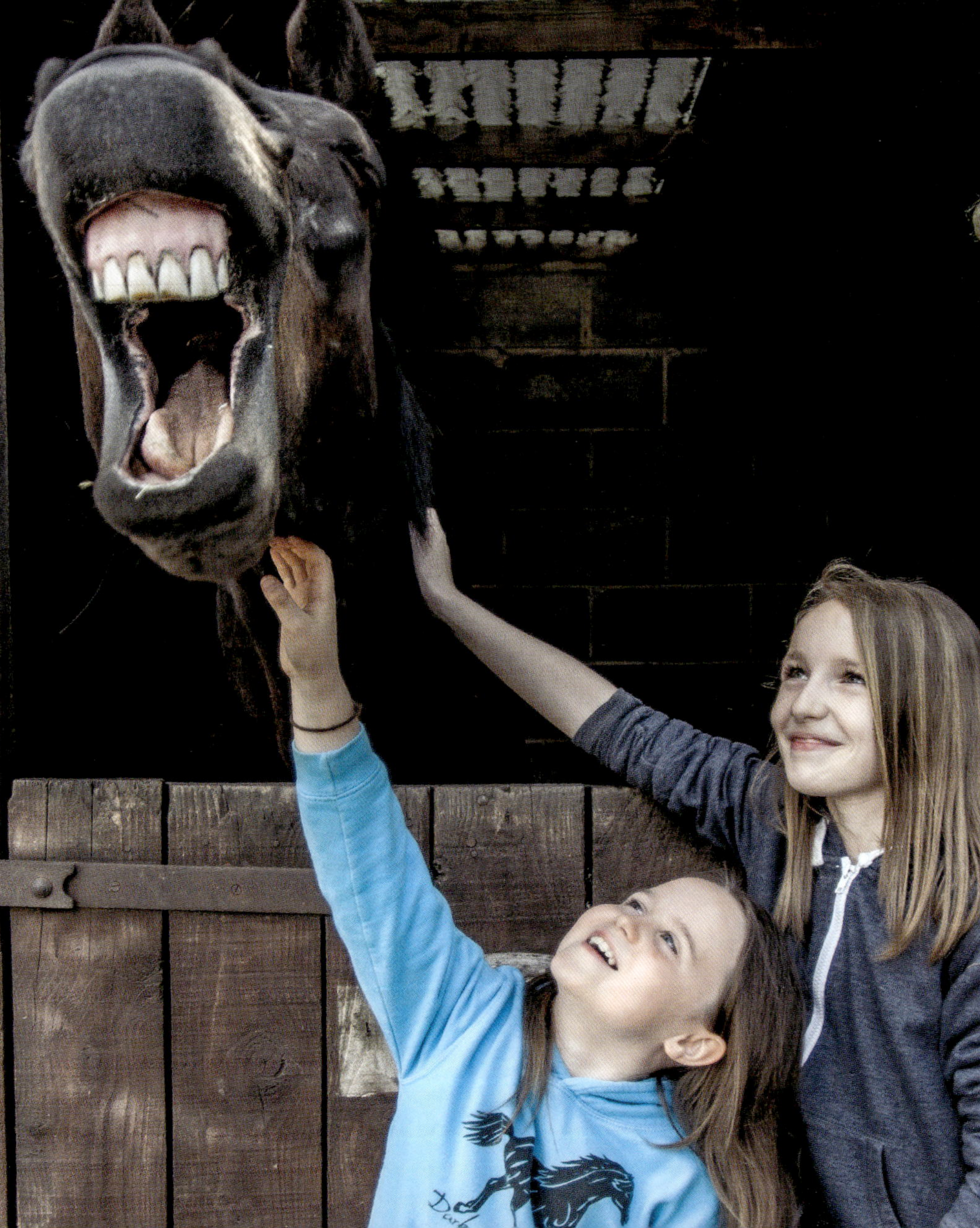

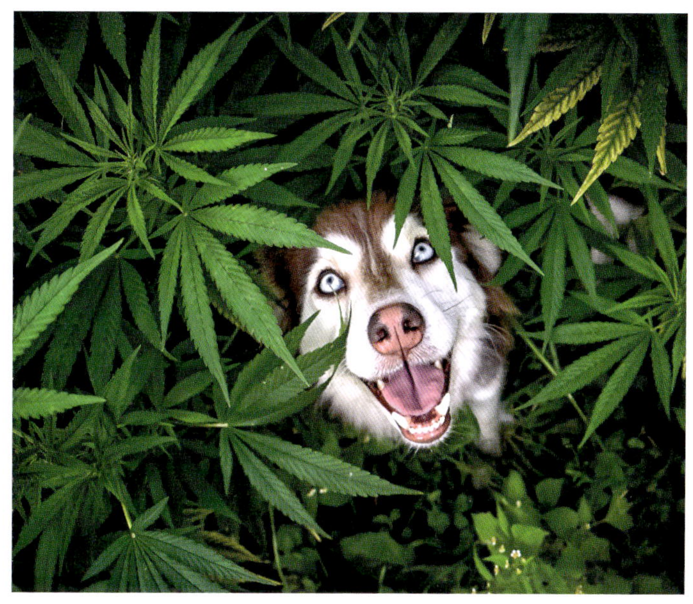

LOCATION: UNITED KINGDOM
Stop it – I'm ticklish!
PHOTOGRAPHER: Bob Moore

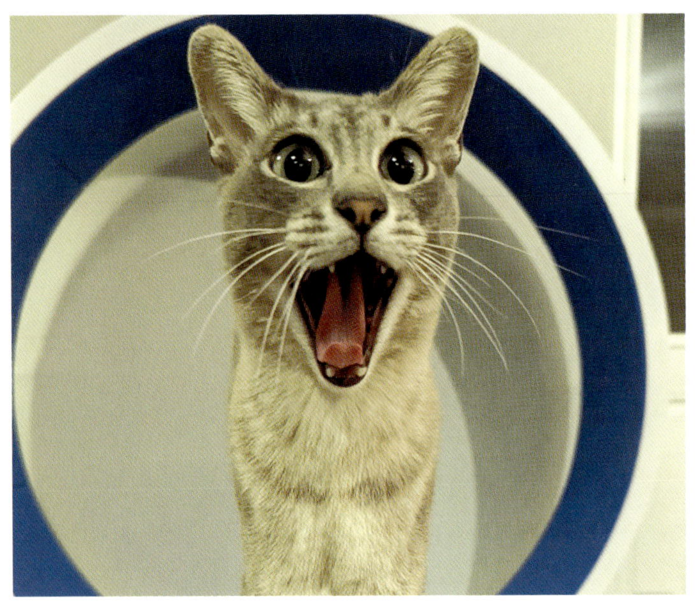

LOCATION: UNITED KINGDOM

Well, you don't need to put this picture through an animé filter!

PHOTOGRAPHER: Beth Noble

LOCATION: GERMANY

Life's a drag.

PHOTOGRAPHER: Stefan Brusius

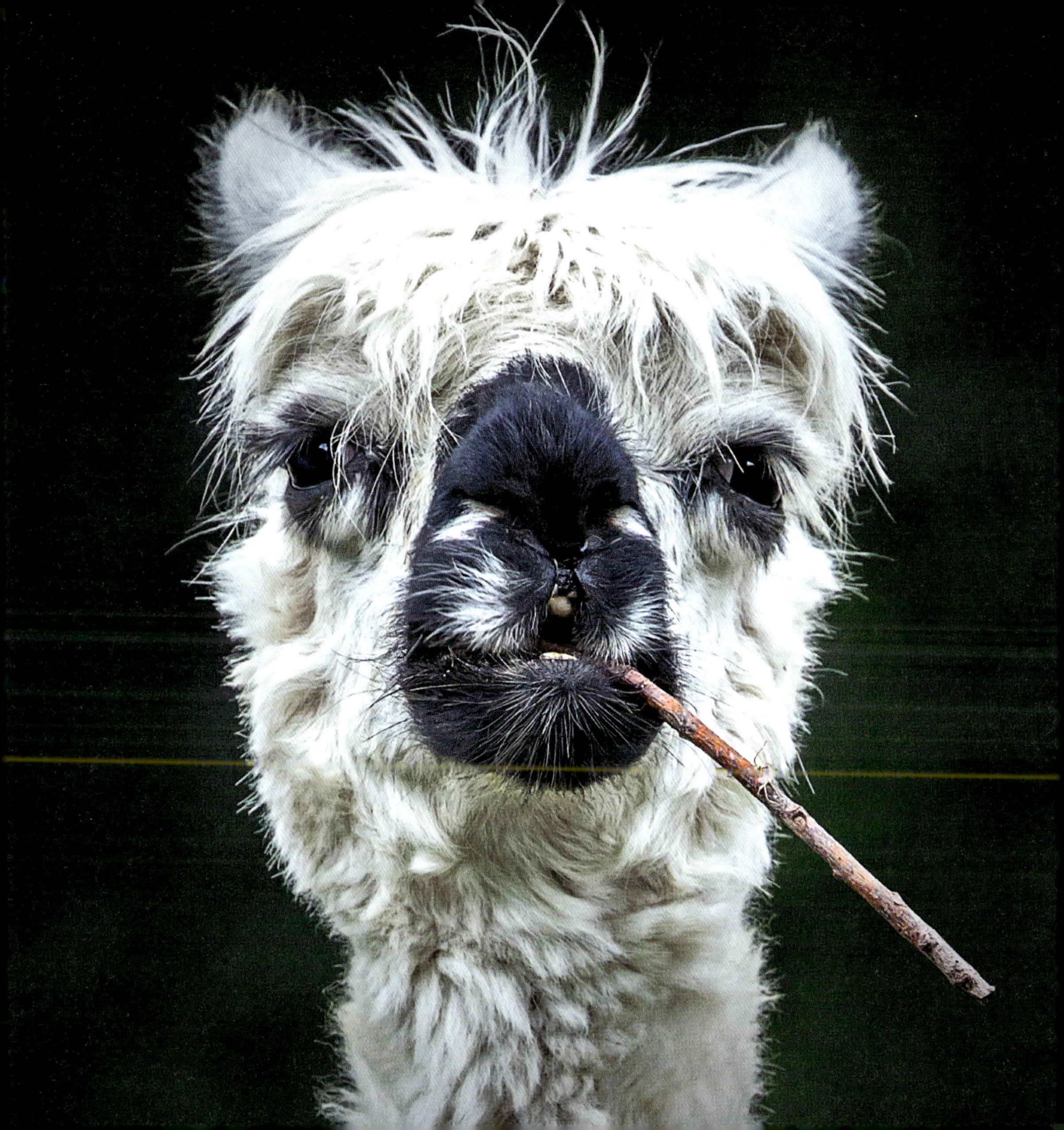

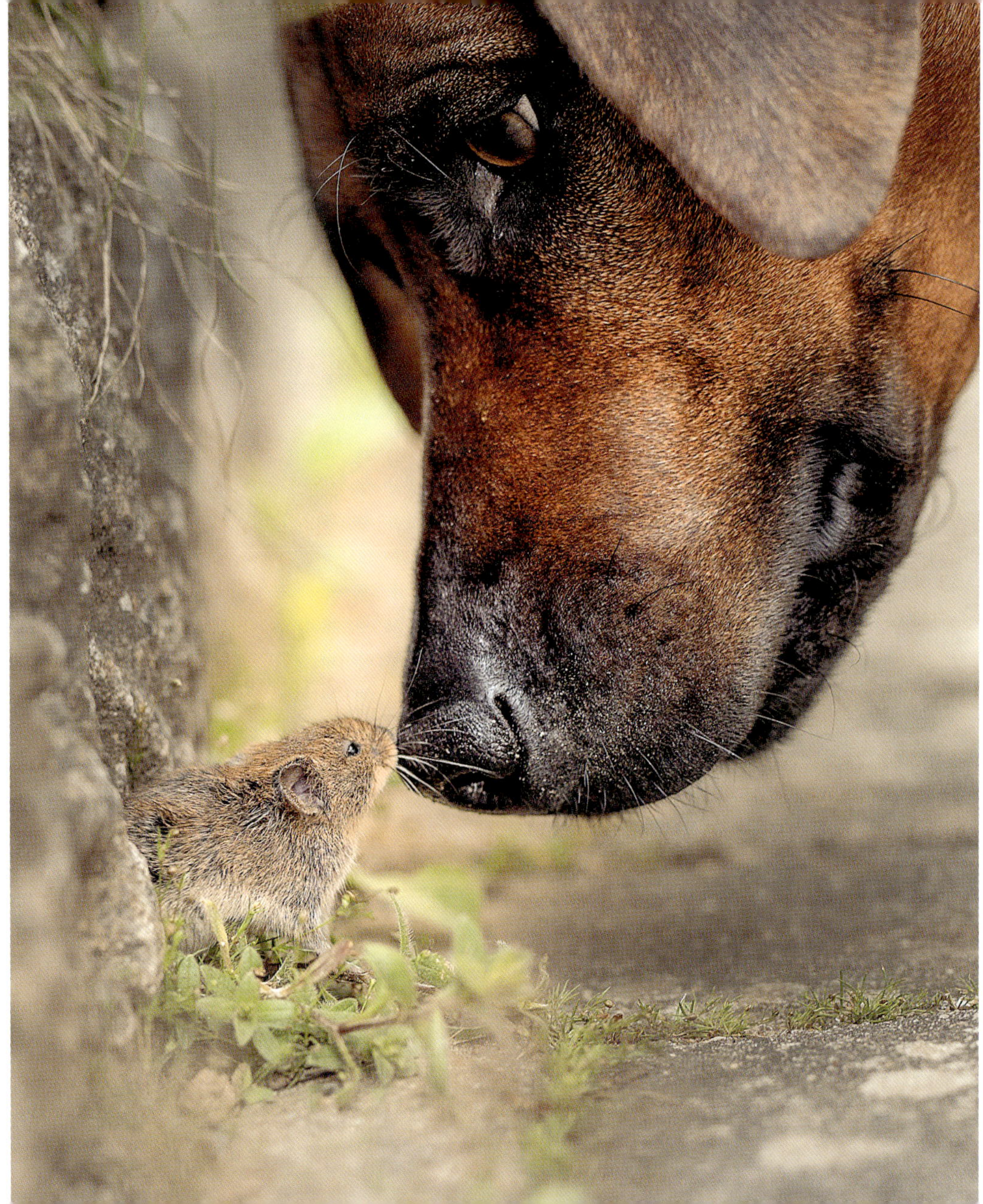

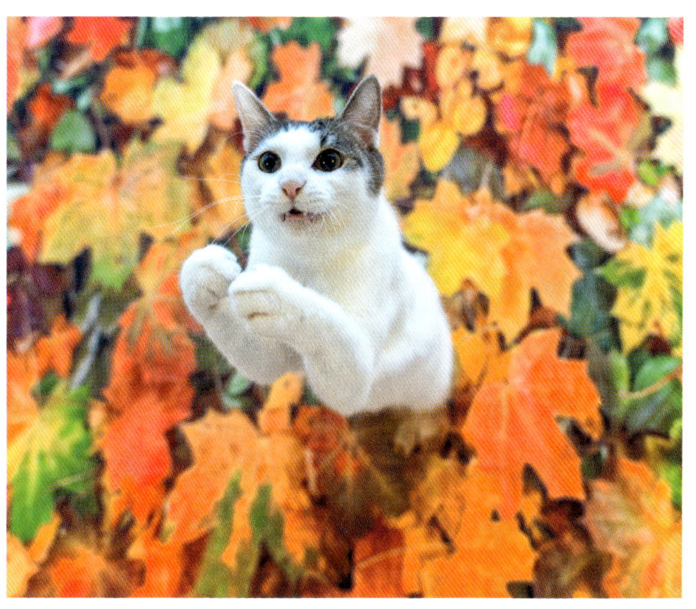

LOCATION: JAPAN
In training for the Brawl in the Fall.
PHOTOGRAPHER: Kazutoshi Ono

LOCATION: GERMANY, BAVARIA,
Mice to meet you.
PHOTOGRAPHER: Udo Krauss

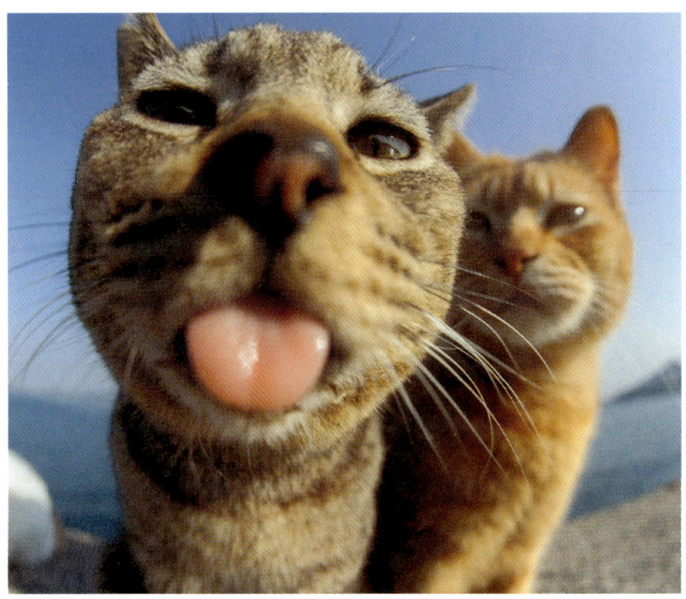

LOCATION: KAGAWA, JAPAN

I'll clean that lens for you, no problem.

PHOTOGRAPHER: Masayoshi Yamamoto

LOCATION: GERMANY

I'd love to see the dog groomer's face when this guy comes through the door.

PHOTOGRAPHER: Tammo Zelle

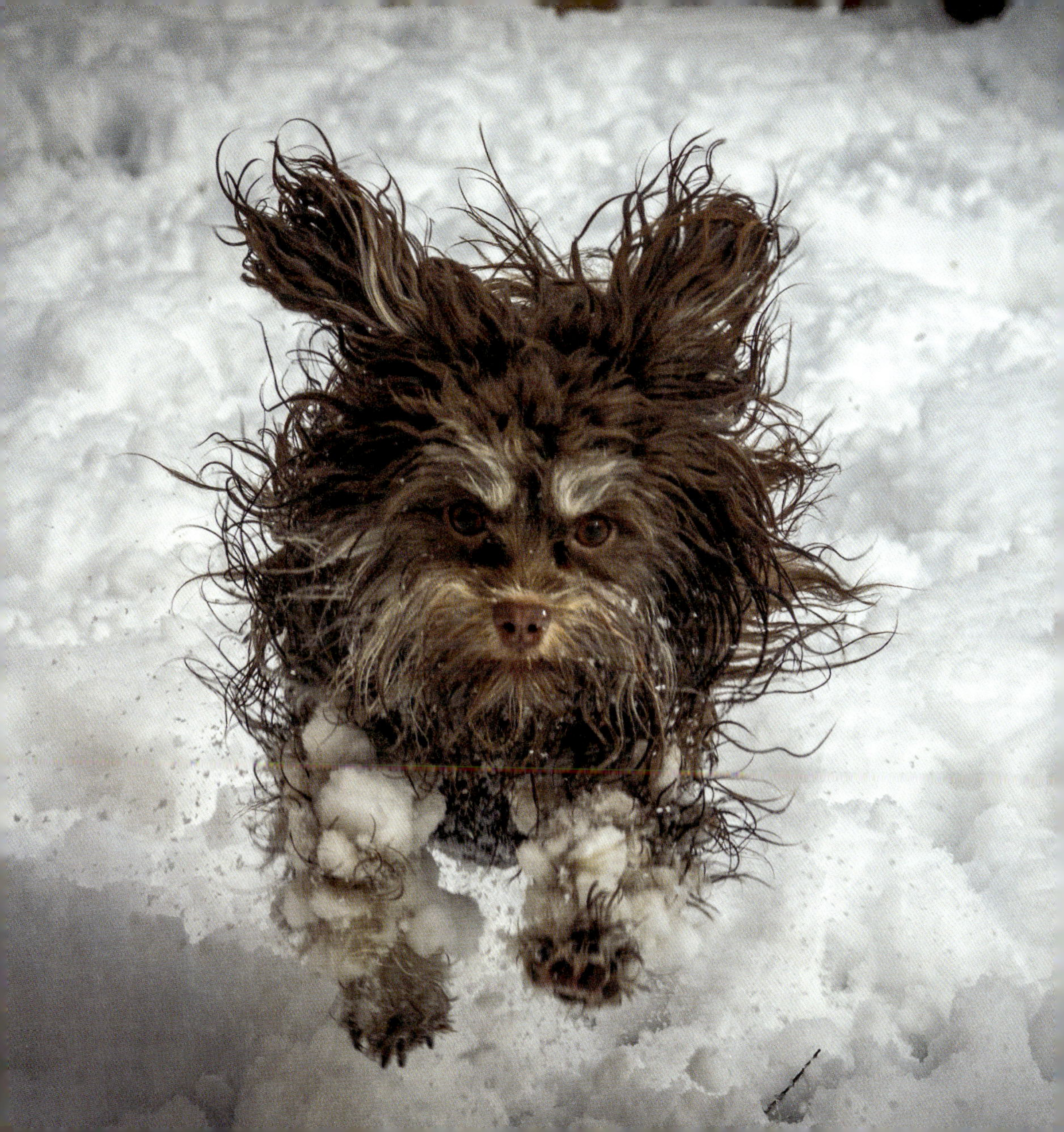

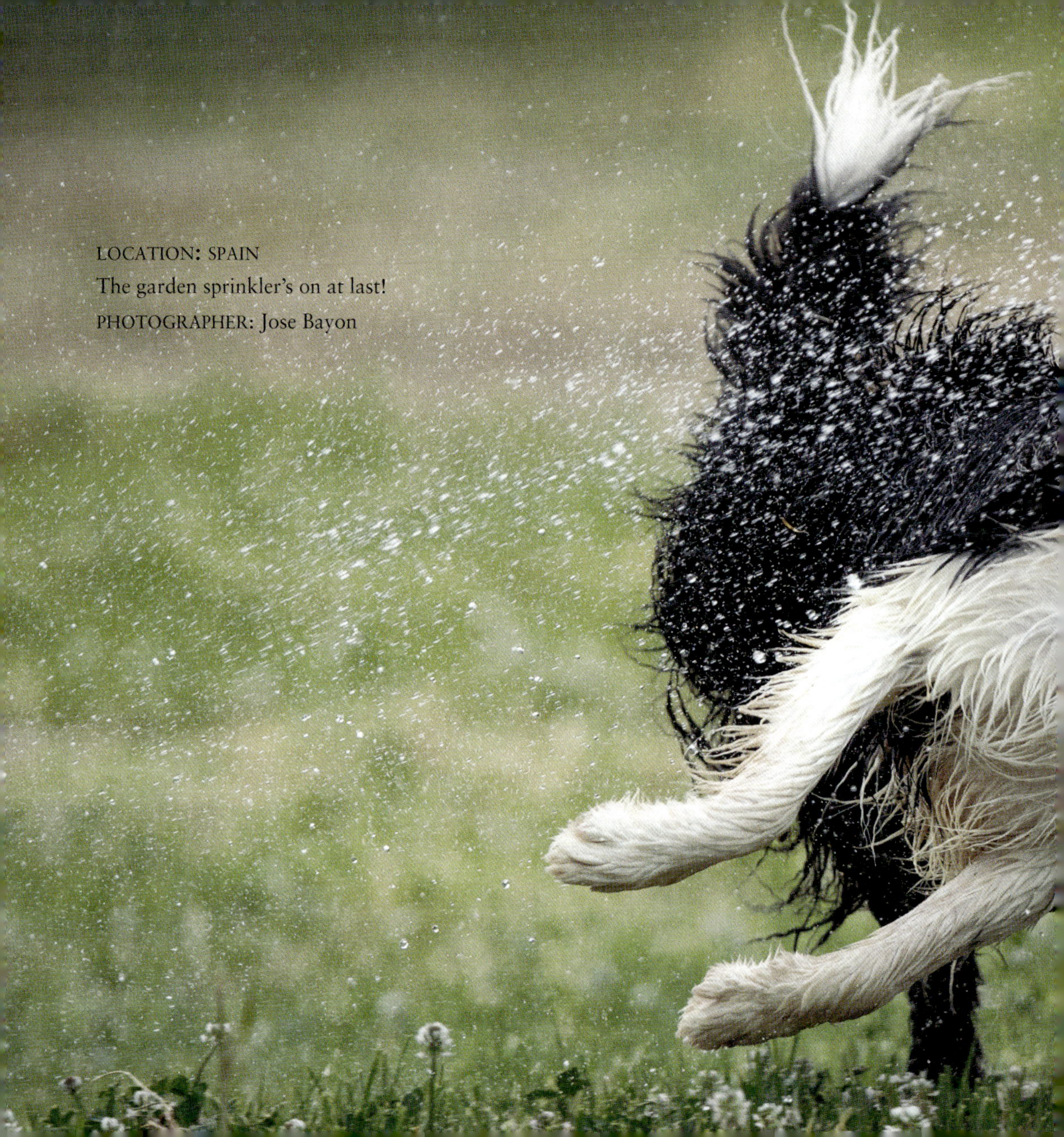

LOCATION: SPAIN
The garden sprinkler's on at last!
PHOTOGRAPHER: Jose Bayon

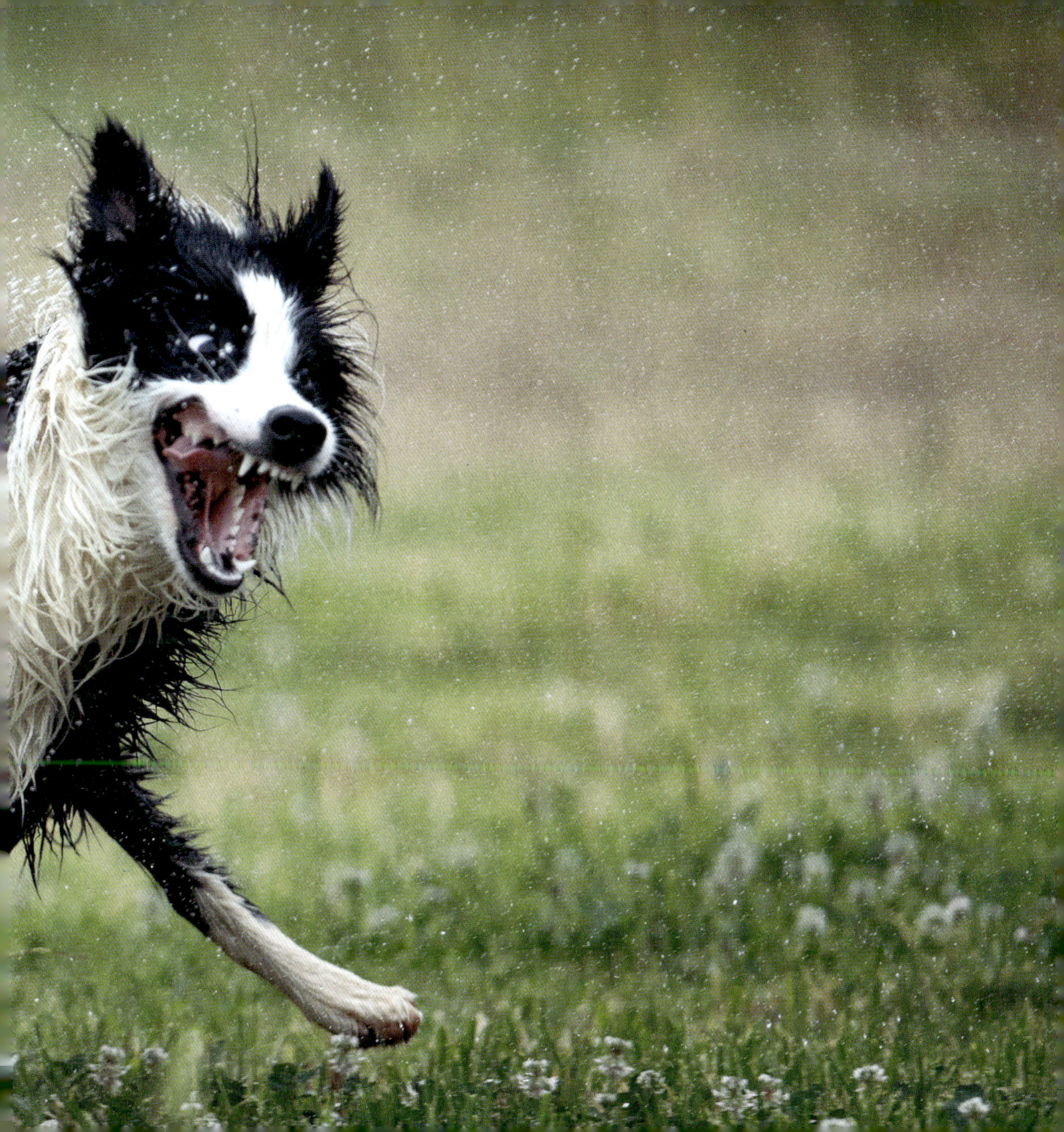

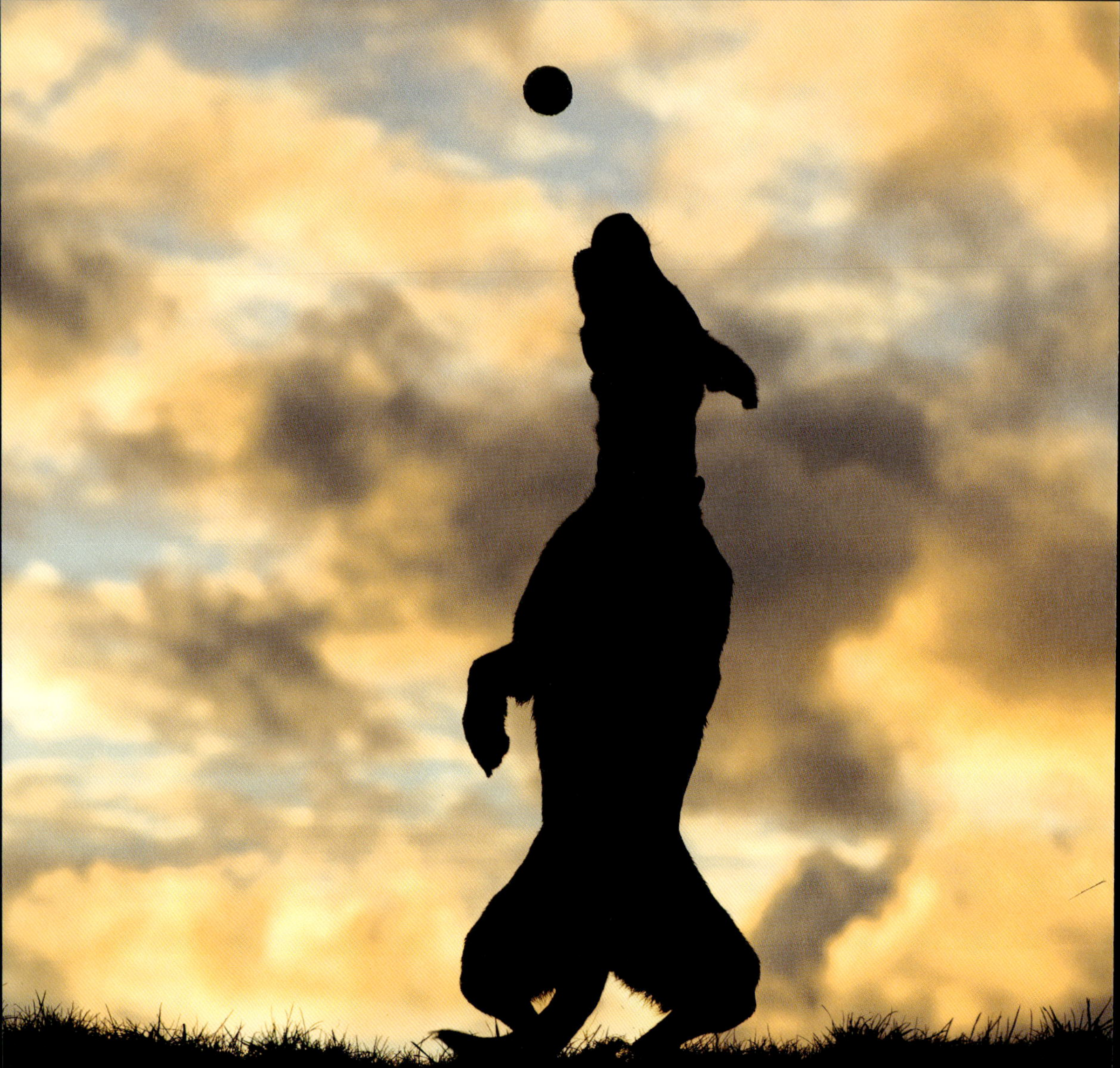

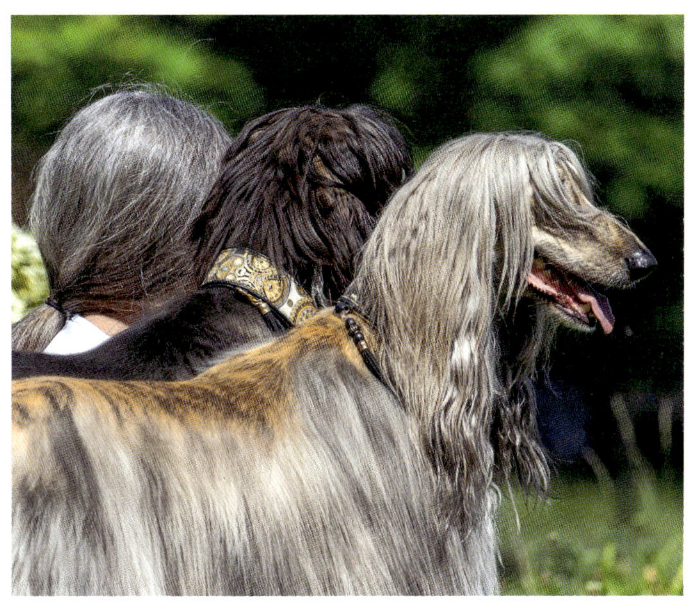

LOCATION: WARRINGTON, UNITED KINGDOM
I see a little silhouetto of a ball.
PHOTOGRAPHER: Christine Johnson

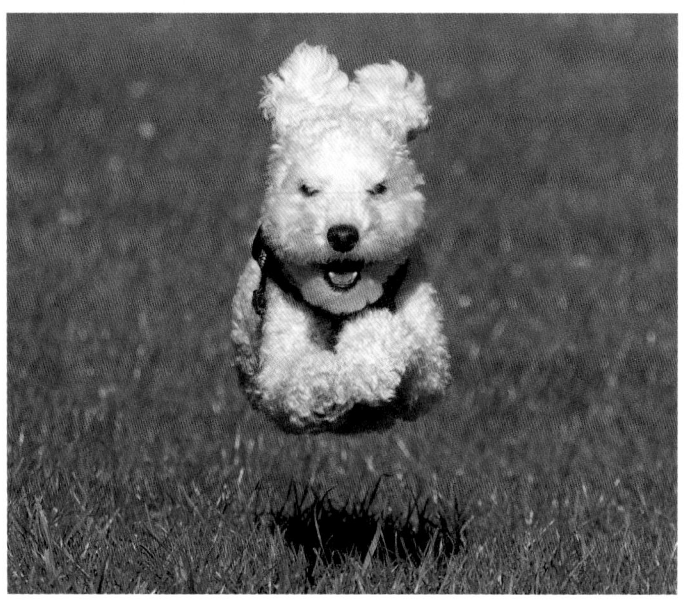

LOCATION: AYCLIFFE, COUNTY DURHAM, UNITED KINGDOM
Super Poodle!
PHOTOGRAPHER: John Young

LOCATION: BRAZIL
Look what I found down the back of the sofa!
PHOTOGRAPHER: Monyque Macedo Dos Santos

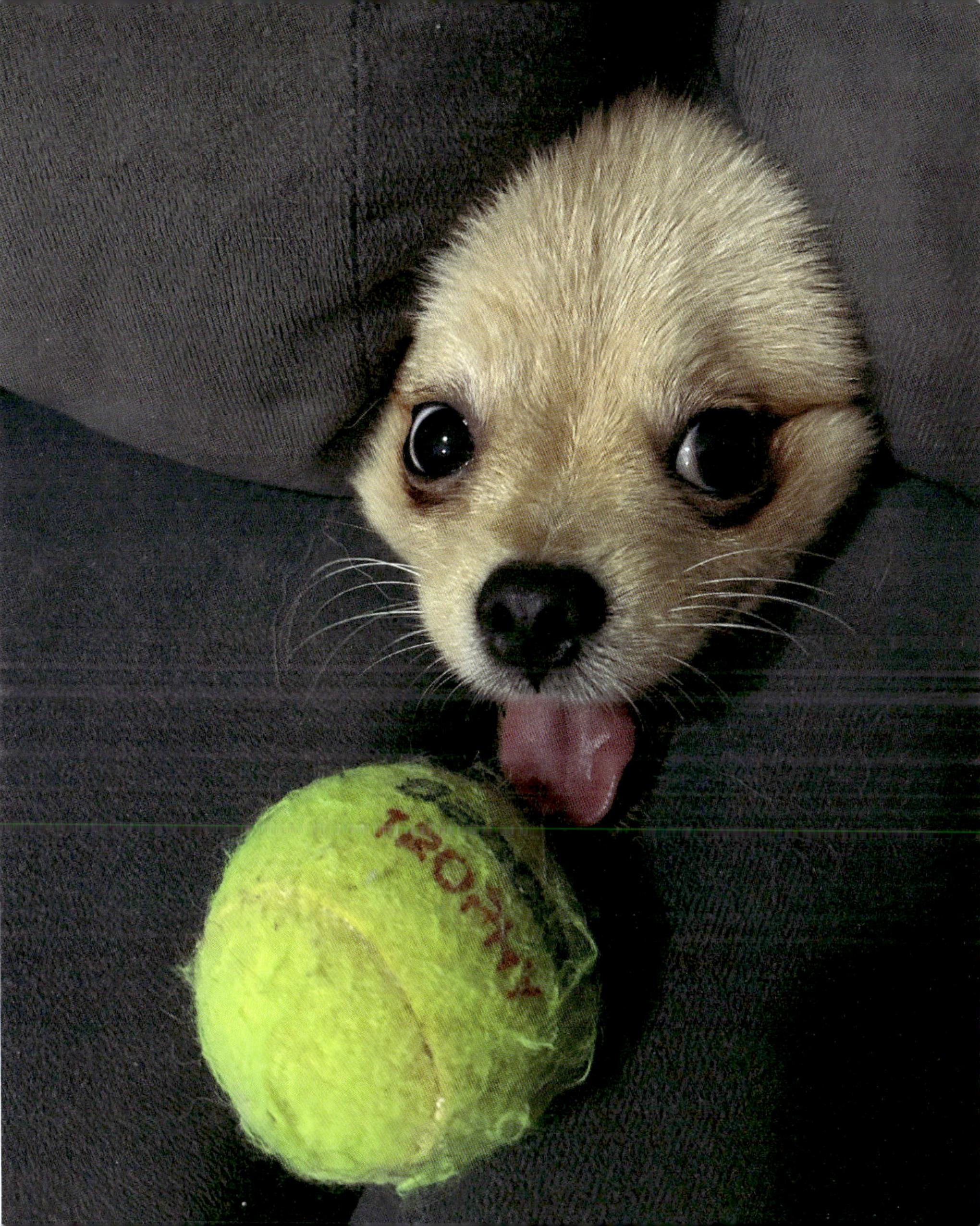

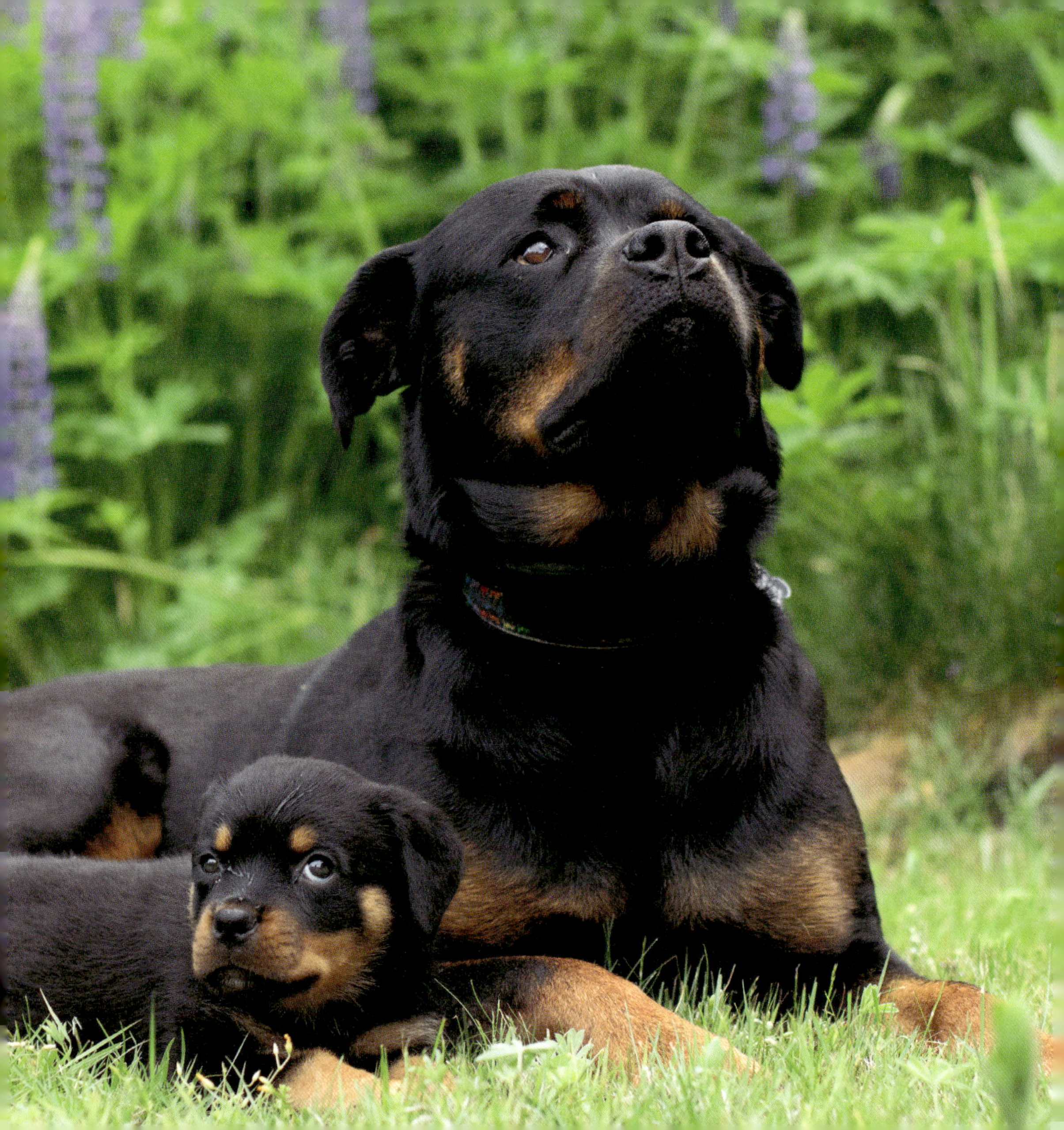

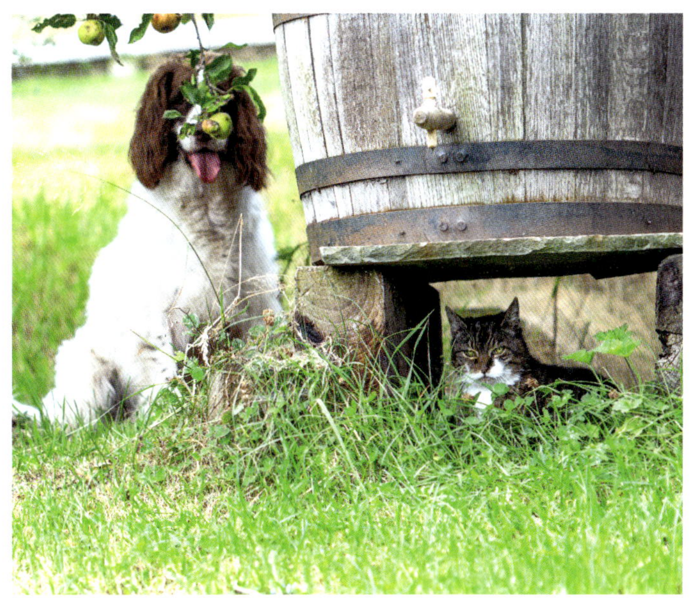

LOCATION: AMHERST, MASSACHUSETTS, UNITED STATES
Oh no, mum's doing her regal pose again.
PHOTOGRAPHER: Darya Zelentsova

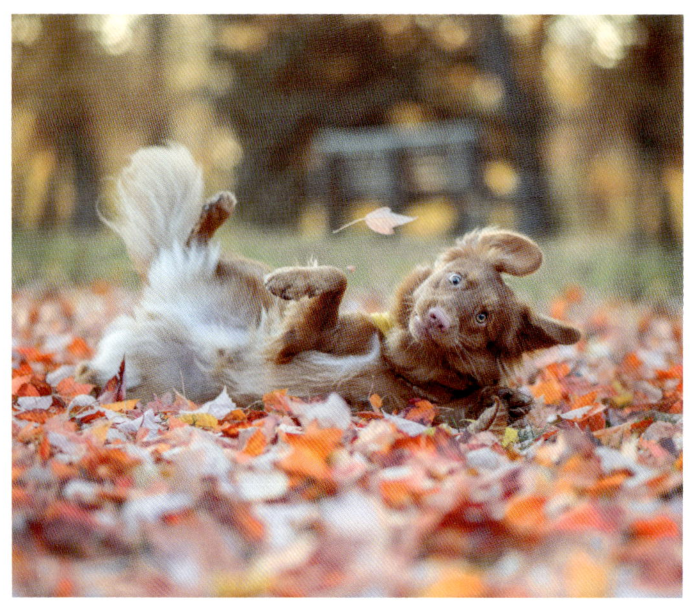

LOCATION: AUSTRIA

Tell me honestly – have I died and gone to doggie heaven?

PHOTOGRAPHER: Kerstin Leichtenmuller

LOCATION: AMHERST, MASSACHUSETTS, UNITED STATES

Hay fever really isn't ferret all.

PHOTOGRAPHER: Darya Zelentsova

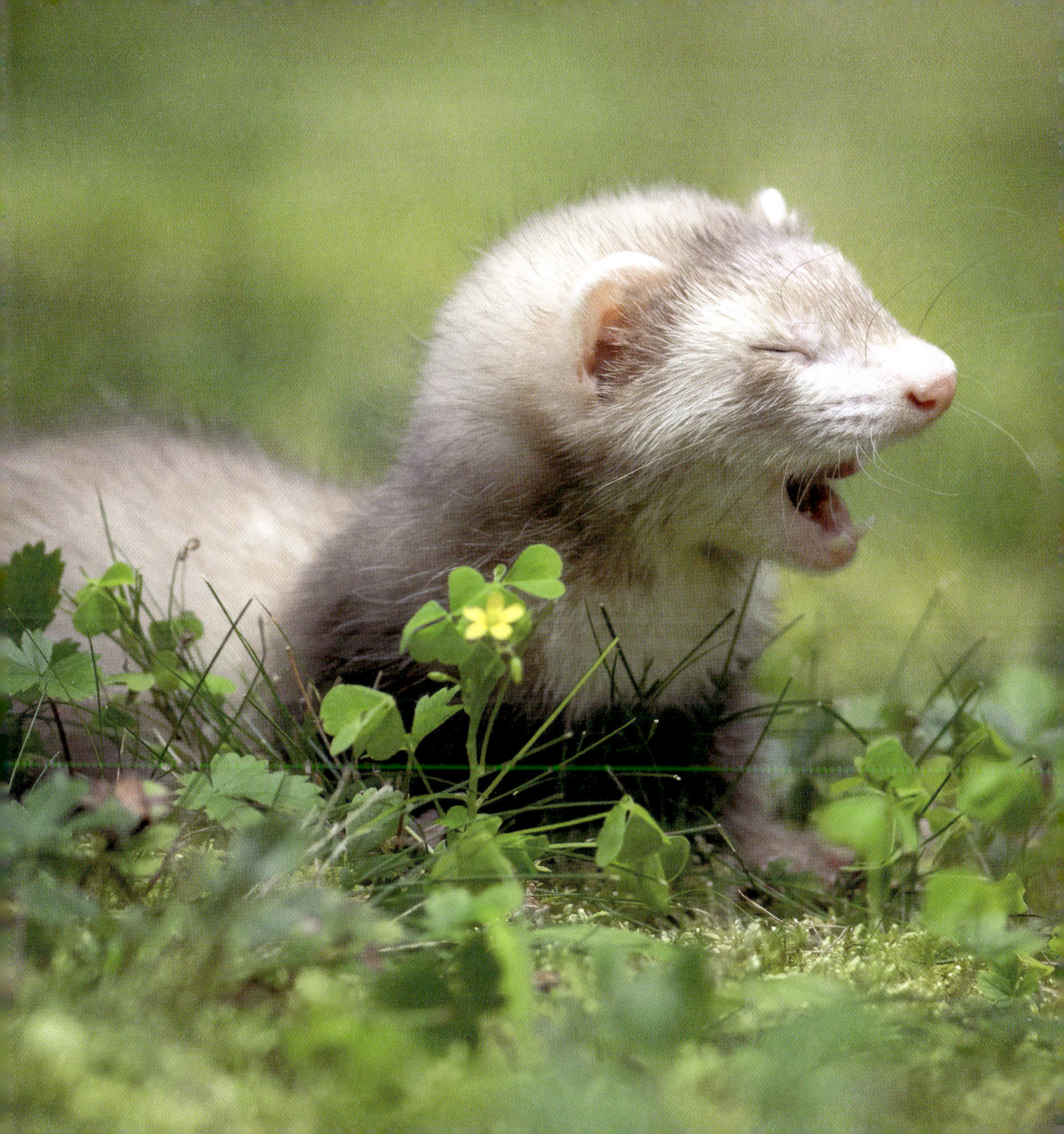

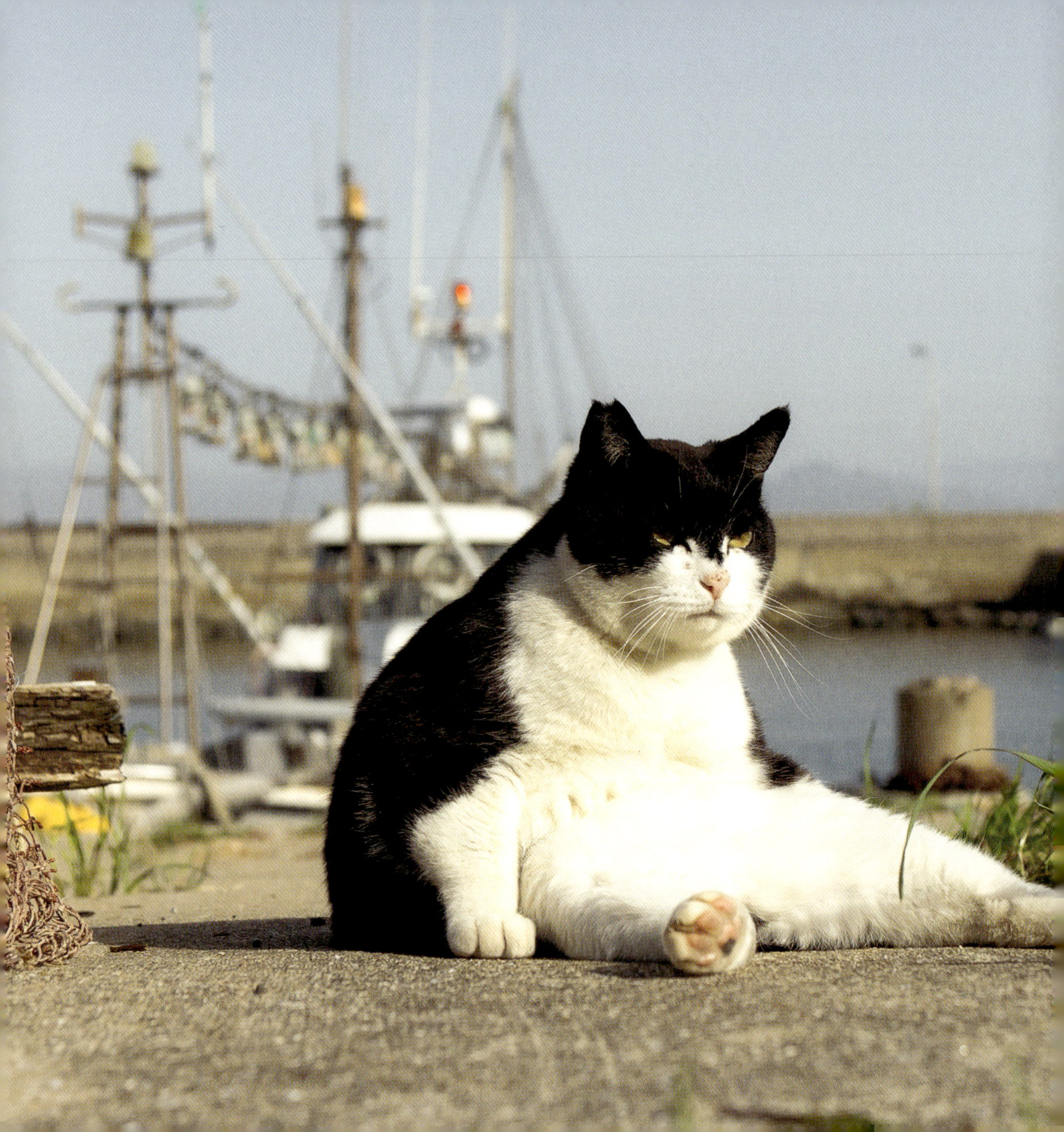

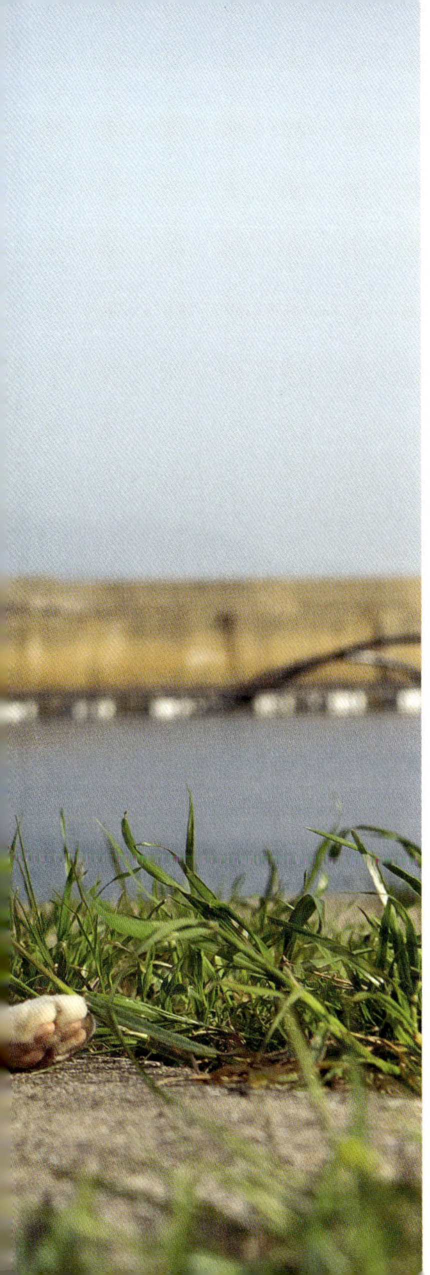

LOCATION: FUKUOKA, JAPAN
Don Clawleone.
PHOTOGRAPHER: Kenichi Morinaga

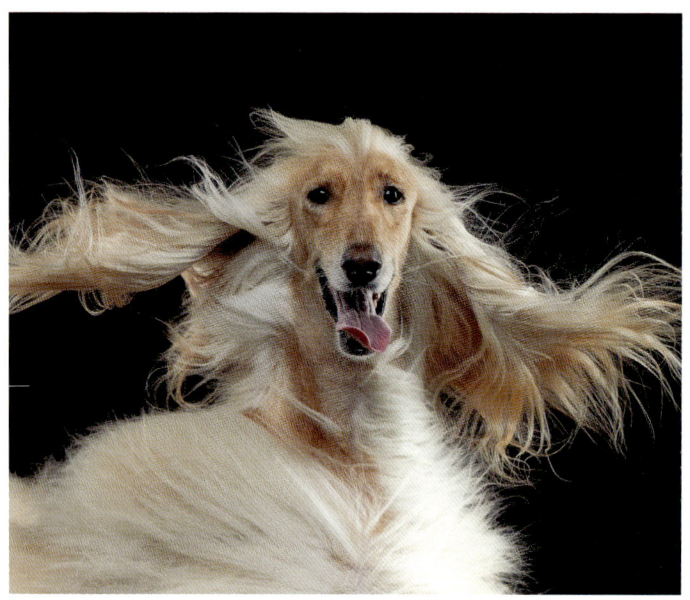

LOCATION: RUSSIA

Maybe she's born with it.

PHOTOGRAPHER: Lana Polyakova

LOCATION: JAPAN

Celebrating a purrfect 10 on the Balance Beam.

PHOTOGRAPHER: Kazutoshi Ono

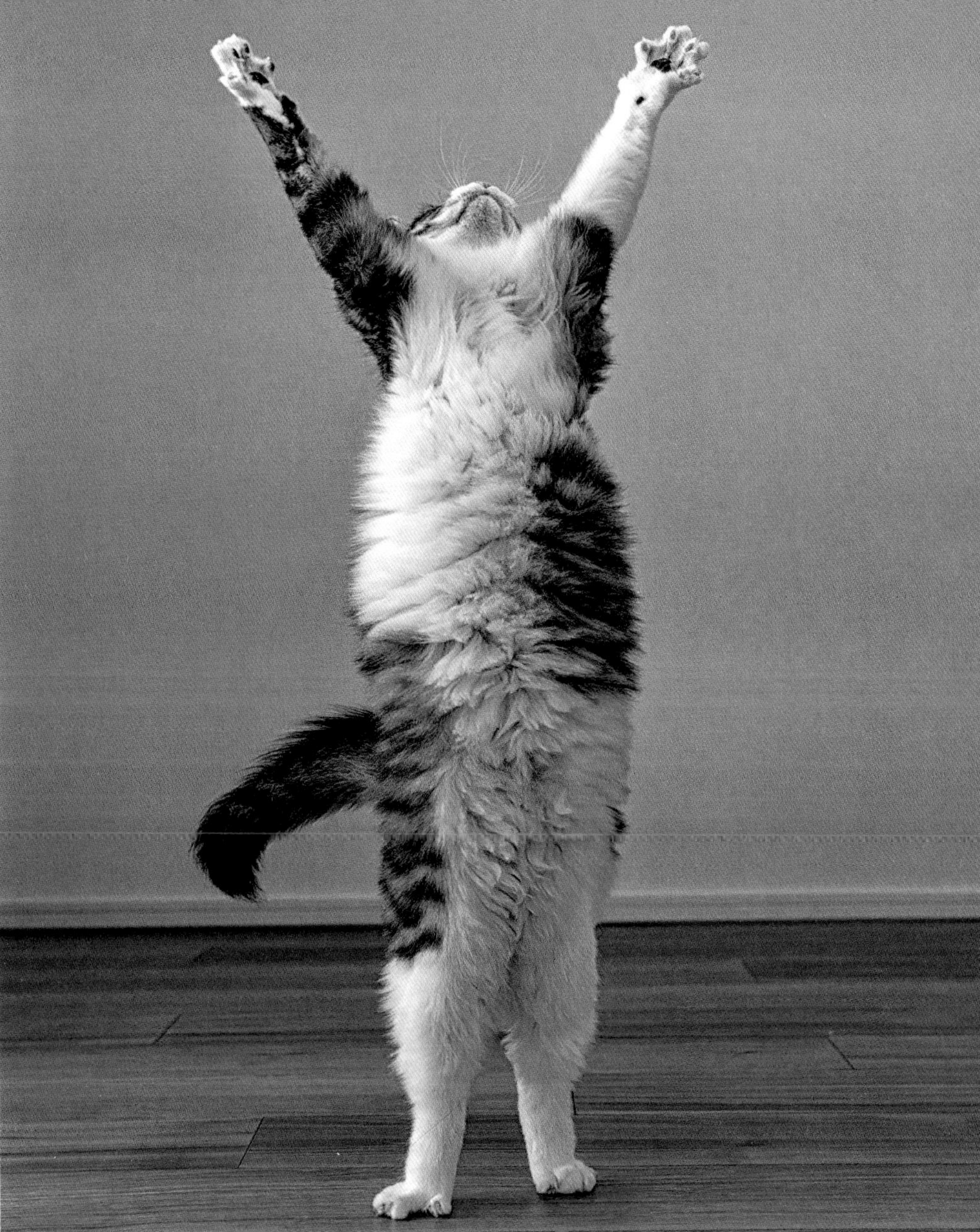

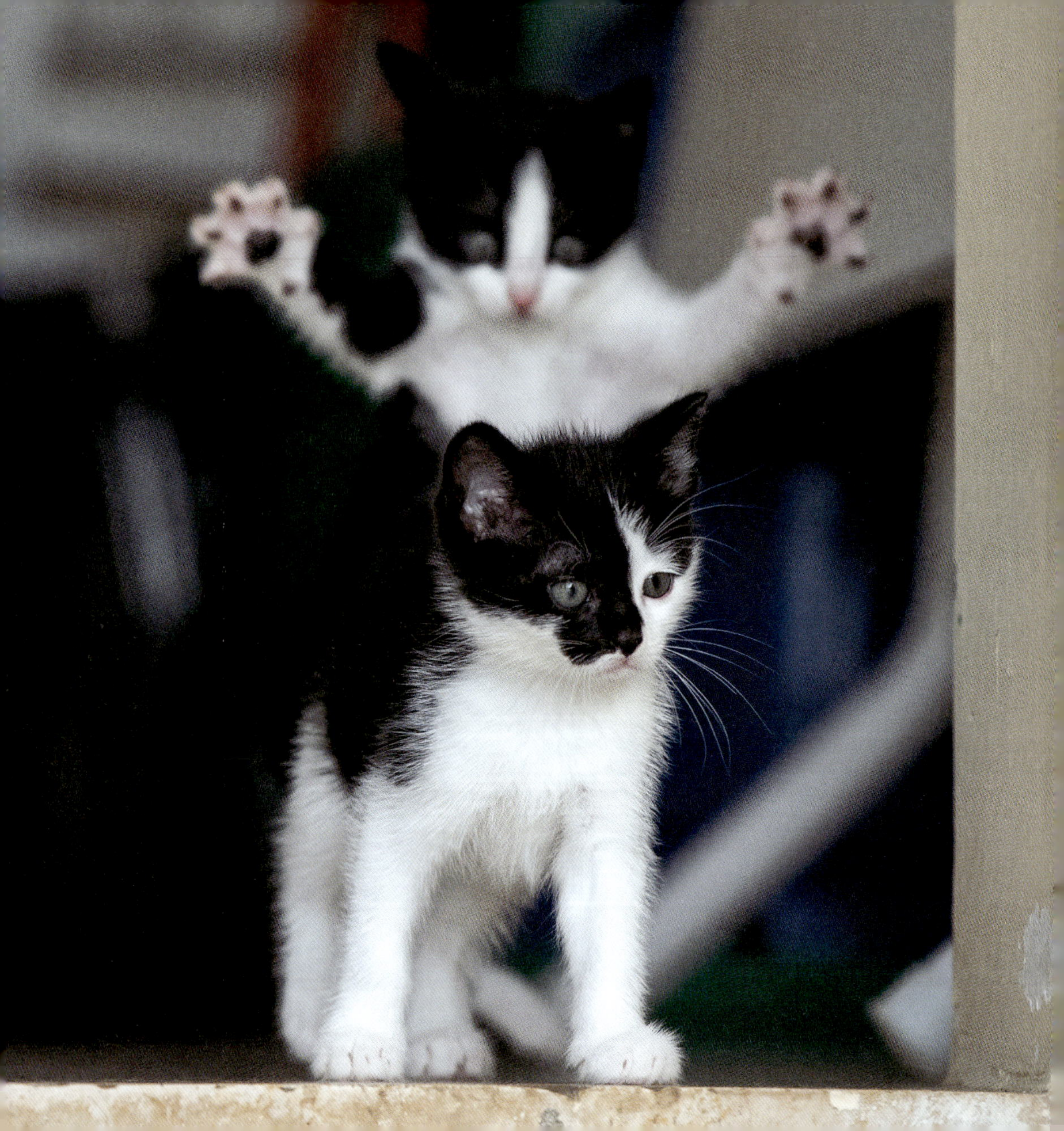

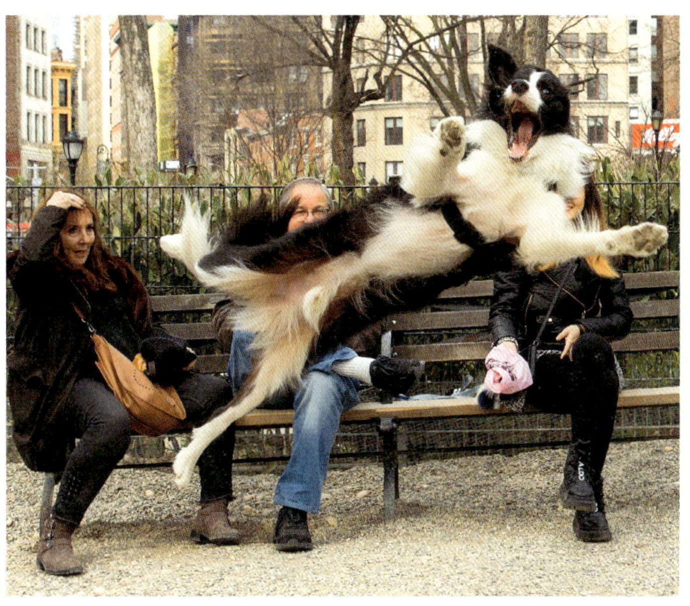

LOCATION: NEW YORK, UNITED STATES

The dog bodyguard recruit was really proving his woof.

PHOTOGRAPHER: Chris Porsz

LOCATION: LEBANON

You gotta be kitten me.

PHOTOGRAPHER: Michel Zoghzoghi

OUR ANIMAL WELFARE MISSION

One of the main reasons the Comedy Pet Photo Awards was thrust into this world was to support and champion positive animal welfare. Through the competition we want to laugh and cheer with these wonderful creatures but also encourage people to start supporting small grass roots animal welfare charities. And every year as our competition gets a little bigger, the message is getting a little louder and we can help more and more organisations. We all lead busy lives BUT ... by doing a few simple things, we can start to make a difference. We have listed a few things here you can do that in themselves are teeny tiny steps but if everyone takes one, there will be a stampede!

- *If you are thinking about getting a pet and the situation is right to be able to give a rescue animal a new home, then please, please do consider it. You could make a real difference to an animal's life – plus think how smug and wholesome you'll feel!*

- *If you have time, why not volunteer at your local rescue centre? There is bound to be one near you and they are always looking for help to mend a fence, clean out kennels, walk a dog or two or just be another pair of hands. You might even get a T shirt.*

- *Help with the fundraising. Lots of welfare centres and shelters rely on donations, so why not bake and sell some cakes, ride a bike to work for a week (to work off the cake), do a 12hr danceathon or get the kids to do it – you choose the music! Every penny helps.*

- *Fostering an animal can really help give a cat or dog a break from kennel life or a temporary home when things don't work out as planned. And you get to meet some wonderful characters without the full-time commitment of adoption.*

- *Why not volunteer to be a dog walker? Lend a hand and a leg or two with pets whose owners can no longer walk them for whatever reason. This will instantly propel you to the number one spot of the most popular person in the entire universe!*

- *And lastly, and only if you can – donate, donate, donate! In fact, you've started already – by buying this book you've already helped us give to charities that help support animals around the world. Keep it up!*

ACKNOWLEDGEMENTS

I don't normally get to write anything for the books, but I've managed to sneak this one under the radar without anyone noticing. And as nobody ever reads to the end, I think I might get away with it.

First up, I want to say huge thank you to Paul and Tom for setting up this whole competition caper. It really was an amazing and brilliant idea. Pure gold in fact. Now knowing you both like I do, I honestly don't know how you did it. But you did, and I am very glad and very proud to be a small part of it. It is one of the best jobs in the world and I am ever grateful that our paths collided somehow. I will definitely be hanging around for when you come up with the next big idea!

Right, next up, and this is the really important bit, we want to thank all our supporters who actually make Comedy Pets happen. Our awesome judges who have had the enviable job of casting their votes in the last five years in some form or another; the wonderful, energetic and absolute rock that is Kate Humble, who has been there right from the start and is a constant champion and supporter for us; Emma Milne, another Comedy Pet lifer and our super vet, who makes sure no animals are harmed in the making of these photos and in whom we trust completely; Elke Vogelsang, top pet photographer and all round excellent person, who steps up whenever we ask her to do absolutely anything; Mel Giedroyc for giving up her precious time and for writing little notes against each finalist entry to make us laugh even more and Gerard and Jarvis Gethings, newbies this year and whom we're hoping to hoodwink into staying forever (but don't tell them). You're all fabulous!

As you can imagine, running the competition means we rely on a lot of kind and patient people, so a big thank you to Ronny and Andrew at Amazing Internet for looking after our website (and continuing to open and read my emails) and to ThinkTank Photo for the awesome camera bags that you donate, we are beyond grateful.

Those of you that follow us will know that animal welfare is very close to our heart and thanks to some great partnerships over the years, including Mars Petcare and Animal Friends Pet Insurance, we have been able to make substantial donations to the following charities: Blue Cross, Dean Farm Trust, London Inner City Kitties, Guide Dogs, Wild at Heart Foundation, Animal Support Angels and Cat Welfare Group. It's a lovely side hustle, that as well as making us smile, the Awards can directly help improve the lives of animals having a hard time through these wonderful and hard-working organisations.

Big round of applause to Ciara Lloyd and Joe Hallsworth and the awesome team at Bonnier Books for putting together this gorgeous book and keeping the faith. And finally, the biggest thank you of all to everyone who has ever entered the Comedy Pet Photo Awards. You make the competition the success that it is and keep us all giggling till the cows come home. This book is for you lot and your pets … now go and buy 10 more immediately!

Michelle Wood
Head of all things involving any detail whatsoever, allowing the founders to absolve themselves from all blame and do what they do best

ABOUT THE TEAM

PAUL JOYNSON-HICKS, MBE. Paul started the Comedy Pet Photo Awards alongside his great pal, (no, really, they are friends) Tom Sullam. It was, of course, Paul's inspired idea, although Tom still says it was his. The jury are still out. Paul is a wildlife photographer, (recently 'award-winning' to his great relief, although Tom still out 'awards' him, much to his delight) a humungous animal lover, a passionate wildlife conservationist and a domestic animal welfare advocate. He grew up with dogs and now has his own slightly mad pair of English Springer Spaniels, as well as chickens and three cats at his home in Arusha, Tanzania.

Having spent the first part of his professional life working in financial services in London, TOM SULLAM realised the error of his ways and decided to quit everything to pursue a career in photography. Much to Paul's annoyance, Tom then won the prestigious Fuji Photographer of the Year award, along with the One Vision prize and then turned his hand to commercial photography. Having lived in Tanzania (where he met Paul) he now lives in Surrey with his family, an unbelievably handsome Labrador and a feline legend called Slinky.

Grateful not to be a professional photographer, MICHELLE WOOD likes pootling around with jpegs, pngs and pixels and has spent much of her life researching, commissioning and choosing art and photography for many different projects. She lives in Oxfordshire with her family, a patient and dear labrador called Joey and two beautiful but crazy whippet puppies in the house she grew up in ... perfectly situated between The Cotswold Distillery and Hook Norton Brewery. Nope, we wouldn't move either!

Dr. EMMA MILNE, BVSc FRCVS. is our competition super vet, who checks every single entry and whose animal welfare knowledge is impressive and boundless. Emma used to be pretty famous after being on a TV show back in the late 90s and yet in spite of this A-list superstardom, she does completely LOVE the animal welfare backbone of the competition and has been involved since the very small beginnings. Her grown-up job is mostly spent trying to educate the whole world not to buy pets they cannot look after and pets that breeders have deformed over the years by choosing ridiculous bodies that don't work anymore. A worthy mission indeed!